Trust in an Age of Arrogance

Trust in an Age of Arrogance

C. FitzSimons Allison

WIPF & STOCK · Eugene, Oregon

TRUST IN AN AGE OF ARROGANCE

Wipf & Stock
An imprint of Wipf and Stock Publishers
199 W. 8th Ave., Suite 3
Eugene, OR 97401

www.wipfandstock.com

ISBN 13: 978-1-60608-555-4

Manufactured in the U.S.A.

I am grateful to Houghton Mifflin Harcourt for permission to quote excerpts from *J.B.: A Play in Verse* and to Virginia Theological Seminary, the Charles Price Fund, for permission to quote the second verse of Josiah Condor's hymn.

For

James Parker Allison

and

Allston Allison Kitchens

and

John DeSaussure Allison

Charles Dickens claimed that pride for one's children is not a sin for it is
a mixture of two great Christian virtues: faith and hope.
I thank God that these virtues have produced a love for which I am
inexpressibly grateful.

Contents

Acknowledgments

L IKE THE PROVERBIAL FROG in the slowly heating frying pan, we are not sufficiently aware of the serious consequences of replacing Christianity with secularism. The literature on the subject of secularism is voluminous. Something new and important is published almost daily. The temptation to read and not write can result in eschatological postponement. Without the persistent expectations and aid of Paul Briggs to help break my pattern of delay the task would never have been completed.

The Beeson Divinity School scholar, Fran Cade, has been especially helpful and encouraging as was her mother before her. Together with Jane and Alex Dickson they show why the very word for encouragement (*parakaleo*) is the name of the Holy Spirit.

I am in great debt to Grayson Carter who read the whole manuscript and made valuable suggestions and corrections. Maxie Dunnam's magnanimity is especially appreciated as his help and encouragement were not deterred by his disagreeing with some portions of the book. Of the many who have given me valued assistance are Jim Basinger, David Brannon, Linda and Tom Hall, Andy Morgan, Steven Paulson, Paula Sevier, Matt Stillman, Phil Thrailkill, William Witt, and Rod Whitaker, although they should not be blamed for what I have done or failed to do with their aid.

The fine line between denominational loyalty and denominational idolatry exposes critics of any tradition to reproach, censure, or anger. Coleridge once warned: "Truth is a good dog but beware of barking too close to the heels of an error, lest you get your brains kicked out." I am barking quite close to some serious errors, but I would like to point out to those who might kick in return that I have not spared my own beloved Anglican Communion from criticism and would ask if any tradition should be seen as immune to Jesus's warning: "Take heed! Beware the yeast of the Pharisees and the Sadducees!"

One of my most perceptive critics has raised the question whether my presentations themselves are not yet untainted with inadequate compassion for Pharisees, Sadducees, and the world. If so I pray that the reader will be on guard lest my sin become contagious.

As tough-love critic and companion in faith my wife, Martha, is as much a part of this book as she is of my life. No words are adequate to express my gratitude and love.

Preface

FOR THOMAS CRANMER, THE human heart was both the heart of the human problem and the heart of all hope for human beings. As the first Protestant archbishop of Canterbury, Cranmer understood that we follow "too much the devises and desires of our own hearts" and as a result "there is no health in us."[1] Yet, he also believed that "if the profession of our faith of the remission of our own sins enter within us into the deepness of our hearts, then it must kindle a warm fire of love in our hearts towards God, and towards all others for the love of God."[2] For Cranmer the three Rs of Anglican pastoral care were: realizing the power of sin; relying on the power of unconditional love; and remembering the power of Scripture to make the first two abundantly clear.

Such clear-eyed honesty about both the pitfalls as well as the potential of human nature has all too often been forgotten in the modern era. As Perry Miller, the famous Harvard expert on Puritanism, recognized, both the religious and rationalist heirs of the Reformation have seemed to suffer from a "failure of nerve." Too "sentimental" in their estimation of human ability, they have simply "lacked the stomach for reality."[3]

Not so C. FitzSimons Allison. First as a noted scholar, then as the XII Bishop of the Episcopal Diocese of South Carolina, he has been formed by Cranmer's three Rs of pastoral care. Consequently, he has devoted his life to reminding Christians cosseted by illusions of human perfectibility that the power of sin merely twists such smug pretensions into crude moralisms justified by cruel heresies. For human self-centeredness will always seek to make religion the ultimate sanction by which to prove ourselves better than other people. And human reason will always seek to rewrite God's revelation so as to gloss over rather than illuminate our own destructive impulses.

Bishop Allison has taught generations of clergy and laity that the waywardness of the human heart is the human condition's real tar baby from which only our Creator can deliver us. He has stressed over and over again that the heart of the Gospel of Jesus Christ is not what we have to

1. Joseph Ketley, ed., *Two Liturgies, A.D. 1549, and A.D. 1552.*
2 J. E. Cox, ed., *Miscellaneous Writings and Letters of Thomas Cranmer.*
3. Perry Miller and Thomas H. Johnson, eds., *The Puritans.*

do to please God, for all we do remains tarred by self. Rather, the heart of the Gospel of Jesus Christ is what God has been pleased to do for us. Humanity finds peace only with God and power for new life in the cross of Christ. For only God's unconditional love shown there can birth grateful love in our hearts, and only love is stronger than sin.

Yet, deluded that the educated human will makes the difference, too many contemporary preachers, whether conservative or liberal, end up relying on the old standard goads to better human behavior. Whether the aim is to discourage sexual immorality or to encourage the acceptance of sexual diversity, the pastoral means is almost always the same: duty and pride in compliance, shame and fear in failure. Modern preachers may proclaim their moralisms and even their heresies in the name of God's love. Nevertheless, they all too often fail to rely on the Gospel of grace to transform their own hearts, let alone those to whom they preach. As aptly expressed by Bishop Allison, they mount their pulpits merely to "fuss" at people.

To cut through all such sentimentality and sloppy thinking, the bishop has taken up his pen one last time. With insight gained from a lifetime of critical scholarship and the cure of souls, he has written a book that lays out for us with unfailing clarity the regularity with which the leaven of self has worked its way through the thought of both secularist and sacred writers in the modern period. He challenges us to heed Perry Miller's warning and steel ourselves to stomach reality. For Bishop Allison knows that only when our eyes have been opened to the destructive yeast of the Sadducees and Pharisees at work in our history and in our own hearts can we begin to appreciate afresh the Gospel of grace. Only when we recognize the power of sin can we learn to rely on Scripture to make clear the even greater transforming power of the unconditional love of God revealed in Christ Jesus our Lord. Only when we inwardly digest the pastoral wisdom of the Anglican Reformation can we begin to lay a solid foundation for a new reformation in our own era.

May God so use this book in our hearts that it will be said of us once again that they know we are Christians, not by our fussing, but by our unconditional love.

Ashley Null
Humboldt-Universität zu Berlin
Ascension Day 2009

INTRODUCTION

The Center

I am Not, and God Is

> When we open our eyes as babies we see the world stretching out
> around us; we are in the middle of it . . . I am the center of the
> world I see; where the horizon is depends on where I stand . . .
> Some things hurt us; we hope they will not happen again; we call
> them bad. Some things please us; we hope they will happen again;
> we call them good. Our standard of value is the way the things
> affect ourselves. So each of us takes his place in the center of his
> own world. But I am not the center of the world, or the standard of
> reference as between good and bad; I am not, and God is.[1]
>
> —Archbishop William Temple

AT A RECENT FAMILY gathering my wife was greeted by two of our small
grandchildren who live in different cities. They ran to her shout-
ing, "Grandma! Grandma!" One of them burst into tears crying, "She's
not your Grandma! She's my Grandma!" William Temple (1881–1944),
Archbishop of Canterbury, accurately described the universality of our
human situation.

The implication of Temple's assertion is that the source of our conflict with others resembles our grandchildren's perspective. We are the
center of our world and they are the center of their worlds. This is true
not only for individuals but for families, political parties, tribes, cities,
and nations. Our self-centeredness creates the need for laws, locks, police,
prisons, and time-out places for children. This self-as-center is the cause
of divorce, litigation, corruption, murder, war, genocide, and terrorism.

---

1. William Temple, *Christianity and the Social Order*, 52.

Human self-centeredness ultimately puts us in an adversarial posture not only with others but with God himself.

We attempt to civilize this self-centeredness by seeking some exchange that seems advantageous to both. Huge systems of qualifications, paper trails, legal agreements, regulations, and constant vigilance must be in place to avoid unfair, ruinous, and self-centered abuse. Although we seek to harness and domesticate our self-centered perspectives and desires, human ingenuity for taking unfair advantage of others always seems to get ahead of regulations and regulators. As long as we are the standard of reference between good and bad we will be in conflict with another's different standard of reference. Self-interest is an ever-present, potentially destructive force even when interests and goals unite us in mutuality and cooperation.

Although this human condition may be treated and modified in an infinite variety of ways, history and personal experience have taught us that, no matter what common alliance, mutual agreement, inhibition, or limitation of our wills we attempt, self-interest rises to the top as a potentially destructive force. Admirably, we often try to see things from the other's point of view, but our empathy is limited. I recall saying to my wife, who had sprained her ankle two years before I sprained mine, that I remembered how awkward and inconvenient it was for her, but "I don't remember it hurting like this!"

The most workable solution to this universal difficulty is to commit oneself to a center greater than the individual self. But what center? Today's postmodern, post-Christian culture would answer unity in diversity. But unity or solidarity based on what? Tyranny has produced much unity (e.g., the 600-year Ottoman Empire and the union of the Soviet Socialist Republic in the twentieth century) but at a great cost to freedom. A business partnership can provide a higher claim on our time and energy as long as one subordinates oneself to the partnership's economic goal. Unity based on family alone squelches individuality and independence. Unity based solely on kinship produces clan warfare. Unity founded on a community results in tribal warfare. Unity based on personal loyalty to an institution can produce uncorrected corporate and political dishonesty and corruption. Unity based only on national identity is constantly threatened by unchecked power, chauvinism, and wars with other national entities.

The twentieth century saw at least two examples of collective resolutions to human self-centeredness. National Socialism (i.e., Nazism) in Germany claimed the nation as the center and Communism gave the Soviet Union the hope of an international classless society. Each amounted to radical subordination of self-interest to national or classless interest.

Another alternative is Ayn Rand's philosophy of objectivism, the pursuit of one's own rational self-interest and one's own happiness as the highest purpose of life. The influence of her philosophy, *The Virtue of Selfishness,* and of her novels, *The Fountainhead* and *Atlas Shrugged* can scarcely be exaggerated. Leading business executives in the twenty-first century, including Alan Greenspan, long-time Chairman of the Federal Reserve, are among her most ardent admirers and followers.[2] He called himself one of Rand's acolytes, but when the economic bubble burst he acknowledged that self-regulation by Wall Street had failed: "Those of us who have looked to the self-interest of lending institutions to protect shareholder equity, myself especially, are in a state of shock disbelief." Rational self-interest interpreted by a self-centered self will exploit the weak and disadvantaged, is susceptible to greed, and will produce regularly occurring scandals such as the Dutch Tulipomania (1634–1636), the South Sea Bubble (1711–1720), the collapse of the American corporate giant Enron, and the meltdown of the banking industry in the twenty-first century. Two modern hopes attempt to resolve the problem of human self-centeredness: the loss of self in a secular collective, as in Nazism or Communism, and the commitment to rational self-interest, as in the philosophy of Ayn Rand that underlies much of modern capitalism. Each has been shown to be not only inadequate but dangerously destructive.

The simple point that William Temple makes is that we are not only born self-centered and are in rivalry and conflict with others who are also born self-centered, but we are naturally at enmity with the true center, God. In a secular world stealing someone's pen is merely a crime against its owner but it is a much deeper offense. In God's world the pen belongs to Joe and if Bill steals it he is attempting to create a world in which it belongs to Bill. It is an offense against the real center: God. If Bill kills Joe it is not simply a crime against Joe. Bill is trying to create a world in which Joe does not exist. The crime, the offense, the sin is an antagonism against God, the true and final reality. "Against thee, thee only, have I sinned, and

2. Doherty, *Radicals For Capitalism.*

done this evil in thy sight . . ." (Ps 51:43). To ignore this reality and put our confidence in either some communal center or our own rational self-as-center is a false and malignant hope. Jesus warned us long ago about such hopes:

> "Take heed. Beware the yeast of the Pharisees and the Sadducees."
> (Matt 16:6)

We desperately need a new center, a commitment beyond our own selfish nature, the state, or a classless society. Things of this world will inevitably fail. Only in rediscovering the true center can we hope to have justice, mercy, and freedom in a culture where Christianity has been distorted almost beyond recognition. In this book, we will explore the simple text of Jesus's warning that is capable of clarifying myriad complexities that obscure a clear view of the world and of the Christian promise.

Justice Oliver Wendell Holmes is said to have observed that he cared nothing for "simplicity this side of complexity," but would give his life for "simplicity on the other side of complexity." Simplicities before complexities are to be avoided because they cannot recognize, acknowledge, or encompass the infinite aspects of reality. Such simplicity as "people are good" cannot acknowledge and treat the fact of human destructiveness. "People are bad" is a simplicity that cannot perceive the reality of human ingenuity, creativity, and love. It would be easy to simply dismiss the Pharisees and Sadducees as bad people and keep ourselves in the category of good people. Such assumptions blind us to reality and to our own need to heed Jesus's warning. What is it about the teaching of the Sadducees and Pharisees that we need to beware of in our lives today? A fresh and unclouded view of our culture and our churches can show us how we have ignored the warning and have fallen under the spell of these erroneous teachings.

SADDUCEES

The biblical Sadducee is a near equivalent of today's secular humanist who believes that this world is all there is. Sadducees did not believe in the resurrection, spirits, or angels. The modern Sadducee attempts to resolve our human predicament by depending solely on ingredients of human invention restricted to this world. The results are in vain and the consequences destructive. With no final and transcendent hope, the Sadducee yeast renders each historical commitment as the final and ultimate last word. The vain hope for justice in history alone will break our hearts as each commitment proves inadequate, corrupt, or ineffective. Without God's judgment upon it, immorality or evil done in this life becomes the final injustice when any perpetrator of evil dies with no accountability. According to the Sadducee, the perpetrator has no final reckoning for his evil deeds and is thus rarely able to receive justice or mercy.

Let us ponder a fictional story of a bank robbery and murder. A man came into a bank with a gun. He demanded that Agnes, a clerk, give him all the money in her drawer. She pushed the alarm. He shot and killed her and ran out of the bank into a waiting car and escaped. Sometime later Bernard James, a suspect, was arrested, tried, and on the testimony of Susan, (Agnes' fellow cashier), was found guilty and executed. However, Susan's testimony was false; she only wanted revenge and for someone, anyone, to pay for her friend's death. She knew when she testified that James was not the murderer. Years later Susan died peacefully in her sleep. For the Sadducee, truth and justice are forever denied and buried in the graves of Susan and James. The inescapable trust of the secularist is that injustice and the grave are the end.

Peter T. Forsythe is credited with the observation that when within us we have nothing above us we soon succumb to what is around us. We are surrounded by the beckoning call of self-centeredness. Whether manifest in a call to baseless unity or endless self-glorification, evidence would suggest that churches are no longer looking up but around for direction. When lost people come to church many find only a reflection of the world and go away empty. Sadducean yeast relegates us to being no more than the self-centered creatures who continue in rivalry, conflict, and self-destruction beneath a veneer of constant compromise and endeavors to control.

PHARISEES

Unlike Sadducees, the Pharisees agree with Jesus about eternal life; however, they see this not as a gift, but as what they have earned and deserve. Self-righteousness is the product of the Pharisee yeast. It feeds the very self-centeredness that Jesus Christ came to heal. When found in the church, it represents Christianity to the world in a singularly unattractive and undesirable way. A common expression: "heaven for the climate, but hell for the company" is an indication how people react to Pharisaical

Christians. They would rather be in hell with other sinners than in heaven with those who thought that they were good enough to be there.

Perry Temno, a leader in the community and generous contributor to the Episcopal Church and local charities, was proud of the fact that he had lost friends and business because of his stand for integration. He was sincerely grateful that he was not a Baptist or Methodist and despised talk about being born again. With several generations of his family buried in the churchyard and a degree from Yale, Temno considered himself a faithful, though somewhat imperfect, Christian—not a sinner—one who believed he had kept the Ten Commandments. In comparing himself with his friends he considered himself a far better citizen and church member. He believed that Jesus was a good teacher, though often impractical, and generally a good example for his children to follow. His inescapable trust, as an example of a contemporary Pharisee, was in his own goodness, especially when compared with others.

The Pharisaic alternative to the Sadducee yeast is that when within us we have nothing above us we soon succumb to what is within us. The Pharisaic yeast will not let us humbly admit either our need for forgiveness before God, who alone is righteous, or that we have fallen far short of the persons we were intended to be. Thus, we are left with the singularly unattractive burden of reliance upon our own flawed goodness and our endeavors for self-esteem.

Jesus's warning to his closest followers concerning these two cancers is the simplicity that explains enormous complexities. His teaching helps us to see with a clearer vision and then begin to receive, hear, and appropriate the love that these cancers have obscured and forced out of our vision. Today's Sadducee is characterized by a low view of God, an unconcern with heaven or hell, and a commitment to self-esteem at the expense of transformation, salvation, and true unity with God. The other yeast finds Pharisees in the church with a higher view of God but one reduced to the level of their own worthiness. This means justice without grace, redemption without repentance, and assurance of salvation by one's own goodness. The discrepancy between God's justice and our goodness is rectified by lowering the awesome righteousness of God while at the same time inflating one's own self-worth.

No one can claim immunity from this cancerous yeast. Even among the most astute theologians the temptation is there: "When [Karl] Barth was working up his *Church Dogmatics* during summers in the Swiss Alps, he wrote to a friend that he had to guard himself every moment from slipping back into the old way of making the self both center and standard."[3]

We live and breathe in an age that does both. Such assumptions make it impossible to appreciate fully the wisdom and power of Jesus's teaching concerning the Pharisees and Sadducees. Our arrogance, as seen in the church as well as in the secular world, makes it increasingly necessary to heed Jesus's warning concerning the yeasts. Both yeasts relentlessly attack the faithful. Looking over the history of the church we see in every age the results of not heeding Jesus's warning: "Beware the yeast of the Pharisees and Sadducees."

Our secular arrogance and our religious self-righteousness are in our heritage as well as in the very air we breathe. This spiritual asthma chokes our civilization and counterfeits the Christian faith, leaving the gospel's hope and promise largely unknown.

In order to open our hearts and minds to the warning as well as to the promise of Jesus, we must first establish grounds for humble trust in God, in spite of the arrogance of our age. Only with such trust will we be able to sing the Lord's song in our increasingly strange land.

> My Song is Love unknown
>   my Savior's love to me,
>   love to the loveless shown
>   that they my lovely be.
> O who am I that for my sake
>   my Lord did take
>   frail flesh and die?[4]
>
> —Samuel Crossman (1624–83)

---

3. Forde, *Captivation of the Will*, 21.

4. Samuel Crossman, *Hymnal*, no. 458.

Trust in an Age of Arrogance

". . . I came to understand that sin is not a matter of morality or conduct, but a state or orientation of a man's entire consciousness which does not make God its center."[1]

—Arthur McGill

C. S. LEWIS HAS diagnosed the arrogance of our age in his essay, "God in the Dock."

> The ancient man approached God (or even gods) as the accused person approaches his judge. For the modern man the roles are reversed. He is the judge, God is in the dock. He is quite a kindly judge: if God should have a reasonable defense for being the god who permits war, poverty and disease, he is ready to listen to it. The trial may even end in God's acquittal. But the important thing is that man is on the Bench and God in the Dock.[2]

What was true in Lewis's day, the middle of the last century, is even truer in post- modernity. We who live in modern (and post-modern) times have traded our role with God's role. God is no longer the judge of us but we of him. We have arrogated to ourselves the attributes of deity and given to God the responsibility to justify himself, repent, change, or disappear as irrelevant. Lewis's prophetic and diagnostic description, written in 1947, has clearly come to pass. At no time in the history of either Christian or pagan religions has a people shown such hubris toward God or to the gods. Even pagans believed that hubris in the face of the gods would bring judgment and destruction. Awe, fear, trembling, dread, rever-

1. McGill, *Sermons*, 149.
2. Lewis, *God in the Dock*, 245.

ence, and even respect are almost absent today from the human posture before God.

Barbara Tuchman, the eminent historian, writes: "In the search for meaning we must not forget that the gods (or God, for that matter) are a concept of the human mind, they are creatures of man, not vice-versa."[3] This voice of arrogance can clearly be heard also in the writings of Karen Armstrong, the widely praised and rarely criticized ex-Roman Catholic nun and formidable scholar. She claims that the deity is a product of humankind's creative imagination. Her book, *A History of God*, ends with this comment: "if we are to create a vibrant new faith for the twenty-first century we should, perhaps, ponder the history for some lessons and warnings."[4] She has examined in this much praised book the deity whom humans have imagined and recommends the lessons she has learned as we "create a new faith" for the current century. Like a black cat in a dark night this example of arrogance is hardly noticeable.

And Armstrong is not alone. Another ex-Roman Catholic author, Jack Miles, claims in *Christ: A Crisis in the Life of God* (2001) that Christ died not for our sins, but for God's sins! Our cultural leaders often take these assumptions and judgments as worthy reflections of Judaism and the Christian faith. Responsibility for our actions is removed as well as our hope for repentance, redemption, and transformation. Miles panders to our self-centeredness by placing blame on God who must change to meet our needs and desires.

Miles is no offbeat exotic scholar but a seriously respected and reviewed author, another black cat in the dark night of cultural arrogance. His book, a best seller, not only received a Pulitzer Prize but also the John Templeton Prize for Progress in Religion. "If I were God, I do not think I would want to be studied by most contemporary theologians" is the understandable response by Alasdair MacIntyre, Professor at Notre Dame.[5] This role reversal between us and God is characteristic of our age. No longer is it "he who made us and not we ourselves" (Psalm 100) but we who have made him.

Another example of our age's arrogant treatment of God can be seen in Harold Kushner's *When Bad Things Happen to Good People*. His

3. Tuchman, *March of Folly*, 45–46.

4. Armstrong, *History of God*, 399.

5. MacIntyre, "Books and Culture," 5.

sensitive and poignant reaction to his son's fatal illness is a needed and convincing demonstration that all tragic things that happen to people are not to be understood as punishment for sins. Jesus clearly taught us in Luke 13:1–5 and John 9:1–3 that those upon whom the tower of Siloam fell or the man born blind were not instances of punishment for sin. But at the end of this reassuring message about false guilt, Kushner resolves the profound mystery of iniquity (2 Thess 2:7 KJV) by exhorting us to love God "and forgive Him despite His limitations."[6] Here the inexplicable matter of innocent suffering is resolved by this condescending gesture to an imperfect God who is reduced to an object of our forgiveness. In other words, our knowledge of right and wrong is superior to God's.

Perhaps the epitome of this arrogance is Norman Mailer's autobiography of Jesus, *The Gospel According to the Son*. A reviewer described the work:

> In recent years, Mr. Mailer has tried to dress his all-too-human subjects, Lee Harvey Oswald and Pablo Picasso, in the garments of heroism. This time he has tried to do the reverse, with equally distressing results. In trying to describe Jesus and God as accessible novelistic characters, Mr. Mailer has turned them into familiar contemporary types; he has knocked them off their celestial thrones and turned them into what he knows best, celebrities.[7]

The best comment on this was a cartoon in *The New Yorker*. A man, standing before the eternal throne of judgment, is screaming, "Wait a minute! Wait a minute! I just look like Norman Mailer!" Our cultural arrogance has changed God and Jesus into mere celebrities. Another age would have called this blasphemy. That we will all appear for judgment before the throne of almighty God becomes a subject for humor in contemporary journalism. Trust in God has been replaced by trust in man, the hallmark of secularism. The air we breathe is saturated with such hubris.

Although not widely recognized as such, secularism is a faith in "this-world-is-all-there-is-ism," as Reinhold Niebuhr termed it. Western civilization has no evidence for this confidence, historically, empirically, or scientifically, but this hope and trust rests on assumptions that have replaced those of the Christian faith. God is no longer a player among the many changes and disappointments of hope and trust.

6. Kushner, *Why Bad Things Happen to Good People*, 148.
7. Kakutani, review of *Gospel According to the Son*, April 14, 1997.

Nor is the church immune to our current proclivity or tendency to secularism. As Christians we, too, tend to replace confidence in what is perfect with what is imperfect. Trust in self-centered humans has resulted in an inflation of confidence in autonomous humanity to arrogant proportions. We must come to accept the existence, and understand the nature, of this secular dogmatism in our culture in order to comprehend the extent to which it has captured our churches. If God is not to be trusted, what or whom can we trust?

SECULAR PSYCHOLOGY

The substitution of secular psychology for trust in God was perhaps best illustrated in the works of Philip Rieff, especially his *Triumph of the Therapeutic* (1966). Rieff claimed that these psychotherapeutic religiosities represent a failure of nerve by both psychotherapists and clergymen. One of the most influential psychotherapists, Erich Fromm, writing in the middle of the twentieth century, claimed:

> If man gives up his illusion of a fatherly God, if he faces his aloneness and insignificance in the universe, he will be like a child that has left his father's house. But it is the very aim of human development to overcome infantile fixation. Man must educate himself to face reality. If he knows that he has nothing to rely on except his own powers, he will learn to use them properly.[8]

The assumption that one can educate oneself to reality, and know that there is nothing to rely on but one's own powers, and that one will learn to use them properly, is a confidence (a faith, a trust). As a substitute for Christianity, it is an example of hubris begging for judgment.

The psychiatrist Allen Wheelis, in his book *The Quest for Identity*, gives another example of replacing trust in God with trust in human beings. He describes his approach to a hypothetical clergyman:

> If the clergyman remains intellectually and emotionally open, his work may provide him with such insight as will force him eventually to relinquish belief in a personal God, in life after death, and in other absolutes which had guaranteed his security.[9]

A symptom of secular society is its unexamined and gratuitously assumed dogma that this world is all there is. Especially noteworthy is

8. Fromm, *Psychology and Religion*, 126.

9. Wheelis, *Quest for Identity*, 109.

the claim that: "Psychoanalysis provides no value system, nor should it."[10] But Wheelis is clearly carrying into his therapy his unacknowledged na-ïve secular value system. "Everyone has values and dogmas but me. My beliefs are not beliefs but truths" seems to be the arrogant assumption of the new therapeutic age. At the same time the therapist who claims to have achieved objectivity "knows" that his patient's value system is not true and that he must relinquish the beliefs that nurtured some of the most creative and productive individuals throughout history—not only Dante, Shakespeare, Handel, and Bach but T. S. Eliot, W. H. Auden, and C. S. Lewis, among millions of other believing Christians throughout the centuries. Wheelis assumes that Christian beliefs do not correspond to reality but reality is inaccessible to those whose hubris limits their trust to an encapsulated history. A person cannot trust simultaneously in the ultimate sufficiency of human ingenuity and in God.

The belief that we have controlling power over our wills is another symptom of secular dogma. Wheelis claims: "Whether or not [the clergy-man] can survey the damage, salvage those elements which are sound, and build a new structure of belief depends upon the courage, tenac-ity, and creative ability which he alone can mobilize to meet the crisis."[11] Behind this statement is the clear but unacknowledged secular dogma that the clergyman's historic faith must give way to a trust in his ability to "build a new structure of belief." His client is being taught to leave the "structure of belief" of 2,000 years and build another one to resolve the human condition described earlier by William Temple. Laying aside the essential question of truth, Wheelis here dumps on his client the burden of having the courage, tenacity, and creative ability that he alone can mo-bilize. If his client could do that he would not be in therapy in the first place. This belief that our wills have the power of themselves to do what we should—to love others as ourselves—is called the Pelagian heresy in Christian teaching. Belief that my heart can be changed by my will alone is an arrogant, cruel, and misplaced confidence.

Wheelis's book contains much wisdom and numerous examples of self-effacing humility. He is no straw man but rather an outstanding ex-ample of a whole generation of therapists who have had an incalculable influence on our age. His popularity and talent is such that his works have

10. Ibid., 50.
11. Ibid., 110.

been printed in *The New Yorker*. He has authored some fourteen books and was one of the most respected and admired therapists of his generation. At issue, however, is the gratuitous assumption, now the unacknowledged dogma of the times, that we alone can resolve the condition of our destructive selves. Those who look to transcendent hope are regarded by Wheelis (and others) as neurotic or pathological. "Modern man cannot recapture an identity out of the past; for his old identity was not lost, but outgrown. Identity is not, therefore, to be found; it is to be created and achieved."[12] This dogma claims to solve the great mystery of human identity by our ability to be our own creator and thereby become just, loving, and merciful by our own endeavors. Yet in his mature years he shows a commendable humility: "I have not found in psychoanalysis the meaning I sought. I function as a guide to the lost, but do not myself know the way."[13] Wheelis is obsessed with the idea, as T. S. Eliot put it, that human kind cannot bear very much reality. He is unpersuaded by his previous attempts to render death as a meaningful conclusion rather than a fated, inescapable end. "A symphony has a climax, a poem builds to a burst of meaning, but we are unfinished business. No coming together of strands. The game is called because of darkness."[14] Darkness of death is the final secular word. Arrogance leads to darkness and it is in this darkness that we now live.

THE CLIMATE OF OPINION

The historian, Carl Becker, in his book, *Heavenly City of the 18th Century Philosophers* (1932), coined the phrase "climate of opinion." He taught scholars that it is well nigh impossible for a historian to escape the climate out of which he or she writes. Inevitably the object of study will be influenced by the assumptions of the historian's own period. He illustrates this, on the one hand, by the example of Edward Gibbon writing out of the eighteenth century's confidence in reason. Gibbon attributes the fall of the Roman Empire largely to religion and particularly to Christianity. He treats Christianity with some surprising respect, but then dismisses it on the basis of his pre-Freudian and optimistic eighteenth-century confidence in reason.

12. Ibid., 205.
13. Merkin, "Neurotic's Neurotic," 47.
14. Ibid., 48.

On the other hand, Professor Michael Rostovtzeff, a twentieth–century White Russian, expresses his century's particular concerns in the title of his work, *The Social and Economic History of the Roman Empire* (1926), in which the object of his study of the fall of the Roman Empire is narrowed to social and economic factors. Each historian looks at the same material through the lens of the concerns of his own times, his own climate of opinion that determines much of the result. This emphasis of concern, and consequent distortion of reality, describes not only historians, but everyone.

An accurate diagnosis and understanding of our age is necessary to free us from the limitations and false assumptions of our own climate of opinion, the lens by which we unconsciously view reality. Reinhold Niebuhr calls the study of history "the fulcrum of freedom" because only by the perspective of another age can we get purchase or a clear view of our own. Only then can we begin to have some objective questions and choices concerning our ideas and beliefs. Otherwise, we will be carried blindly along by the unacknowledged and unconscious opinions of our time. This is especially true in an age where hopes are limited to transactions and developments among self-centered human beings.

As Gibbon's views were molded by confidence in human reason in the Age of Enlightenment and Rostovtzeff's by trust in the social and economic preoccupations of the twentieth century, our views are inevitably influenced by the dominant beliefs of our present age. In response, we need a critical perspective on our own time if we are to begin to be free from its inhibiting, although largely unconscious, influences. The following works help verify this diagnosis of arrogance:

Paul Vitz, *Psychology as Religion: The Cult of Self-Worship*

D. W. McCullough, *The Trivialization of God: The Dangerous Illusion of a Manageable Deity*

W. C. Placher, *The Domestication of Transcendent Thinking About God*

E. Brooks Holifield, *A History of Pastoral Care in America: From Salvation to Self Realization*

Vitz shows what is happening as Christianity is diminished to meet the modern person's perception of his or her self-centered psychological needs. McCullough gives us a bracing criticism of the trivialization of God in the current search for a manageable deity. Placher traces the roots of this reductionist tide to the seventeenth and eighteenth centuries. Holifield's subtitle shows the lamentable departure from Christianity in the training of American clergy. Where this present-day hubris prevails, evangelism is a stillbirth. Churches thus corrupted become impotent to speak to the culture whose prevailing hope, amid the dissolution of the therapeutic trust, is that of inevitable progress

PROGRESS

One trust left to a world without God is a future of progress. Before we simply dismiss the idea of progress, we should appreciate how much actual progress has been made and what makes this hope tempting. We humans are not naturally grateful. We tend to overlook much that is good. We have better teeth than George Washington and live in a society whose defeated party in presidential elections acquiesces even in exceedingly close contests. In the history of civilization and in many contemporary countries, such peaceful transitions of power are rare indeed.

As Stephen Moore and Julian L. Simon have pointed out:

> Over the course of the 20th century life expectancy rose from 47 to 77 years of age. Deaths from infectious diseases fell from 700 to 50 per 100,000 of the population . . . auto ownership rose from one to 91 per cent of the population and patents granted rose from 25,000 to 150,000 a year. Controlling for inflation, household assets rose from $6 trillion to $41 trillion between 1945 and 1998.[15]

Progress in communication, engineering, technology, and medicine has produced undreamed of accomplishments. I recall leaving the Bodleian Library in Oxford one day in considerable discomfort from the effects of a kidney stone. I wandered into a nearby medical museum and looked at some non-flexible seventeenth-century catheters. Any temptation to romanticize my love for the seventeenth century was somewhat diminished by my gratitude for the progress made by modern medicine.

Contemporary reports of the lack of discipline in schools, the accelerating population of prisons, high incidences of abortion, divorce,

15. Moore and Simon, "Greatest Century that Ever Was."

and suicide highlight the limitations of progress as a religious hope. The Heritage Foundation released a study of trends between 1960 and 1990. These thirty years showed a 560 percent increase in violent crimes, 400 percent increase in illegitimate births, a quadrupling of divorce, a tripling of children living in single-parent homes, a 200 percent increase in teen-age suicide, and a drop of 75 points in the average SAT scores. In 1940 teachers identified top problems with their students as talking out of turn, chewing gum, making noise, running in the hall, cutting in line, dress code infractions, and littering. When asked the same question in 1990 teachers identified drug use, alcohol abuse, pregnancy, suicide, rape, robbery, and assault.[16] Now this trend has extended to increasing sexual pathologies, terror, violence, and rampages of murder in schools and colleges.

Professor John Witte of Emory Law School quotes Don Browning concerning the dangers that result from:

> increased separation of love from sexual exchange, sexual inter-course from marriage, marriage from conception, marriage from childbirth, childbirth from parenthood, sexual intercourse from parenthood, child-rearing from marriage, child-rearing from bio-logical parenthood, and the economic viability of individuals from the economic dependencies of marriage.[17]

Witte goes on to point out that sex may be free but children are not.

> Aside from moral and spiritual decadence the economic cost to the culture is devastating. Thirty-eight percent of all American children are now born out of wedlock, and it costs American taxpayers $112 billion per year. Those are the sobering numbers recently reported by the U.S. Census Bureau and by the Institute for American Values. The Census Bureau numbers break down as follows: 25% of all Caucasian, 46% of all Hispanic, and 69% of all African-American children were born to single mothers in 2007. Compared to children born and raised within marital households, nonmarital children, on average, impose substantially higher costs on society in lost tax revenues and for antipoverty, criminal justice, and education programs. According to the Institute for American Values, those costs exceeded $1 trillion this past decade.[18]

16. Bennett, "Getting Used to Decadence," Lecture 477.
17. Witte, "Emory Law Journal," vol. 58, p. 90.
18. Ibid., 98–99.

Our technological achievements seem to be negatively matched by homegrown terror and cultural decadence. General Omar Bradley's comment is not irrelevant: "We have grasped the mystery of the atom and rejected the Sermon on the Mount . . . The world has achieved brilliance without conscience. Ours is a world of nuclear giants and ethical infants."[19] With the failing trust in inevitable progress many signs indicate that this trust is being replaced by a recognition of decadence.

DECADENCE

We are only beginning to realize, especially after 9/11, that the future may not be one of progress but of decadence. Richard Weaver's book, *Ideas Have Consequences*, describes it well.

> Yet to establish the fact of decadence is the most pressing duty of our time because, until we have demonstrated that cultural decline is a historical fact—which can be established—and that modern man has about squandered his estate, we cannot combat those who have fallen prey to hysterical optimism.[20]

The fact of decadence is impressively established by Jacques Barzun in his work *From Dawn to Decadence, 1500 to the Present: 500 Years of Western Cultural Life* (2000), 900 pages produced by an authority on history, education, art, music, science, philosophy, drama, and religion. These 500 years of life in the West are characterized by a cultural decline. His work is a salutary antidote to "hysterical optimism": All the modern technological achievement cannot hide the alarming trend in Western society. The reality of civilization's slide, illustrated so impressively, does not mean that one would prefer to live in the sixteenth century, which had its own share of difficulties. It does mean that secular hope of inevitable progress is no longer tenable. The hope that education and other cultural accomplishments will provide inherent progress as a substitute for Christian trust in Providence is obsolete. Barzun's book may justifiably be called the epitaph on the grave of the doctrine of progress that has largely replaced the Christian concept of Providence. A whole chorus of thoughtful scholars echoes his dire warning.[21] A growing realization that something is terribly wrong is a sobering mirror to our arrogance.

19. Bradley, "Patriot Post," vol. 3.

20. Weaver, *Ideas Have Consequences*, 10.

21. Budziszewski, *What We Can't Not Know*; Wells, *Losing Our Virtue*; Schlesinger, *Disunity of America*; Bennett, *Index of Leading Cultural Indicators*; Sykes, *Nation of Victims*;

Richard Weaver's insistence in 1948 "that cultural decline is a historical fact—which can be established" is amply verified by the literature and subsequent events. The twentieth century exceeded all centuries in genocide, persecution, and war. This, however, is not to claim that those in the persistent state of denial, who have "fallen prey to hysterical optimism," have acknowledged this degeneracy and the need for grace and transcendence. On the contrary, trust and hope confined to secular limits has resulted in a presumptive and growing dismissal of the religious beliefs of others.

NAIVETÉ

Madeleine Albright in her book, *The Mighty and the Almighty: Reflections on America, God and World Affairs*, exposes this failure. The former Secretary of State and UN delegate admits that on her watch U.S. foreign policy made every effort to ignore religion. Under the influence of the secular contempt for religion (or the assumption that religion is merely a matter for private consumption in civilized societies like our own), America's leaders assumed that religion was not an important force in the world, and that the Balkan crisis, the Israeli-Palestinian conflict, and al-Qaida-sponsored terrorism were "not about religion."

This distorted vision stems from the compulsive hope that humans, with reason, education, and new scientific discoveries, have progressed beyond any need for religion. The pervasiveness of secular commitments is indicated by the fact that Albright wrote this critique "against the advice of friends." Neither the commitment of suicidal terrorists nor the commitment of medical missionaries in Rwanda can be comprehended by those limited to a truncated secular trust. Trust in inevitable progress helped bring about the rise of secularism as a substitute for the Christian trust in Providence. Providence, "making provision for" or "providing," had gradually begun to be used as a term for God. It was a favorite phrase of America's founding fathers. "Divine Providence" appears in the last sentence of the Declaration of Independence.

The very idea of Providence came to Britain with Christianity. Before Christianity the pervasive idea that corresponded to personal destiny was

---

Hendershott, *Politics of Deviance*; Bloom, *Closing of the American Mind*; Cheney, *Telling the Truth*; Bork, *Slouching Towards Gomorrah*; Carter, *Culture of Disbelief*; Himmelfarb, *Demoralization of Society* and *Marriage and Morals Among the Victorians*.

the term, "Weird." This Anglo-Saxon term was a near equivalent of the Greek term *moira*, the word for fate. If people drowned fording a stream, or died of consumption, it was their Weird or fate, their assigned lot or fortune. Providence gradually supplanted the pagan concept of Weird. Providence was a product of the Christian gospel. It gave a radically different lens through which to see one's life and one's end, one's blessings and one's calamities. One's fate, or apparent end, was not seen as the last word. All things, even disasters were regarded as clouds hiding the provision of God. "We know that in everything God works for good, with those who love him . . ." (Rom 8:28). This hope is no natural idea, but something revealed in Scripture.

Over centuries a people's hope was transformed from Weird to Providence. One result of this confidence provided by Providence was that nature came to be regarded as a source of knowledge and power, rather than superstition and magic. Creation was believed to be the handiwork of the second person of the Trinity, the *Logos*. This gave confidence in the logic of cause and effect and helped take the spooks out of the woods. Unfortunately this, in turn, was gradually seen not as a provision of God but as a work of man. The unprecedented power, which resulted in knowledge of nature and man's ingenuity to use it, gradually replaced trust in Providence with trust in Progress.[22] Thus, over the centuries, to perceive reality the pagan lens of Weird was replaced by the Christian trust in Providence and that in turn was replaced by trust in inevitable Progress.

This latter belief, the pervasive hope for Western people for more than a century, was deeply undermined by the events of the twentieth century. Confidence in inevitable Progress, as a hope that gives meaning to life, is expressed by the figure Bildad in Archibald MacLeish's play, *J.B.: A Play in Verse*. Bildad, the modern Job comforter, responds to J. B.'s claim of innocence and cry for justice:

22. Lloyd, *Providence Lost*.

History has no time for innocence.

. . .

One man's suffering won't count, no matter
What his suffering; but All will.
At the end there will be justice!

. . .

On the way—it doesn't matter.[23]

Reducing Christian belief to a trust in an impersonal future sacrifices any meaning for an individual's suffering in this life. "On the way—it doesn't matter" is a disconsolate substitute for divine Providence. We have returned to something very Weird indeed as a replacement for the dashed reliance on progress. The result is a crisis of confusion devoid of meaning.

Not unlike the rulers of Renaissance Europe who were profoundly influenced by Machiavelli's famous work, *The Prince*, the present-day leaders in universities and churches have replaced the search for truth with the acquisition of power.[24] Consequently, art has become ugly and music has become noise; worship has become entertainment, while poetry now laments the loss of meaning and confidence. Surely something Weird has come upon us when the most quoted serious poem of our times is that of W. B. Yeats' "The Second Coming," which ends with these lines:

And what rough beast, its hour come round at last
Slouches toward Bethlehem to be born?[25]

One can hope that Yeats is wrong about the coming of the rough beast and that Progress will continue, but we cannot trust that it will be so. Weird, Providence, Progress, and Weird again describe our history. Like the people of Israel during the Babylonian captivity we must learn to sing the Lord's song in an increasingly strange land. The issue before us is how we can bring the trust in Providence to these Weird times.

23. MacLeish, *J. B.: A Play in Verse*, 121.

24. Marsden, *Soul of the American University*, and Sommerville, *Decline of the Secular University*; also Russell's early perception of power replacing truth in *Scientific Vision*, 262 ff, and MacIntyre, *Three Rival Versions*.

25. Yeats, *Collected Poems*, 215.

TRUST IN THIS AGE OF ARROGANCE

The word trust comes from the Greek word *pistis* and is translated as faith, belief, and trust. Its essential meaning is to rely on, or depend upon, something or someone. It is quite different from mere acknowledgment that something exists. Unfortunately both the words, faith and belief, have (for popular usage) too often been reduced to a mere recognition of existence. One can believe that God exists without trusting him. In regard to the word, faith, certain propositions can be written down, bound in a book and called *The Faith of the Church*. Hence, the words belief and faith can be used even when they lack the essential biblical meaning of personal reliance on and dependence upon. Trust, on the other hand, still seems to carry the essential meaning of *pistis*. I will therefore use the word trust for the most part rather than faith or belief.

TRUST AND HOPE

The relationship between trust and hope is important but difficult to describe precisely. Hope is an essential part of life: *dum spiro spero*: while I breathe I hope. A doctor friend observed the opposite: "When my patients cease to hope they cease to breathe." Bishop William Frey expresses it well: "Hope is the ability to hear the music of God's future. Faith (trust) is the courage to dance to it today."[26]

Peter Kreeft has a wonderfully picturesque way of describing how essential hope is to life.

> No one can live without hope . . . we creatures of time are constant-
> ly moving into the future, and our eyes are usually facing forward.
> Hope is like headlights. It is not easy to drive without headlights
> in the dark.[27]

Hope is vital to humans and cannot successfully be amputated nor should it be. When facts and reality contradict our hopes, facts and reality are often deflected to keep a false hope alive. Hope is inevitable but its objects are various and are often inappropriate. Job denies that his hope is in gold. In the book of Esther the Jews' enemies hope to have power. Felix, in the book of Acts, hoped Paul would give him money. Hope in false objects or ideology can be devastating.

---

26. Frey, *Dance of Hope*, 1.
27. Kreeft, *Fundamentals of the Faith*, 176.

I once asked a friend about someone I had just met. He replied with a picturesque, old-fashioned expression, "He's a nice guy but he's about a half bubble off plumb." A carpenter's level has a bubble to indicate whether something is level or plumb. No one is exactly level or plumb. The Greek philosopher Protagoras wrongly claimed that "Man is the measure of all things." When we measure ourselves by others, or others by ourselves, we are using flawed instruments. Building hope or confidence in this off plumb human nature results in a crooked foundation. When we fail to appreciate the fact that all are flawed, much hurt, both personally and socially, results. In a secular, post-Christian world, we are left with no objects for our hope other than off plumb crooked humanity. As hope is essential to life, in the absence of the Christian gospel, a compulsive and blind commitment to a fatally flawed humanity often results.

Trust is different from hope in several ways. Hope can often express merely a desire or a wish about something in the future, something not seen. "I hope the Redskins will win the football game." "I hope my daughter gets into Oxford." In contrast, trust exposes us to a vulnerability and disappointment more serious and sometimes more devastating than hope. In 1952, I hoped Adlai Stevenson would defeat Dwight Eisenhower for President. Fortunately I did not trust or rely on this. Credulity is not a synonym for trust. No one wishes elderly parents to be victims of fraud because of misplaced trust. W. C. Fields wisely taught us: "Trust everybody and cut the cards."

A theological student working in a hospital oncology ward was said to have made the common mistake of new trainees: premature reassurance. A ministry to cancer patients in a hospital needs more substance than mere optimism. Patients need to be given a hope beyond physical survival. Not everyone recuperates. Much of Western culture is making the same mistake on a grander scale in its premature reassurance about human nature. What is needed is recognition that humans are impotent to cure themselves and that they need to know the reality and power of a deeper hope accessible only by a right placed trust. We hope the cancer patient will not die. What is our hope if she dies? Trust enables deeper hopes. We trust that death is not the end because we trust God and his promise.

Another difference between hope and trust is that the latter is more dangerous. Although some hopes can approach the commitment level of trust, the latter's biblical meaning carries the sense of "you bet your life" dependence. This exposes us to a vulnerability to suffering that is not often present in our hopes. Trust penetrates the armor of shyness with which we protect ourselves from exposure and hurt. Without trust there can be no friendship, love, or community, but the risks of embarrassment, disappointment, or betrayal are there.

Trust opens our hearts to both love and hurt. This is true regarding Christian trust. Christian discipleship promises no safety. William Alexander Percy's hymn speaks of John dying homeless on Patmos and Peter being crucified head down. Paul is thrown in prison, beaten with rods, stoned, and shipwrecked. Luke's Gospel tells us that Christians "will be delivered up even by parents and brothers and kinsmen and friends, and some of you they will put to death; you will be hated by all for my name's sake" (Luke 21:16–17).

We are too often reassured by the lie that nothing can harm our churches. It is true that "the gates of hell shall not prevail" (Matt 16:18), but that does not mean that congregations (and souls) will not be lost. Even in a war whose victory is assured, soldiers and whole armies perish. Similar losses can be seen in the churches of Constantinople, Cappadocia, Ephesus, Egypt, Tripoli, and in the abandoned ecclesiastical edifices in metropolitan cities today. We live in an age where both culture and church give us premature reassurance. We badly need the bracing honesty, together with the promised endurance, that comes with suffering and deliverance.

We are invited to trust Jesus Christ who has promised us final and eternal justice that even we can endure because of his dearly bought mercy; that courage and honor in this life are not forever lost; that freedom and joy are begun here and consummated in his kingdom. All we lose is our self-centered self, although this loss is a bigger price than we naturally want to pay. The words of Robert Penn Warren show us that this loss of self is the only door to authentic hope and trust.

> The recognition of the direction of fulfillment is the death of self,
> And the death of the self is the beginning of selfhood. All else is
> surrogate of hope and destitution of spirit.[28]

Warren is speaking here of baptism—the death to self and the beginning of a new center. As we abandon this hope we are in danger of becoming victims of an age in which we swap roles with God. Arrogance is truly

28. Warren, *Brother to Dragons*, 214–15.

a substitute, a replacement (surrogate), of hope and leaves us with a spirit destitute of the trust needed to relinquish our center to the true Center. Such trust is stifled in an age of arrogance. But it is recoverable by letting Jesus's warning remove the barriers to this trust: "Take heed! Beware the yeast of the Pharisees and the Sadducees."

2

The Yeast of the Sadducees

The Church expected or professed to Christianize the world, but in effect the world secularized the Church.[1]

—James Bryce

AUTHENTIC TRUST SHOULD BE recognized in a journey marked by disappointments, warnings, and serious dangers. Jesus gives us a warning about counterfeit trusts when He tells his disciples, following the feeding of the multitude, "Take heed! Beware the yeast of the Pharisees and the Sadducees" (Matt 16:6, 11). His use of the word, yeast, puzzled them. The disciples thought they were being rebuked because they had brought no bread. But they later realized "that he was not telling them to beware the yeast of bread, but of the *teaching* of the Pharisees and Sadducees" (vs. 12) (italics mine).

If he meant teaching why did he say yeast? Teachers have long exhorted pupils to "say what you mean" but Jesus deliberately used the puzzling term yeast (or leaven) instead of teaching. Why? We can understand something of his choice of yeast by the following story from *Parade* magazine.

> In Chippewa Falls, Wis., it got so hot that a traveling load of yeast filled pizza dough expanded, breaking out of the back of a truck and creating a 25 to 35 mile oozing blob on Highway 29. "We had everything from bread-loaf size droppings to some about half the size of a car," said Sgt. James Barnier of the Wisconsin State patrol. They used snowplows to get it off the highway.[2]

1. Bryce, *Modern Democracies*, 90.
2. *Parade*, Dec. 29, 2002.

Although the effects of yeast in this illustration were visible for miles, yeast itself is often invisible to the naked eye. We do not normally notice its power and influence and some yeasts, like cancer, carry a malignant power. Jesus wanted to impress upon His disciples, and on us, that the teachings of the Pharisees and Sadducees would have deadly effects.

People today rarely see the action of yeast because they buy pre-packaged bread and wine. But the disciples lived in an era when everyone was aware of the remarkable qualities of yeast for good or for ill and most of us today realize that some forms of yeast (or mold) can be dangerous and destructive. Bread or wine can be ruined if the wrong yeast is present. Those who have experienced the effects of a hurricane or a flood are familiar with the destructive character of mold, which is a type of yeast.

A friend once showed me how he made wine. He had a five-gallon glass jug that contained water, sugar, grape juice, and yeast. A tube at the top of the jug ran through a stopper and into a glass of water that was bubbling with released air. I asked the purpose of the glass of water with the tube in it and he explained that it was an air lock. If the air were not released it would break the glass jug. I asked, "Why don't you just let the air out of the jug instead of using the tube and stopper?" "Without the air lock," he said, "unseen yeasts in the surrounding air would ruin the wine and make it undrinkable."

Jesus is telling us, as well as the disciples, that the air we breathe is full of malignant yeast, such as false teachings like that of the Pharisees and Sadducees. These teachings distort and spoil the good news making it inaccessible. Scripture's warning about doctrine (Eph 4:14; 1 Tim 1:3, etc.) and the church's use of creeds, confessional statements, and catechisms are the functional equivalent of the air lock. We must concede at the outset that those of us, who believe in the necessity of boundaries and limits, creeds and catechisms, and the importance of sound doctrine, must resist the temptation to give people water from the air lock to drink rather than the wine it protects. The power is not in the air lock of creeds and confessions but in the Gospel they protect. Creeds, essential as they are, did not hang on the cross for us. They are essential in pointing to, guarding, and preserving the unique love that God has given us.

We make two mistakes: first, we believe we have no need for air locks and, second, we substitute air lock water for the wine it preserves. Sound doctrine should never be devalued. Sadducees would like to substitute correct political strictures for Christian doctrine and secular assumptions for the air lock. The wine is too precious and dearly bought to be confused with the contents of air locks of creeds and doctrine, whose function is not to be a substitute for the wine but to be a guard to protect it from the heresies of contaminating yeast.

Of the two yeasts against which Jesus warned us we look first at the yeast of the Sadducees and deal with the Pharisees in chapter 5. The little we know about the Sadducees' teachings comes from the synoptic Gospels, Acts, the writings of Flavius Josephus, and later rabbinic compilations.[3] Clearly their teaching denied the resurrection and any sense of accountability or trust in life after death (Matt 22:23–24; Mark 12:18–27; Luke 20:27–38). The trap they tried to set for Jesus, which is recorded in each of these synoptic passages, invokes the injunction (Deut 25:5) in which a man is enjoined to marry his deceased brother's widow. Seven brothers succeeded each other as each husband died. The Sadducees asked Jesus, "In the resurrection whose wife shall she be?" The spirit of this question reflects contemporary pre-adolescent materialism like Bishop Spong's assertion, "If Jesus had ascended he wouldn't have gone into heaven but into orbit."[4]

Sadducees denied the resurrection and they seemed to do so through the lens of materialism. "For the Sadducees say that there is no resurrection, no angels, nor spirits" (Acts 23:8). Such teaching is bereft of any spiritual dimension. Their logic seemed to be based upon the false premise that material is the only reality. Consequently, in the resurrection life, the same conditions must prevail as in the earthly life. Hence, the absurdity of having seven husbands is offered as evidence against belief in the resurrection. Jesus's response was unequivocal: "You are wrong, because you know neither the Scriptures nor the power of God . . . have you not read what was said to you by God, 'I am the God of Abraham, and the God of Isaac, and the God of Jacob'? He is not God of the dead but of the living" (Matt 22:29–32).

Scripture deals with what would be called secular (or worldly in contrast to sacred) in some quite deferential ways. Jesus's reply to the Pharisees, "Render to Caesar the things that are Caesar's and to God the things that are God's" (Mark 12:13–17) shows a legitimate and necessary

---

3. See Saldarini, *Pharisees, Scribes and Sadducees*; and Kendall and Rosen, *Christian and the Pharisee*.

4. Spong, *London Times*, August 4, 1989.

place for the secular. He tells those who followed him that the centurion's faith was more than he had found in Israel (Matt 8:10). St. Paul appealed to his rights as a Roman citizen and appealed to Rome in his legal case when he writes, "Let every person be subject to the governing authorities. For there is no authority except from God" (Rom 13:1) he is speaking about what we would call secular authorities.

The writings of scholars, such as Bernard Lewis and Michael Nazir-Ali, stress the virtual absence in Islam of any concept of secular as a neutral category ungoverned by religion.[5] As we live under an increasingly non-Christian authority in matters of ethics, freedom, and justice, it is well to recall Jesus's statement about what is Caesar's, his illustration of the Roman centurion, as well as Paul's appeal to Roman law. We need to remember, however, that the assumptions of secularism will lead any society without God to replace him with idols of their own choice and to impose non-Christian values and morals in the name of those idols. This trajectory of secularism is also seen in Scripture in the difference between Romans 13:1 (see above) and the Book of Revelation's description of persecution under the Emperor Domitian. Here, even Scripture seems to have a different approach to the secular in different contexts.

Underneath this complex issue of the secular is the Christian approach that excludes coercion as a weapon to induce faith. Although reprehensible attempts to coerce faith have been made in times past, love and redemption will never be a result of force. Jesus let the rich young ruler walk sadly away (Matt 19:22). Love can only elicit and evoke. The cross is the supreme example of love's drawing power: "And I, if I be lifted up from the earth will draw all men unto me" (John 12:32).

---

5. Lewis, *What Went Wrong?*, 96–116. Nazir-Ali,*Conviction and Conflict.* The matter of how Christianity looks upon the secular is quite different from that of Islam but is itself a complex issue. St. Augustine's distinction between the *City of God* and *City of the Earth* is the subject of much important scholarship. How is a Christian guided by his dealings with non-religious authorities who do not share Christian ends? Markus's *Christianity and the Secular*, O'Donovan's *Desire of the Nations*, Hauerwas's *After Christendom?*, Milbank's *Theology and Social Theory* approach this complex but unavoidable subject differently. Milbank's insistence that, because the "secular ends" are false, all means to penultimate ends are flawed and therefore sinful. But that does not deny that imperfect and even sinfully tainted justice has a quality of justice congruent with a Christian's cooperative (and also tainted) endeavors. Reinhold Niebuhr's willingness to cooperate with Communists against the Nazis is a case in point. Nevertheless, Milbank's point prevents surprise when the trajectory of decent values of the secular turn demonic (e.g., revolutions against Latin American dictatorships that in turn become tyrannical themselves).

However, our contemporary secularism has a unique aspect about it. Canon V. A. Demant of Oxford University pointed out:

> The ancient paganisms, the Bible and the Christian Church all have this in common that they hold the source of all things to be a divine reality which transcends the world as well as operating in it. The secularisms of today have this in common, that they hold the meaning of the world to lie within it itself.[6]

This new yeast of a self-contained, autonomous world had its beginning in the early Renaissance. Petrarch (1304–74) insisted that "Whatever the validity of the claims of the other world simple human joys and loves on this side of the grave have a legitimate right to a large part of man's endeavors."[7] What was merely a claim to a large portion in the fourteenth century has become an exclusive portion in the twentieth century.

This claim was encouraged in America by the reaction to the ecclesiastic tyrannies of Europe. Our founding fathers were unwilling to perpetrate those mistakes. They wanted to deny any coercive control by either state or church. That wise concern, however, has been gradually interpreted to mean the conscious exclusion of any religious influence on affairs of state and public education. "A wall of separation of church and state" is the popular phrase read into, but absent from, the Constitution. The phrase originated in a private letter from Thomas Jefferson to the Danbury Baptist Association. But Jefferson here did not mean to separate altogether politics and religion. As Professor John Witte of Emory University has pointed out: "In the very next paragraph of his letter, President Jefferson performed an avowedly religious act of offering prayers on behalf of his Baptist correspondents: 'I reciprocate your kind prayers for the protection and blessing of the common Father and Creator of man.'"[8] This non-constitutional phrase, separation of church and state, has replaced in the popular and judicial mind the original and wise but quite different first amendment sentence: "Congress shall make no law respecting an establishment of religion." The consequent misuse of the term has resulted in a separation of faith from the state, schools, universities, and media. This separation has quarantined religion from public endeavors and relegated faith to merely private concerns leaving public morals bereft of religious

6. Demant, *Religion and the Decline of Capitalism*, 113.
7. Lucas, *Renaissance and the Reformation*, 199.
8. Witte, *Religion and the American Constitutional Experiment*, 56.

roots. Many of our leaders, including some of the Supreme Court justices, are thus largely ignorant of the beliefs that spawned the great institutions of our country.[9]

FACTORS IN THE RISE OF SADDUCEE TEACHING

We need to understand why the Sadducees believed as they did even if we disagree with them. In spite of Jesus's firm denial of their contentions and his agreement with the Pharisees on the matter of the resurrection, his confrontations with the Pharisees are far more numerous and severe. Pharisees are prime agents in the rise of Sadducees as shall be explained more fully in a later chapter.

The Pharisaic misuse of belief in an afterlife ("pie in the sky when you die") must have been present in biblical times, too. Karen Armstrong tells us how this use of heaven and hell led her out of the Christian faith:

> I think I can safely say that as a child my religious life was ruined by the notion of the afterlife. I was obsessed with the fear of Hell. The nuns at my convent school instructed me in the Catholic doctrine of mortal sin, which seemed perilously easy to commit. If you died with one unshriven and unrequited mortal sin on your soul, you would languish in Hell for all eternity. Religion, as far as I could see, was chiefly concerned with "getting into Heaven."[10]

She thought that to avoid hell and attain heaven one must acquire merit. To acquire merit one must obey the rules and the law. The compulsive need for confidence in one's own righteousness, a particularly unattractive characteristic, is the consequence of the teaching she received. It is not only spiritually dangerous but singularly unbecoming. This doubtless was a factor in the Sadducee reaction against some Pharisees and their holier-than-thou witness. One can imagine a context in which the Saducean ideals seem quite attractive when contrasted with the self-righteousness of Pharisees. The apparent threat to human freedom by the existence and intervention of spirits and angels would likewise be off-putting to intellectual and aristocratic citizens with materialistic as-

9. A much needed correction to this widespread mistake is being done through the scholarship of Berman, Witte, and Alexander. Witte and Alexander, eds., *Teachings of Modern Christianity in Law, Politics, and Human Nature*. See also their *Festschrift* for Berman, *Weightier Matters of the Law*.

10. Karen Armstrong, "Is Immortality Important?," *Harvard Divinity Bulletin* 34 (2006) 20.

sumptions about reality. The position of the Sadducees was also delicately balanced between limited Jewish freedom and totalitarian Roman rule, which made them suspicious of (and hostile to) Jesus and his destabilizing band of followers.

Since the eighteenth century, Sadducean secularism has had an unprecedented cultural atmosphere in which to thrive. Materialistic inferences, including Newtonian physics and the rejection of divine revelation during the Enlightenment, the development of power over nature during the Industrial Revolution, the invention of the silicone chip and artificial intelligence during the computer age, and the emergence of embryonic stem cell research and genetic cloning in the age of modern medical research have all stimulated our human tendency to autonomy (being a law unto itself) as perhaps never before in human history.

Whatever the factors influencing the rise of Western secularism, the notion of human autonomy tends to make Christian faith irrelevant. However, it also leaves a wistful sadness in the human heart as illustrated by Matthew Arnold's "Dover Beach."

> The sea of faith
> Was once, too, at the full, and round earth's shore
> Lay like the folds of a bright girdle furled;
> But now I only hear
> Its melancholy, long withdrawing roar . . .
> Ah, love, let us be true
> To one another! For the world, which seems
> To lie before us like a land of dreams,
> So various, so beautiful, so new,
> Hath really neither joy, nor love, nor light,
> Nor certitude, nor peace, nor help for pain;
> And we are here as on a darkling plain
> Swept with confused alarms of struggle and flight,
> Where ignorant armies clash by night.[11]

Some theologians in England now applaud the sucking sound of this long departing faith. Those of us who live in "Its melancholy, long withdrawing roar . . ." need to attend to Jesus's warning even more than the disciples did. In spite of the enormous scientific advances of the twentieth century, this yeast has produced unprecedented tyranny and death in the name of hopes limited to the confines of this world. These

11. Priestly and Spier, eds., *Adventures in English Literature*, 544–45.

hopes are based not on facts but on opinions and conjectures. Anyone living near the ocean knows that tides go out and also return. The tide that carried out the Christian faith is returning, but it is composed of a complex and lethal mixture of neo-pagan and yet unknown dark powers. Under the influence of this contemporary yeast, whatever hopes men and women might have for justice and for what is right are to be found within history alone.

That remarkable man, Thomas Jefferson, is an example of commitment to a limited hope. He was deeply influenced by the French Enlightenment and for too long remained a supporter of the French Revolution even in the face of its horrors. He compiled his own version of the New Testament by eliminating all miracles and passages that might suggest that Jesus Christ was more than a mere man, and he ended his gospel with Jesus's dead body in the sepulcher. Modern secular historians err in calling all the early leaders of our country deists. Jefferson, however, does more closely represent that closed clockwork view of the universe than does George Washington, Benjamin Franklin, James Madison, John Adams, James Wilson, Gouvernor Morris, Alexander Hamilton, or John Witherspoon.

The issue of faith held by the founding fathers is complex and reading contemporary secular assumptions into the eighteenth century is unhelpful. Human nature is remarkably capable of holding inconsistent views. Even Thomas Jefferson could say: "When I consider that God is just, I tremble for my country," even if it did not lead him to tremble for himself.[12]

IGNORANCE AND NAIVETÉ CONCERNING THE DEEPER ROOTS OF EVIL

Jefferson's denigration of theism, with his hopes confined to this world, carried with it a concomitant naiveté about sin. His blindness to the fallibility of man is nowhere better disclosed than in Robert Penn Warren's long poem, *Brother to Dragons*. Jefferson had two nephews, Isham and Lilburne Lewis, sons of his sister, Lucy. In December 1811, these young men committed an unspeakable murder of a slave, George, who had accidentally broken their mother's pitcher. Their act is a matter of record.

---

12. A good short description of this matter with references can be found in McDougall, *Freedom Just Around the Corner.*

The murder occurred just prior to the horrendous earthquake that shook the entire Mississippi valley.

The brothers were arrested and released on bond. In a suicide pact they agreed to shoot each other over their mother's grave. Lilburne was killed but Isham's fate is unknown. Robert Penn Warren takes poetic license in this work to ask Jefferson why he had never mentioned in any of his writings, public or private, this horrible event that occurred in his own family. "Did you not care?" Warren asks. The poem leaves no doubt that Jefferson cared greatly and felt deeply but he could only cling to his Enlightenment assumptions: "And my heart crunched like a chick in a sow's jaw. I said I must cling more sternly to the rational hope" (an example of man's need to cling to hope).[13] This inability of the rational hope to acknowledge the evil in man and the world was a lie that Meriwether Lewis later claimed made him unprepared for the world.

Meriwether Lewis was Jefferson's kinsman, secretary, and indomitable, courageous explorer with Captain George Clark. Some years after their heroic trek across the continent and back he apparently took his own life in Tennessee while on his way to Washington to face criticism as Governor of the Louisiana Territory. Warren pictures Lewis confronting Jefferson, calling his too rosy picture of human nature a lie:

> Had I not loved, and lived your lie, then I
> Had not been sent unbuckled and unbraced
> To find, in the end—oh, the wilderness was easy!
> But to find, in the end, the tracklessness of the human heart[14]

Not the wilderness of the West but the tractless wilderness of the human heart left Lewis defenseless against reality.

THE KEY THAT SECULARIZES THE WORLD

Owen Chadwick's *The Secularization of the European Mind in the 19th Century* (reprinted four times since 1975) discloses the crucial assumption in Sadducee teaching by a quotation from the English historian and writer, John Morley (1838–1923), himself one of the major influences on the secularization of Western culture. "Human nature is good. This, said

13. Warren, *Brother to Dragons*, 135.
14. Ibid., 184.

Morley, is the key that secularizes the world."[15] The goodness of human nature is one of the half-truths that is the foundation of secularization. We are indeed made in the image of God, but we have rebelled against him and are at odds with each other. Human beings are distressingly fallible, corruptible, self-justifying, and self-damaging.

F. W. Dillistone, the Oxford scholar, makes a similar point in his description of how the reality and depth of human sin led T. S. Eliot to a deeper sense of Christian hope than that held by Jefferson. Dillistone describes Eliot's perception of what is unknowable and unacknowledged through the lens of the Sadducees:

> It was not enough to focus attention, as his Puritan and Unitarian forebears had tended to do, upon particular moral offenses which could be defined and condemned and avoided. There were deeper roots of evil in the human condition, a *negativity* expressed by symbols of loneliness, numbness, purposelessness, meaninglessness; a *futility* expressed by symbols of sterility, aridity, vacuity; an *impurity* expressed by symbols of disease, infection, contamination. No system of external rules and punishments could deal with this deep-seated ailment. Only some form of death . . . could bring it to an end and in so doing make possible a new beginning (italics mine).[16]

As there is a correlation between the Sadducees' naïve trust in human nature and their reliance on inevitable progress, so there is a correlation between the realization of our tragic and intractable condition (sin and death) and the trust in the Easter resolution. Eliot's confidence was, in large part, in this correlation of a profoundly realistic perception of our flawed human condition with the liberating trust in the death and resurrection of the Savior.

The Sadducee's trust is credible only if one defines the world as without negativity, futility, and impurity. Or if such things are recognized, confidence must be placed in the power of human will to overcome them. St. Augustine called it the Pelagian's "cruel praise" of human nature that the self-centered flaw in one's nature can be repaired by a determined will. The fundamental confidence of the Sadducee is this Pelagian hope. One must be naïve about the fact of sin and cast a blind eye on the reality of evil in order to embrace this hope.

15. Chadwick, *Secularization of the European Mind in the 19th Century*, 152.

16. Dillistone, *Religious Experience and Christian Faith*, 63.

An example of this naïveté concerning human frailty is seen in the pervasive influence of Ayn Rand. She writes:

> My philosophy, in essence, is the concept of man as a heroic being, with his own happiness as the moral purpose of his life, with productive achievement as his noblest activity, and reason as his only absolute.[17]

She rejects any belief in the supernatural and insists that man's reason is fully competent to deal with reality. She is oblivious to the inability of reason to overcome human bias or distortions of justice or reason's ability to justify evil. Where was she when the atrocities of the twentieth century were perpetrated and justified by man's reason? She knew nothing of Luther's wisdom about the capacity of reason to be "the devil's whore." Denying any transcendence leaves her and her devotees bereft of any superior hope than human reason.

Leaders of our economy, following the incredibly naïve trust in "rational self-interest" as taught by Ayn Rand, were blindsided by *ir*rational greed on the part of bankers, brokers, mortgage lenders, and mortgage holders as well as the utopian dreams of politicians. The god of Rand's "reason as the only absolute" died in the recession of 2008, leaving myriad victims, both guilty and innocent. Ideas do have consequences.

Milton Friedman and other influential economists, along with Ayn Rand, are victims of this naïve trust in "rational self-interest" with little or no government regulations as that which fuels our economy. At the same time trust in regulations can be equally naïve given the inefficiency of bureaucracies and human nature's ingenuity in finding loop holes. Under the influence of Sadducean yeast, Christian teaching of selflessness in the use of power or the pursuit of greed is not an option. The irony is that Christianity is usually dismissed as naïve by the ultra naive secularists who trust in "human rational self-interest," a trust that has brought financial calamity to the nation and world.

Certainly, rational self-interest was not the motivation of those who risked life and livelihood to found this country. Nor did they have any such trust in "reason as the only absolute." They were led by the learned Presbyterian divine, John Witherspoon (1723–1794), president of Princeton, signer of the Declaration of Independence, and teacher of James Madison and others, who insisted on the separation of powers

17. Rand, *Atlas Shrugged*, 1074.

because human reason is not a reliable trust. Eric McKitrick and Stanley Elkins describe him as "the greatest teacher of his day in America" and exhibiting "a judicious pessimism about most aspects of human nature."[18]

Professor John Witte, commenting on the loss of balance between human dignity and human capacity for evil, writes:

> Such views take too little account of the radicality of human sin and the necessity of divine grace. They give too little credibility to the inherent human need for discipline and order, accountability and judgment . . . They give too little insight into the necessity for safeguarding every office of authority from abuse and misuse. A theory of human dignity that fails to take into account the juxta-posed depravity and sanctity of the human person is theologically deficient, and politically dangerous.[19]

Andrew Delbanco's *The Death of Satan* is a disturbing history expressed in the subtitle: *How Americans Have Lost the Sense of Evil*. Delbanco's concern is that with the loss of such old words and moral concepts as "Satan, sin and evil" an atmospheric vacuum is left into which "Satan, always receding and always sought after"[20] is bound to return. If he does return as a fundamentalist, demonized force external to human nature, it will be truly diabolical, according to Delbanco. On the other hand, if he is perceived, as in the thought of "Edwards, Emerson, Niebuhr, and King," as a symbol of "our potential for envy and rancor toward creation," it can result in "the miraculous paradox of demanding the best of ourselves." Delbanco's attempt to recover an appropriate awareness of evil in American history is much needed but it ends with no deeper solution to counter evil than a Pelagian hope of "demanding the best of ourselves."[21]

One of my most embarrassing experiences occurred while teaching an adult class several years ago at Grace Church in New York City. I had been given M. Scott Peck's book, *The Road Less Traveled*, and I had read, with great approval and excitement, much of it. The author, an articulate and thoughtful psychiatrist, had "slipped the surly bonds" of psychological determinism and begun to appreciate the spiritual realities of grace.

---

18. Elkins and McKitrick, *Age of Federalism*, 85–86.
19. Witte, *God's Joust, God's Justice*, 58.
20. Delbanco, *Death of Satan*, 234.
21. Guinness, *Unspeakable: Facing up to Evil in an Age of Genocide and Terror*.

He even quoted the whole of John Newton's powerful hymn, "Amazing Grace."

I had heartily recommended the book to the class without having read the last third of it. The next Sunday I was pinned to the wall with quote after quote from the class as to Peck's astonishing identification of our unconscious self with God (e.g., "Since the unconscious is God all along we may further define the goal of spiritual growth to the attainment of godhood by the conscious self.").[22] He uses all the religious words of grace and God but his trust was that our unconscious is God and is trustworthy. This book became one of the all-time best sellers while Peck himself, in the face of the tragic realities of his own patients and his own life, found he could no longer trust in human nature's unconscious, much less see it as God. Our unconscious is every bit in need of healing as our conscious self.

In 1983, Peck published *People of the Lie: The Hope for Healing Human Evil* in which he describes the lies and evil that often come from the very "unconscious self" that he had previously trusted as God. In the preface he describes his baptism in 1980. "My commitment to Christianity is the most important thing in my life and is, I hope, pervasive and total."[23]

His Sadducee trust in human nature (our unconscious as God) could not withstand the clinical reality of our destructive capacities for evil. Unfortunately, this more hopeful and realistic book has not enjoyed the uncritical popularity of his previous work that encouraged trust in one's deeply flawed unconscious.

Shortly before Peck's death he was interviewed by David Neff of "Christianity Today" and offered this observation:

> You know, we look at young children, and we rejoice in their smooth skin and spontaneity, but they're also all born liars, cheats, thieves, and manipulators. And it's hardly remarkable that many of them grow up to be adult liars, cheats, thieves, and manipulators. What's much more difficult to explain is why some of them grow up to be honest, God-fearing people. Saint Paul talked about "the mystery of iniquity," and this is all mysterious stuff. Evil is a great mystery. But it pales, as far as I'm concerned, before the mystery of goodness, which is the even greater mystery.[24]

22. Peck, *Road Less Traveled*, 283.
23. Peck, *People of the Lie*, 11.
24. Peck, *Christianity Today*, 85.

Having raised four children, as well as having a mirror and a memory, it is clear to me that our nature desperately needs to be domesticated but, even more so, to be transformed. As G. K. Chesterton observed: "Certain new theologians dispute original sin, which is the only part of Christian theology which can really be proved."[25] Yet the Saducean faith in this world tends to infect and blind the eyes of even the most intelligent and scholarly people. *Suffering* (1975), written by Dr. Dorothee Soelle, emeritus professor at Union Theological Seminary in New York, deliberately excludes any consideration of hope or grace from outside the boundaries of history, or anything that transcends the conditions of our natural lives. With the jettisoning of the Christian trust, she has certainly warranted her place in the Sadducee ward and left us with a pale trust in human nature (and, in her case, the hope of Karl Marx). She is not alone. The erstwhile official publishing company of the Episcopal Church, Seabury Press, produced a number of books written by clergy, which deny any hope of eternal life.[26]

"For historians (and that includes a number of Christian historians as well) supernaturalism is simply not a live option."[27] These are the words of Van A. Harvey, professor emeritus of religious studies at Stanford University and the author of *The Historian and the Believer* (1996). The Saducean atmosphere is so pervasive that he presumes to speak not only for himself but for everyone else, too.

Such prominent theological scholars as Gordon Kaufman, Schubert Ogden, Rosemary Radford Ruether, and others not only deny the hope of resurrection, and the very idea of heaven, but also claim that such hopes are deplorable machinations of self-interest. Trust in Jesus's resurrection and in life after death, the source of moral perseverance and enduring trust of Christians for centuries, has now been cast aside and replaced by skepticism. This trust has become, in the yeast-infected eyes of many modern theologians, an unworthy escape from responsibilities in this world into the selfish haven of heaven. Justification is claimed for relinquishing hope of an afterlife because such hope might deter the efforts toward justice in this world. This claim has been ably countered by C. S. Lewis:

---

25. Chesterton, *Orthodoxy*, 115.
26. E.g., Adams, *Sting of Death*; Rogan, *Campus Apocalypse*; Gatch, *Death*.
27. Harvey, *Christian Century*, 91–92.

> If you read history you will find that the Christians who did most for the present world, were just those who thought most of the next . . . It is since Christians have largely ceased to think of the other world that they have become so ineffective in this. Aim at Heaven and you get earth "thrown in": aim at earth and you will get neither.[28]

The illustration of William Wilberforce and the evangelical Clapham Sect, with their tireless heroic efforts to abolish the slave trade (and eventually the practice of slavery itself), child labor, and other worthwhile endeavors, comes to mind.

Francis Fukuyama is an example of one who has replaced trust in God with trust in human nature. In his book, *The Great Disruption: Human Nature and the Reconstitution of Social Order* (1999), he declares himself in agreement with the alarming diagnosis of the decadent drift of Western culture as expressed by Bork, Himmelfarb, Carter, et al., listed in the first chapter. He is, however, not at all dismayed because of his optimistic and naïve trust that human nature will correct itself. His hope does not include religion: "Rather than integrating society, a conservative religious revival might in fact accelerate the movement toward fragmentation"; and the "only reason for hope is the very powerful innate human capacity for reconstituting social order. On the success of this process of reconstruction depends the upward direction of the arrow of History."[29]

A small cloud seems to have formed over that confidence in his more recent book, *Our Posthuman Future: Consequences of the Biotechnology Revolution*. He now expresses some dark fears consequent on what a biotechnological revolution can do to our culture and to our species:

> We declared in 1776 this principle that all men are created equal and then we gradually fulfilled it. Genetic engineering has the power to undo all that we have accomplished, in fact creating different classes of people who would not be by nature equal and therefore not entitled to equal rights . . . you don't want to do things that turn people into gods or sub humans, in effect.[30]

28 Lewis, *Mere Christianity*, 134. Wall's *Heaven* is a rigorous Christian claim against the Sadducean hopes of the academic world. His critique of such influential anti-Christians as Hume, Feuerbach, Nietzsche, Russell, and two contemporaries, Sagan and Singer, is exceedingly valuable.

29. Fukuyama, *Great Disruption and the Faith of Our Fathers*, quoted from *Atlantic Magazine*.

30. Cromartie, "Books and Culture."

"Who doesn't want to?" was the question Fukayama was asked in an interview with Michael Cromartie:

> Cromartie: Are there limitations to this idea that human nature can provide the normative ground in the coming age of biotechnology? Fukuyama: Well there's religion. I have a long chapter, which I regard as the central chapter in my book, on human dignity, in which I try to explain what that means in secular terms. But you could do it just as easily by saying that man was created in the image of God. It may have been easier to simply take that line of argument.[31]

As a member of the scholarly elite in America, Fukuyama could not bring himself to include even such a tentative break with the Sadducean assumption as would "explain what that means in secular terms." As the son of a Methodist minister he does seem to have breathed in childhood the air of transcendent trust: "Well, there's religion." (But this higher trust is explicitly absent from his works except when he dismisses it because it will "accelerate the movement toward fragmentation.") Mention of such hope occurs only when interviewed for a Christian publication.

A more thoroughgoing example of the Sadducee is Steve Bruce. His work, *God is Dead: Secularization in the West*, casts doubt on the whole idea that secularization and the decline of religion since the Middle Ages has actually occurred. Bruce gives an overview that goes a long way toward establishing the contemporary fact of secularization, even if the piety and faith of previous generations may be exaggerated. For Steve Bruce, the point is that Matthew Arnold's retreating sea of faith with its melancholy, long withdrawing roar is not cause for lament but for rejoicing.

The accelerating movement of secularism is producing a large fraternity of aggressive atheists denouncing Christianity. In addition to Bruce, Sam Harris's *The End of Faith* (2004), Christopher Hitchens's *God is Not Great: How Religion Poisons Everything* (2007), and Richard Dawkins's *The God Delusion* (2007) are enraged assaults on Christianity. When there was more confidence in the secular hope, the general attitude toward Christianity was a somewhat benign condescension to what was considered a primitive, outmoded, and obsolete belief that is withering away. With the growing loss of secular confidence and the presence of formidable and impressive Christian witnesses, these aggressive atheists

---

31. Fukuyama is the author of *End of History*.

are not content merely to disbelieve. They increasingly have the need to attack something they don't believe exists. These attacks are not new. Blaise Pascal (1623–1662) observed: "Men despise religion; they hate it and are afraid it is true."[32]

On the other end of the spectrum is Edward Norman's book, *Secularization* (2002). Writing (at that time) as an English Anglican, he is profoundly aware of the corrosive acids of secularization (the Sadducee yeast) especially upon Europe and England. Advancing a biblical perspective and exemplifying the best of contemporary theological rigor, he sees the vitality of Christian faith flourishing globally and gives us profound perspectives on our current condition:

> Modern preachers or teachers who are skeptical of miraculous events in the life of Christ rob the religion they seek to serve of its authority—for Revelation is the bridge between time and eternity, the window on another world. In this sense, if in no other, secularized understandings of Christianity destroy the faith from within.[33]

This Christian faith needs to be stated clearly in order to establish its distinctiveness from secularism. Professor Eric Mascall in an earlier work on the subject, *The Secularization of Christianity* (1965), shows that the Christian

> is concerned with man's life as a member of "another world," . . . [and] sees his final destiny as lying in that "other world" and beyond bodily death . . . [The Christian] will associate that "other world" with a beneficent Creator, upon whose will "this world" is dependent for its existence and its preservation and in union with whom his own beatitude will consist.[34]

This is what the secularist/Sadducee has given up.

Mascall saw, before many of us did, the cancer of the Sadducee yeast, not merely in the culture but also in the Church.[35] Secularization "is not a reinterpretation of the Christian religion but a substitute for it" and he deplores the "failure of nerve which has stamped many contemporary theologians into a total intellectual capitulation to their secular

32. Pascal, *Pensees*, 52.

33. Norman, *Secularization*, 70.

34. Mascall, *Secularization of Christianity*, 191.

35. Especially in such theologians as Van Buren, Robinson, and Knox.

environment."[36] We cannot say we were not warned when Jesus told us to "take heed, beware the yeast of the Sadducee."

An outstanding treatment of secularism is Christian Smith's *The Secular Revolution: Power, Interest, and Conflict in the Secularization of American Public Life*. This remarkable critique is, ironically, the product of scholars in sociology, a field originated by Auguste Comte (1798–1857), one of the fathers of secularism. Its eleven authors acknowledge that the secularization of American public life has long been considered an inevitable outcome of modernization. However, they reject this assumption. They show that the declining authority of religion was not some necessary product of modernization but rather the intentional achievement of cultural and intellectual elites who sought to gain control of social institutions, thereby increasing their own authority and control. Human tensions (self-as-center), conflicts, and decisions, instead of some impersonal inevitability, have brought about the Sadducean cancer in education, science, politics, religion, the judiciary, journalism, and medicine.

A most comprehensive treatment of secularism is *The Secular Age* by Charles Taylor. In more than 800 pages Taylor describes in carefully balanced descriptions the different forms of the secular, its contributions and weaknesses. He shows how Christianity produced a non-religious form of secularism and also how the latter has never altogether disentangled itself from the religion that gave it birth. Taylor himself is a Christian and he shows the crippling effect in all human endeavors when transcendent reality is denied or lost. Capitulation to secularism, what Jesus warned us against, has become an almost universal assumption of Westerners. Its believers rarely acknowledge that their belief is based solely on materialistic conjecture or that nothing exists beyond this world.

The examples of blinding arrogance and culture-destroying yeast of the Sadducee presents biblical Christians with a serious temptation to overlook the great text in John 3:16: "For God so loved the world that he gave his only Son, that whoever believes in him should not perish but have eternal life." Although we must not take our agenda from the world and merely reflect it, we must not forget it is the world that God loves. As parents love their unruly and self-damaging teenagers, Christians are to be the very instruments of God's love to this very needy world.

---

36. Mascall, *Secularization of Christianity*, 282.

One small but telling illustration of the sadness of the Sadducee is the reaction to a little known classic about a young Jewish woman in a Nazi concentration camp, Etty Hillesum's *Letters From Westerbork*. It is reminiscent of the better known *Diary of Anne Frank;* although, Etty was older than Anne. Etty's diary and letters, written under the cloud of her impending execution, are truly inspiring. They exude a depth of faith in God in the midst of horrifying historical hopelessness. Her help to others, encouragement, perseverance, comfort, and even episodes of joy show a remarkable and explicit faith in God. Her story is deeply moving.

The reviewer of this book in the *Times Literary Supplement* acknowledges the extraordinary life of this woman whose faith surmounted the indescribable horrors of the Nazi holocaust. He wrote the following:

> It is an extraordinary human document, so extraordinary in fact that I had to pause every now and again to ask if it could be authentic. By the end I felt it didn't matter for if this is a work of fiction it is a work of such imagination and power as to have the validity of fact . . . I have been torn by conflicting emotions in reading this book, but finally put it down with a feeling of awe. Like Job, Etty revives one's faith in man, though it diminishes one's faith in God.[37]

The reviewer of this remarkable story of a young woman's ministry and faith in God is so blinded by the Sadducean yeast that this moving story of a martyr among Nazi atrocities evokes not faith in God but faith in man. This comes close to doing what Job did not do: curse God (consign to oblivion). Were the Nazis not men? Certainly Etty's faith was not in men but in the God who gave her hope, in spite of man's horrifying capacity for and execution of evil. The reviewer's sad hope in humanity lies in stark contrast to the trust that characterizes Etty's letters, her faith, her life, and her remarkable joy and selflessness amidst man's perpetration of unspeakable horror.

If our hope lies in human ability to make all things right, the tendency is to believe that some historical action, program or ideal could bring the ultimate victory for which everyone yearns. No matter how commendable and beneficial such programs or ideals, they will inevitably become occasions of dangerous and destructive idols as we shall see in the next chapter.

---

37. Hillesum, *Letters from Westerbork*, quoted on flyleaf.

3

Idolatry

"Man's nature, so to speak, is a perpetual factory of idols."[1]

—John Calvin

WITH THE DENIAL OF resurrection and the loss of transcendent judgment, hopes this side of the grave become final hopes and therefore idolatrous. Jettisoning what Thomas Cranmer called the "sure and certain hope of eternal life" leaves these proximate hopes with no antidote to idolatry.

Idolatry flourishes especially in an age that tends to deny its reality. In today's world we tend to think of idolatry as primitive people making molten images and bowing down to them. But idolatry is often more subtle and sophisticated. The hope for a classless dictatorship of the proletariat became an idol for millions in the twentieth century. Human reason has become the idol of the followers of Ayn Rand.

As Lutheran theologian Gerhard Forde shows, when we trust an idea or construct an image that is amenable to our expectations and desires, it "is no different from making a god of wood or stone or bronze; it is simply idolatry, and it is born of unbelief."[2] Andre Malraux, war hero, scholar, novelist, French intellectual, and statesman, writes under the influence of the Sadducean yeast:

> The greatest mystery is not that we have been flung at random
> among the profusion of the earth and the galaxy of the stars, but in

1. Calvin, *Institutes of the Christian Religion*, 108.
2. Kimel, *Speaking the Christian God*, 114.

37

this prison we can fashion images of ourselves sufficiently powerful to deny our nothingness.[3]

To fashion images of ourselves is precisely what Scripture means by
idolatry. With such a pervasive temptation no wonder the first two of the
Ten Commandments are about idolatry. Scripture is replete with warnings against idols and idolatry.

The *Cambridge Biographical Encyclopedia*, in its article on Madonna
(the entertainer, not the mother of Jesus), says: "Her defiant and raun-
chy stage appearances became an important role model for teenagers in
the 1980's and 1990's, and her international success has been secured by
clever promotion and image-making." Words like role model and image
making contain unacknowledged religious content concerning human
identity and carry a virulent option for idolatry. A *New York Times* article
cited the widespread and growing use of surgery to improve appearances.
A reporter asked, "Who do all these surgically enhanced people want to
look like?" The surgeon replied, "Our religion is celebrity, and our gods
are celebrities . . . When we conform to the dictates of taste, that's who
we look to."[4] So-called celebrity idols are those whose lives and clothes
become models for thousands. Having Arnold Palmer's name on a set of
golf clubs, or Michael Jordan's name on basketball shoes, enhances their
sales enormously.

". . . they made idols for their own destruction." (Hos 8:4)

Herbert Schlossberg used this text to write an exhaustive and perceptive treatment of idols: *Idols for Destruction: Christian Faith and Its
Confrontation with American Society.* He skillfully shows the permutations
of our current idolatry of history, humanity, mammon, nature, power, and
religion. One of his many telling illustrations is that of August Comte, the
nineteenth-century father of sociology, who gave that discipline not only
its name but also its major assumptions that advocated the worship of the
Great Being, defined as humanity past, present and future.[5]

Schlossberg does not spare religion, pointing out the constant
refrain of the [biblical] prophetic message that the priests, prophets,
and teachers had prostituted themselves and turned to the service of

3. Friedman, *To Deny Our Nothingness.* Quotation from title page.

4. *New York Times,* May 2, 2004.

5. Schlossberg, *Idols for Destruction,* 41.

evil. He quotes Alexander Schmemann, who pointed out that people tend to be unaware that their normal Sunday worship service repudiates the culture they daily uphold as their way of life. The attempt to be contemporaneous, or relevant, ensures the irrelevance of theologies and churches. The warning attributed to William Inge, the Dean of St. Paul's Cathedral, is important: "He who marries the spirit of the age will find himself a widower in the next."[6]

Idolatry can be very subtle, and we are understandably tempted by it when it contains something good. Great and wonderful ideals have seduced whole nations into idolizing proximate hopes with devastating results. Reason is one of the most subtle idols. Jacques Ellul claimed that it became the god of this world. A critique of the idolatry of reason is not to disparage it but to see its limitations, a human faculty as flawed as any other faculty.

We can examine four illustrations of societies that suffered the consequences from failing to acknowledge reason's limitations (or as Luther observed in his characteristic earthiness: "reason is the devil's whore"). Consider, for example, the very birth place of rational knowledge: classical Greece, especially the Athens of Socrates, Plato, and Aristotle. Describing the Golden Age of Pericles, Professor P. R. Dodds writes:

> The next thirty-odd years witnessed a series of heresy trials which is unique in Athenian history. The victims included most of the leaders of progressive thought at Athens—Anazagoras, Diagoras, Socrates, almost certainly Protagoras, also, and possibly Euripides . . . All these were famous people. How many obscurer persons may have suffered for their opinions we do not know. But the evidence we have is more than enough to prove that the Great Age of Greek enlightenment as also, like our own time, an Age of Persecution—banishment of scholars, blinkering of thought, and even . . . burning of books.
>
> This distressed and puzzled nineteenth century professors, who had not our advantage of familiarity with this kind of behavior. It puzzled them the more because it happened at Athens, the "school of Hellas," the "headquarters of philosophy," and, so far as our information goes, nowhere else.[7]

6. "Context," March 15, 1997.

7. Dodds, *Greeks and the Irrational*, 189.

Another example comes from the center of rationalism—France in the eighteenth century, the Age of Enlightenment. "Liberty, Equality, and Fraternity" is an invigorating and refreshing ideal in any age, but it was especially so in eighteenth-century France. The context of monarchial tyranny, ecclesiastical corruption, aristocratic arrogance ("Let them eat cake."), and rigorous social structures was a mixture into which the volatile idea came and ignited the explosion of the Revolution. Who could quarrel with such a goal? Such a good? Such an ideal? But when the Christian symbols, which pointed to transcendent truth, were torn down and replaced by the goddess of Reason, the streets soon ran red with blood in the Reign of Terror.

When the best hopes and ideals of human history have no transcendent light or judgment shed upon them they will inevitably become idols and wreak havoc on their worshippers. Ironically, liberty, equality, and fraternity to be established by the goddess Reason was never even approximated. From the beginning it was denied by the revolution. Liberty was never accorded to any who criticized the revolution. Fraternity was far less prevalent than fratricide. The only equality was that no one, regardless of social rank, could hope for a fair trial.

A recent advocate of trust in reason, who attributes the ills of history and humanity to religion, is Sam Harris, whom we mentioned in chapter 2. His book is a serious 300-page scholarly work devoted, in the most part, to his hope that human reason is a solution to the problem humanity faces. That this hope was expressed and acted upon in the French Revolution is not mentioned. One is tempted to observe that the omission is not reasonable. The ideas and human hopes that spawned the French Revolution are tempting idols for us today.

Idolatry of a good idea in eighteenth-century France was echoed with another good idea in twentieth-century Germany.

> In the first forty years of the twentieth century one single nation enjoyed the acknowledged intellectual leadership of the world. Its language was indispensable to anyone specializing in the sciences, philosophy, or scholarly pursuits generally. Yet in the space of five years this same language had made itself despised in most of Europe as the language of brutes and tyrants who had perverted their brilliant intellectual achievements to the irrational, diabolic service of "blood and soil."[8]

8. Cherbonnier, *Hardness of Heart*, 151.

Idolatry

The Third Reich in Germany promised a rule of law to bring peace to a Europe whose nations had warred with each other over centuries like the self-destructive children in William Golding's *Lord of the Flies* (1954). This ideal of stability was more enticing to Europeans than Americans are apt to appreciate. Only the Roman Empire in reality and the Holy Roman Empire in ideal had promised such peace. The history of Europe is virtually synonymous with warfare. In the Balkan countries peace came only by tyranny. Throughout the history of Europe scarcely have there been two consecutive decades without the outbreak of war. Now the Germans (and who else could?) promised order and peace. Many within the German church, and many German scholars in general, were unable to see clearly because their sight was blurred by secular assumptions. With little perception of God's final justice and accountability, many were paralyzed into doing nothing in the face of Hitler and Nazi atrocities. Only the hope of transcendent justice was adequate to bring light and courage in the face of the horrible Nazi means taken to bring about their ends of rule and order. Those who did protest, such as Karl Barth, Dietrich Bonhoeffer, and the signers of the Barmen Declaration,[9] did so by unclouded trust in a resurrection faith that would judge even the most popular of seemingly worthy causes. Characteristic of Sadducee sickness in people, according to T. S. Eliot, is that they fear the injustice of men more than the justice of God.

"From each according to his abilities, to each according to his needs" (Karl Marx). Was there ever a loftier slogan or a more effective one in seducing the intellectual and scholarly communities of Western civilization and leaders of Asian countries? Arthur Koestler described it in his book, *The God That Failed*:

> The necessary lie, the necessary slander; the necessary intimidation of the masses to preserve them from shortsighted errors; the necessary liquidation of oppositional groups and hostile classes; the necessary sacrifice of a whole generation in the interest of the next—it may all sound monstrous, and yet it was so easy to accept while rolling along the single track of faith.[10]

This proximate hope, made absolute in a climate that believed man would prevail, was, as Koestler called it, a god, a single track of faith and

9. A statement in Barmen, Germany in 1934 by confessing Lutheran theologians objecting to the liberal leaders accommodating Christianity to the age, e.g., Nazism.

10. Koestler, *God That Failed*, 61.

one that failed. It failed largely because of the concomitant blindness of secularism to the pervasiveness of sin. Why do we not give according to our abilities? Because being self-centered we tend to be greedy, selfish, and remarkably able to justify these sins. If people do not give as they are able, they must be made to do so. And who is going to make the makers do so? The fatal flaw in the Communist ideal, which in large part brought down the iron curtain, was its naiveté regarding the flaws in human nature. Our overwhelming self-centeredness meant that dedication to the collective could never compete with dedication to self-interest.

The ideal of Communism was more appealing to many than the ideal of National Socialism. Yet Communism produced more murder and mass destruction than the estimated twenty million deaths as a result of Nazism. In a review of Stephane Courtois' *Le Livre Noir Du Communisme* (1997), Martin Malia makes an impressive case for the fact that Communism's evil far exceeded that of the Nazis, but it still lacks any popular acknowledgment.

> Any realistic accounting of Communist crime would effectively shut the door on utopia; and too many good souls in our unjust world *cannot abandon hope* for an end to inequality. And so, all comrade-questers after historical truth should gird their loins for a very long march indeed before Communism is accorded its fair share of absolute evil (italics mine).[11]

The Sadducees cannot abandon hope and they will inevitably place their trust in this world's aims and not the purposes of God. The academic establishment has been generally described as more tolerant of Communist tyranny than Fascist tyranny. Seeking justification to excuse the former, someone asked Tolstoy to explain the difference between left-wing tyranny and right-wing tyranny. The novelist was reputed to have replied, "Oh, yes, there is a difference—like the difference between cat bleep and dog bleep." Reinhold Niebuhr, himself, is an example of this bias. "It must be admitted, however, that the moral cynicism and nihilism of romantic fascism is more unqualifiedly destructive than the provisional cynicism and ultimate utopianism of communism."[12]

When Western culture is dominated by secularism and pervaded by the yeast of this world-is-all-there-is-ism, idolatry becomes among

11. Malia, review of *Le Livre Noir Du Communism*.
12. Niebuhr, *Nature and Destiny of Man*, Vol. I, 52.

the most ignored and unrecognized of our sins. This idolatry has been especially virulent within the church. After serving for twelve years as Presiding Bishop of the Episcopal Church, John M. Allin made a "confession of sin" in his farewell speech to the General Convention that he had loved the church more than the Lord of the church. In that confession he spoke for many of us who find that we, too, are guilty of the idolatry of putting the church before the Lord of the church.

Any unqualified loyalty to an institution will result in idolatry, but the legitimate claim of the church to transcendence makes it an even more tempting, seductive, and pervasive object of idolatry. Any time a local congregation, denomination, or worldwide communion places the church above the Lord of the church, the result is idolatry and beneficial to none. Bishop Allin's confession should be a graceful example for us all.

THE DENIGRATION OF DOCTRINE

The air-lock, symbol of creeds, catechism, and articles, whose function is to protect us from idolatry, has been neglected and even denied as necessary. The official committee report of the House of Bishops of the Episcopal Church, chaired in 1967 by Bishop Stephen F. Bayne, Jr., was charged with the task of responding to Bishop James Pike's denial of the creedal affirmations of Christ and the Trinity. The committee recommended that "the word heresy should be abandoned" except in the case of controversies in "early formative years of Christian doctrine . . . [The word heresy] presumes to a measure of theological prejudgment which is inappropriate to the mature Christian community."[13] When Bishop Pike denied essential tenets of Christianity he was censured by the House of Bishops for his tone and manner and not for the substance of his teaching![14] The assumption that it was necessary to confront heresy in the early centuries of Christianity, but is unnecessary today because we are now mature, could scarcely be surpassed as a combination of ignorance and arrogance in the history of the church. The ignorance of contemporary examples of ancient heresies is matched by the arrogant assumptions that we mature moderns are not subject to the Bible's warnings about false teachings and wrong doctrine.

13. Bayne, *Theological Freedom and Social Responsibility*, 22–23.
14. Turner, "Pro Ecclesia," vol. 8:1.

The air-lock function is being neglected, not because the old heresies are mere matters of the past or that we are now a mature Christian community, but because the churches today are awash with false teaching. Our vaunted maturity is exposed in all its self-damage on countless psychiatrists' couches and in courtroom litigation. Nor are we immune to our distressing inclination to reproduce the doctrinal distortions of the past. In fact, Scripture warns us that the times will come

> when people will not endure sound teaching, but having itching ears they will accumulate for themselves teachers to suit their own likings and will turn away from listening to the truth and wander into myths (2 Tim 4:3–4; also cf. Heb 13:9; Eph 4:14; 2 John 9; Rom 16:17).

Samuel Johnson's observation that "patriotism is the last refuge of a scoundrel" indicates how a good thing, patriotism, without a commitment higher than one's country, can turn evil. My country, right or wrong, is my country can be a license for great wickedness. Hannah Arendt in her candid but compassionate treatment of Pius XII and his leadership during the Nazi years is quoted to the effect that Pius's legacy symbolizes a truth "that all religions should probably heed. It is that logic of institutional self-preservation may be incompatible with moral clarity."[15] This is true not only for all religions but for every institution: political, commercial, educational, or philanthropic.

An example of this institutional loyalty, which inhibits moral clarity, can be seen in the recent pederasty scandals in the Roman Catholic Church. But the principle extends to all churches and all institutions from hospitals, schools, the military, and Wall Street firms. Exempting institutions from accountability encourages the pervasive idolatry for the Sadducee whose confidence is devoid of any transcendence for judgment. The poet William Langland (1332–c.1400) warned us long ago of this dynamic in institutions:

> When the kindness of Constantine
>   gave Holy Church endowments
>   in lands and leases, lordships and servants,

---

15. Arendt, review of Hochhuth's *Pius XII.*

The Romans heard an angel cry on high above them,
"This day endowed Church has drunk venom
And all who hold Peter's power are poisoned forever."[16]

This venom tends to infect not only churches but all institutions. It can be cruel to an individual as well as an institution. Suppose a man has worked hard to build a successful business only to have some partners, or his son-in-law, take over and run the business into the ground. The disaster would be painful for anyone but particularly so for the Sadducee whose business is his ultimate hope. His hope is dashed as the business fails. A sacrificial loyalty to a business or institution, or even a church, seems heartlessly unappreciated and cruelly forgotten to an individual who is treated as dispensable after a lifetime of loyal service.

As we seek identity through things of this world, we inevitably refer to images of other flawed people: celebrity idols, revered scoutmasters, or favorite aunts. We will use such models for our lives, consciously or unconsciously. Our dignity and identity, however, is unique. Our true identity is not achieved by copying other people.

The "reasonable, religious, and holy hope"[17] enables us to get beyond dependence on other people or on our own accomplishments for our identity. This holy hope connects us to Christ who made us, redeemed us, and is saving us. An anchor is the church's symbol for this hope. Our identity is not defined by a Cambridge degree, a Marine Corps commission, a successful business career, or birth into an aristocratic or wealthy family. All are a half-bubble-off plumb and in need of redemption.

We may use any of these options for guidance and reassurance but none adequately defines us as human beings. Our identity rests on something much deeper. True hope is the anchor hooking us to one who can enable us to ride through the storms of disappointment, heartbreak, and disillusionment, as our idols crack and prove impotent as models for identity.

I recall taking three of my children fishing in a fourteen-foot boat when they were quite young. Most of the afternoon was spent nursing or untangling lines rather than fishing. While I was taking a fish off a line one child dropped an oar overboard. Another speared at it with the other oar and both oars went floating down the creek. We were 100 yards from

16. Tuchman, *Distant Mirror*, 6.
17. *Book of Common Prayer*, 489.

our dock, the tide was going out, and we were without oar or paddle. Fortunately, we did have an anchor with a long anchor line. I was able to throw it some distance in front of the boat, let it sink and catch, and haul in the line. With repeated throws and pulls we eventually reached the dock.

The anchor has been the Christian symbol of hope because it is hooked to a firm but unseen ground. "For in this hope we were saved. Now hope that is seen is not hope. For who hopes for what he sees? But if we hope for what we do not see, we wait for it with patience" (Rom 8:24–25). Sadducees have relinquished any hope for resurrection and eternal life. They have abandoned that which Christians do not see but are hooked to, Cranmer's "sure and certain hope." Christopher Wordsworth, Bishop of London and nephew of the poet, William Wordsworth, tells us why hope and faith lead us to love:

> Faith will vanish into sight;
> > hope be emptied in delight;
> > love in heaven will shine more bright;
> > therefore give us love.[18]

Until that consummation, the only connections we have with the unseen ground and final reality of love are faith and hope.

Medicine has a term, etiology, that refers to the study of causes, origins, or reasons for diseases or conditions. The etiology of human nature's universal tendency to idolatry is this very yeast of which Jesus warned us: the Sadducee denial of hope by which alone we have access to faith and by which we will know the sight, delight, and love promised in Wordsworth's hymn.

Whether a business, a family, an institution, one's own talent, or an ideal, we have seen how each could become for us the ultimate or last word. When that happens we are afflicted with idolatry and will, in time, be disappointed, hurt, embittered, or devastated. The medicine for this malady is a bigger and eternal trust as our hope, the Last Word, the Alpha and the Omega, Jesus Christ risen.

We resist this medicine, however, as long as idols are working for us. When they begin to crumble we defend them by finding scapegoats. Cain's reply to God, when asked about the murdered Abel, was, "am I my brother's keeper?"; Adam's reply to God about eating the forbidden fruit

18. *Hymns Ancient and Modern New Standard.*

was, "The woman whom you gave to be with me, she gave me fruit of the tree, and I ate." Eve's reply was, "The serpent beguiled me, and I ate." The buck stops at the serpent for all of us who are looking for scapegoats.

The larger object of our hope helps us acknowledge, without despair, the flaws and imperfections in the objects of our lesser hopes. The Sadducee in us leads us to defend our lesser hopes by blaming others or ourselves. Christian hope puts all lesser hopes and their inevitable ultimate disappointment in a graceful perspective. Rudyard Kipling showed a grasp of this wisdom in his poem, "If."

> If you can meet with triumph and disaster
> And treat those two imposters just the same; . . .[19]

An imposter is "one who deceives under an assumed identity." After his landslide victory over Barry Goldwater, President Lyndon Johnson carried around in his pocket the results of the Gallup Poll giving him an unprecedented favorable score. This triumph seemed to declare his true identity. It was an imposter.

Only a few years later, as the polls revealed a nose dive in President Johnson's popularity ratings, he sadly announced, as an almost broken man, his unwillingness to run for President again. This disaster was also an imposter that was unworthy of his true identity. He was much more than a popular president and much more than an unpopular president. Each triumph and each disaster in our lives are deceptions masking our true identity. To treat both triumphs and disasters as imposters, as deceivers, does not let either define us. Our identity and worth are anchored to a greater and unseen hope. Treating those two imposters just the same is a defiant claim that the Sadducee's world does not define us.

19. Kipling, *Poems*, 170.

4

Corruption of Morals and Art

If the dead are not raised, "Let us eat and drink, for tomorrow we die."

1 Corinthians 15:32

AESTHETICS AS WELL AS ethics have suffered alarmingly in recent history. Corruption, violence, and ugliness threaten the very concept of culture. Western civilization seems to have lost sight of its destination. The Oxford theologian Austin Farrer asked how we can make sense of the journey if we do not know where the road leads. How can we make sense of this alarming predicament in the light of Jesus's warning about denying the resurrection? Our Christian hope lies in a final and transcendent fulfillment. This, in turn, nurtures, disciplines, and gives meaning to our earthly and proximate hopes.

Forfeiting eternal hope corrupts our human enterprises. If someone is defeated in an election by immoral means, has one's moral striving been in vain and of no ultimate significance? Alabama's segregationist governor, George Wallace, was first defeated as a populist candidate by a segregationist opponent. Wallace's response was that "no one is ever going to out-seg me again." In a secularist society winning is what matters. If nothing exists beyond this world, there can be no final justice, forgiveness, or mercy. How the winning is accomplished is of no consequence. When good causes are defeated by immoral means why not join the wicked to assure success the next time? History has proven to be no reliable arbiter between good and evil. If there is no eternal purpose to our endeavors on the human journey why should they be good rather than evil?

A recent public broadcasting program concerning the current crisis in morals in our society cited the example of a doctor who was suspected of killing patients (later verified). He was given high recommendations in his transfer to another hospital where he continued his killing. Other examples cited were the widespread cheating by students whose parents defended this behavior, unacknowledged corruption in accounting firms and brokerage houses, and falsification in medical and scientific research. Experts spoke exhaustively on the immorality that is rampant in all aspects of society, on its causes, and possible cures. Needless to say, in our secularist culture no mention was made of the culture's loss of any sense of accountability or justice beyond this life.

The panel expressed great wonder at the notoriously unappreciative treatment given to whistle blowers. Reaction can be ruthless toward any who criticize an institution that assumes that it needs no accountability. No matter how accurate, criticism is often seen as malevolent to the institution in which people have placed their loyalty and life's commitment. Those whose ultimate commitment is to an institution are characteristically impervious, or even hostile, to criticism, instead of seeing it as a correction that may be needed for an efficient and healthy organization. Unqualified loyalty to an institution is incompatible with moral responsibility.

The panel is an example of not knowing where the journey leads. Assumption of heavenly judgment, "remembering the account we must one day give," the hallmark of Western civilization through most of its history, has been so eroded by Sadducean yeast or secularism that even a mere echo of St. Paul's warning can no longer be heard: "If the dead are not raised, 'Let us eat and drink, for tomorrow we die'" (1 Cor 15:32). Let us cheat and steal and, if not caught in this life, we will never be held responsible. An uncaught lie becomes the last word. And even if caught in a lie, subsequent accountability in this world is bereft of mercy in the next.

I once pointed out to a friend that if there were no final accounting the only check on misbehavior was the contemplation of being caught. She disagreed, claiming that guilt was still a deterrent; but guilt in contemporary sociopathic times is fast fading, like the smile of the Cheshire cat in *Alice in Wonderland*. She could have mentioned the Stoics.[1] Even Stoicism, with no belief in the resurrection, shares with Christianity an assumption that virtue is an essential aspect of human nature and that its violation diminishes the ultimate health and well being of any person.

---

1. Philosophy of the ancient Greek (Zeno) who taught that one should be free from passion and calmly accept all occurrences as fate.

Virtue (i.e., honesty, loyalty, responsibility, righteousness), to the Stoic, is an inexorable part of human identity as are the laws of nature that affect much that is happening in our bodies. Thus, virtue is ignored or violated at the expense of one's being. Consequently, for the Stoic, humans may possibly be motivated to virtue rather than immorality without any expectation of heavenly accountability. This aspect of Stoicism has long evoked profound respect. But the Stoic pays the price of passion, pity, mercy, and love. Fated necessity rules the world. In the drift of human nature, Stoic virtues are soon supplanted by cafeteria values and all objective standards tend to be drowned in an ocean of moral subjectivity. As virtues are reduced to values, values reduced to mere preferences, all objective standards are lost. Loyalty and morality are no longer seen as solid benchmarks for behavior but only as options for what seems to work for an individual.

Some distortions of Christianity, with their tit-for-tat heavenly rewards as motives for earthly virtue, promises of prosperity, "naming and claiming" material rewards, express a religion of less virtue than that of the Stoic. The latter is willing to do the right thing with no expectation of reward because of this belief in objective, if unseen, reality of virtues that are not mere preferences. But the promise of prosperity is a distressing distortion of the Christian hope. The whole Good Friday/Easter theme is one of utter and complete emptiness of self before God. The sure and certain hope that right will prevail is no longer in our hands or our timing, but in God's. (The treatment of distortions of Christianity will be taken up more fully in subsequent chapters regarding the Pharisee yeast.)

Rewards promised in Scripture are not motives for virtues but expressions of realistic and objective justice, an essential aspect of God Himself.[2] One can get a feel for this dynamic from Larry Doby who played baseball for the Cleveland Indians: "If the front office only knew, I love the game so much I'd play for nothing." "Grant that we may love that which thou commandest . . ." is the Christian prayer we too often forget. We hope that, like Larry Doby, we may love the game enough that we are not lured by rewards. We are merely grateful for the opportunity to play. God is not, however, like a stingy front office. God would not withhold His rewards from those who acted from love with no thought of reward. "For God is

2. Cf. Matt 6:4, 6, 18; 10:41, 42; 16:27; Mark 9:41; Luke 6:35; 2 John 8; Heb 10:35; Rev 11:18; 22:12.

not so unjust as to overlook your work and the love which you showed" (Heb 6:10).

Somehow, the false idea that it is not Christian to seek pleasure or to enjoy some endeavor has crept into popular misunderstandings of the faith. Ayn Rand was misled in this matter by her understanding of Immanuel Kant (d. 1804) and, as a result, rejected Christianity. John Piper, Baptist pastor, corrects the views of Kant and Rand by turning to the Epistle to the Hebrews:

> Every Sunday morning at 11 a.m., Hebrews 11:6 enters combat with Immanuel Kant. "Without faith it is impossible to please God. For whoever would draw near to God must believe that he exists and that *he is the rewarder of those who seek him.*[3]

On rare occasions we have perhaps seen someone completely and totally surprised by being given a well-deserved reward for outstanding service. Awards, given not in expectation or as a result of motives, are surprising byproducts of a life of unself-conscious service. I recall a meeting of hospice supporters where one woman was singled out in the crowd and given an inscribed silver bowl for her tender and untiring work with hospice patients. She was totally surprised. Her work had not had one scintilla of motive for reward other than the joy of serving others. Yet it was indeed deserved. This must be something like rewards in heaven.

An entirely different atmosphere can be seen in the nineteenth century in the effect on morals by the loss of any hope of eternal life. Professor Gertrude Himmelfarb's essay, "A Genealogy of Morals: From Clapham to Bloomsbury," in her *Marriage and Morals Among the Victorians*, traces the genetic descendants of the famous Clapham Sect to literary figures of the early twentieth-century Bloomsbury Group. The former consisted of such influential and leading laymen as William Wilberforce, Henry Thornton, Lord Teignmouth, James Stephen, and Zachary Macaulay who met with the Rev. John Venn in his London parish at Clapham, south of London. These ardent-believing evangelicals, with open Bibles and wet thumbs, worked diligently against formidable odds to secure the abolition of the slave trade and eventually the practice of slavery itself, the enactment of significant public education reforms, and the passage of numerous child labor laws.

---

3. Piper, *Desiring God*, 89–90.

The Bloomsbury Group, on the other hand, was a non-believing literary and artistic group of friends, including Virginia Woolf, Roger Fry, E. M. Forster, Clive Bell, and Lytton Strachey. Astonishingly, those in this latter group are the literal great grandchildren of the famous Clapham members. Himmelfarb traces the heroic but unsuccessful attempts of the two intervening generations to develop an ethic or rationale for morals without recourse to the transcendent conviction of their Clapham fathers and grandfathers. This brilliant essay establishes the fact that God has no grandchildren. Grace and faith are not genetically transmitted. Each generation must be converted anew. The attempt to establish Christian moral norms and ethical duties without the Christian faith has been tried and has failed.

By the fourth generation the Bloomsbury group was described as "not only homosexual and androgynous, but near-incestuous, and polymorphously promiscuous . . . In sex as in art they prided themselves on being autonomous and self-contained, free to experiment and express themselves without inhibition or guilt."[4] E. M. Forster's famous (infamous?) statement: "If I had to choose between betraying my country and betraying my friend, I hope I should have the guts to betray my country."[5] The melancholy, long, withdrawing roar of Matthew Arnold's "sea of faith" leaves behind all loyalties but one: "Ah love, let us be true to one another . . ."

This Sadducee solution of autonomy by the Bloomsbury generation and Forster, in particular, had serious consequences in the next generation. Forster's disciples, Kim Philby, Guy Burgess, and Donald McClain, did precisely what their mentor taught. They betrayed England as spies for the Soviet Union, causing the execution of many Allied agents. Weaver was in no way exaggerating when he titled his book, *Ideas Have Consequences* (1948). The ideas or teachings of the Sadducees have wide-ranging effects and deserve Jesus' warning: "Take heed, beware . . ."

WHAT SADDUCEE YEAST DOES TO PURPOSE

Assuming that all of life can be explained by ingredients within an encapsulated history rules out any appreciation of the wonder of humanity: "What is man that thou are mindful of him" (Ps 8:4). "Heaven is the

4. Himmelfarb, *Marriage and Morals Among the Victorians*, 45.

5. Forster, *Oxford Dictionary of Quotations*, 290.

creation inconceivable to man, earth is the creation conceivable to him. He himself is the creature on the boundary between heaven and earth."[6] He must decide what his destination is and what road he will choose to get there.

The puzzling mystery about human identity evokes a universal thirst for answers. History, literature, and philosophy are full of vain attempts to penetrate this mystery. We are the only animals who wear clothes, who know we are naked ("Who told you that you were naked?" Gen 3:11), and whose nakedness evokes both shame and irrational attention. We are the only animals who blush (and need to, according to Mark Twain). We are the only animals who can exceed, in gratuitous cruelty, all other animals. And yet we are the only animal that it is shameful to call a beast. Only we, of all the animals, laugh and write comedies, tragedies, poetry, and history. Only we pray and are religious. Only we puzzle about what it means to be human. Squirrels don't sit on limbs of trees scratching their heads wondering what it means to be a squirrel. Only we know that we are to die. Only we must decide what sort of animal we will be.

Alexander Pope expressed the mystery of man in four lines:

> Created half to rise, half to fall;
> Great lord of all things, yet a prey to all;
> The judge of truth, in endless error hurl'd;
> The glory, jest, and riddle of the world.[7]

Shakespeare's "Hamlet" eloquently expressed what our culture has excluded from our identity:

> There is a divinity that shapes our ends,
>   rough-hew them how we will.[8]

In a Sadducean world the wonder of this mystery of humanity is squeezed and flattened to the dimension of mere nature. The natural sciences become the Home Depot, the hardware store, for our understanding and edification regarding this mystery. The spectacular success of the natural sciences since the seventeenth century has been due in part to their concentration on cause and effect while setting aside any question of

---

6. Barth, flyleaf of John Updike's *The Centaur.*
7. Ward, *The Poetical Works of Alexander Pope,* 201
8. *Hamlet,* Act V, Scene 2.

purpose. The amputation of purpose from the mystery of human identity is fatal. As Bishop Lesslie Newbigin observed:

> Purpose is a personal word. People entertain purposes and seek to realize them; things, inanimate objects, do not have purposes of their own. An inanimate object, such as a machine, may embody purpose, but it is the purpose of the designer, not its own. If I come across a piece of machinery or equipment and have no idea of its purpose, I can of course take it to pieces and discover exactly how it works. But that will not explain what it is for.[9]

A pipe wrench cannot be adequately described without mentioning its purpose. Names of common things, such as coat hangers, squares, levels, spoons, forks, copiers, and fish hooks, give their purpose. Certainly one of the reasons why the human sciences have not known the same success as the natural sciences is the setting aside of purpose. This loss has spilled over into the humanity disciplines where purpose had been an indispensable ingredient for human identity. A theme of the nineteenth-century theologian, William Porcher DuBose, was that any study involving humans must take into consideration the *ti ev evai* (what was to be—what is our purpose). This question of purpose for humans is generally not asked in today's world.

If we do not know the purpose for which human life was designed, we have no grounds for claiming whether any human behavior is bad or good. Judgments about good or bad become mere personal conjectures. This results in a devastating effect on ethics and morality. On the other hand, if the one who created us and the whole cosmos had told us what our purpose is then what is bad deflects that purpose and what is good effects that purpose.

Paul Tillich correctly claimed that only three alternatives are possible for man: (1) autonomy (auto-nomus—a law unto itself), which if taken alone results in chaos; (2) heteronomy (hetero-nomus—a law outside oneself) which if taken alone results in tyranny; and (3) theonomy —law of God.[10]

---

9. Newbigin, *Gospel in a Pluralist Society*, 16.

10. Tillich, *Systematic Theology*, vol. 3, 249–65. Critics of Tillich's theology should not ignore the orthodox wisdom of these 16 pages. In his book, *Bound to be Free*, Hutter describes the pathology stemming from the pervasive influence of Kant: "Kantian autonomy depends on presuppositions inherently beyond its grasp, and it is by no means just a regrettable accident that autonomy thus conceived has declined into its late mod-

Neither autonomy nor heteronomy has purpose or direction. Autonomy, being a law unto oneself, is a synonym for sin and must be domesticated, inhibited, or controlled for there to be any order in family or society. Heteronomy, law outside of self, has this function of order and domestication, but it is always in danger of becoming tyrannical and destructive of creativity and freedom. It, too, is devoid of purpose for self, except as a mere instrument of a particular collective or the mere pragmatic need for order. We are reminded of William Temple's description of our condition of self-centeredness, with its expression in the heteronymous tyranny of Communism, and the narcissistic autonomous philosophy of Ayn Rand's capitalism.

Critics have pointed out that the plays of William Inge dramatically illustrate this tension between autonomy (self-law) and heteronomy (other law). In both *The Dark at the Top of the Stairs* and *Bus Stop* the masculine figures are attractive and robust but irresponsible and immature. In the process of domestication by the women in their lives they become more civilized and docile but bereft of their previous unmanageable vitality. Domestication, however necessary, is not synonymous with redemption.

The Christian hope of God's rule is not one of mere domestication and consequent loss of virility, but redemption and freedom in the context of purpose. Theonomy transcends the chaos of autonomy and the tyranny of heteronomy. (Theonomy should not be misunderstood as reducing God's law to mere ecclesiastical rules.) Purpose is the crucial element of God's rule. Humans, in their head-scratching wonder concerning their capacity for both grandeur and misery, need to know that they were not only made in the image of God but were made for God (Gen 1:26, 27; Rom 8:29; Col 3:10).

Being a law unto oneself is particularly valued by the Sadducee because of the inevitable threat of tyranny of "other law." But being a law unto oneself still begs the question, what is self? The Christian claims that we are made in the image of the creator of the world who is more and other than creation. He has revealed himself in the law and prophets and supremely in Jesus the Christ, whom to follow is to know him and oneself more fully. Virtually all of that trust is absent from our secularized and Sadducean leavened hope. We are thus left with the question—begging

ern distortions of individual sovereignty, will to power, and license. These three rather, are 'preprogrammed' in the very concept of autonomy itself because . . . the ethics of autonomy depends on resources it ultimately cannot account for," 114.

Polonius's lie: "To thine own self be true and it shall follow as night follows day thou canst not be false to any man." Many quote this as Shakespeare's wisdom but not noticing that Shakespeare put it into the mouth of a silly old man.

To what self are we to be true? The self-centered, narcissistic self described by Temple? The sixty-year-old CEO believes he is being true to himself as he swaps his spouse of thirty-five years for a trophy wife. As Godly purpose and direction are set aside by the climate we breathe we discover ourselves in our feelings, our genes, or in examples of equally flawed others called icons or celebrity idols.

William Temple used the expression, *faux pas*, to describe Rene Descartes's attempt to find an absolute firm base for the self's knowledge.[11] Descartes did this by skepticism: I can doubt everything down to the thought that I doubt. *Cogito Ergo Sum*: "I think therefore I am." But this autonomous foundation for human knowledge was even more influential in the English-speaking world through John Locke: "If I doubt all other things that very doubt makes me perceive my own existence and will not suffer me to doubt that."[12]

The autonomy implied in such expressions as "I doubt," "makes me," "my own," and "suffer me" is served up to be a universal foundation for building knowledge (and has had paralyzing and devastating effect on the professional study of Scripture). The loss of trust, as a means of knowledge in the seventeenth century, combined with the next century's explosive and unprecedented power of the industrial revolution, has done much to define modern man. Perhaps W. B. Yeats had such in mind when he wrote:

Locke sank into a swoon
The Garden died
God took the spinning jenny
Out of his side.[13]

John Locke, the new autonomous (law unto oneself) Adam, asks not for love but for power, mates not with Eve but with the machines of the Industrial Revolution. The mating of autonomy and knowledge without purpose, which is appropriate only to machines, has produced some ter-

11. Temple, *Nature, Man and God*, 57–81.
12. Locke, "Essay Concerning Human Understanding."
13. Yeats, *Collected Poems*, 211.

rible offspring. This dehumanization of industrial workers is poignantly portrayed in Charlie Chaplin films. The general tendency of corporations (where workers are sacrificed to the greater concern of the bottom line) and hospitals (where patients are reduced to being referred to as "the gall bladder in Room 302"), among other institutions, to treat workers and patients as things, is the product of this historical mating. A machine may have a purpose but it is the purpose of the designer, not the purpose of the machine itself. Inanimate objects do not have purposes of their own. People have purposes and build machines to fulfill them.

The magazine, *Progressive Farmer*, occasionally has pictures of some tool of bygone times and readers are asked to identify it. The answer is clearly unavailable until its purpose is shown. Given its purpose we know what it is; we know its identity. Purpose and direction are questions scarcely asked in the modern period. "You are God's workmanship" (Eph 2:10) is a text that needs to be heard in our Sadducean age. If we want to understand a machine short of its intended purpose, we can analyze it, take it apart, and examine how it is made, consider why it is not working, and what makes it work. Assumptions about human nature without reference to purpose have produced the characteristic twentieth-century therapy for humans—analysis (knowledge of a thing learned by taking it apart: Freud: psychoanalysis; Jung: analytical psychology). Analysis is the opposite of synthesis. Synthesis is significantly absent from our secular culture.[14] Therapy based on analysis without purpose has led to such disappointing observations as: After nine years of analysis he was finally able to say "son of a bitch" in front of his m-o-t-h-e-r.

In a secular age the purpose of a person is not brought to bear as a factor in one's identity. We are left to be known only by analysis of what we are and have been but never what we are to be. The promise that, "What no eye has seen, nor ear heard, nor the heart of man conceived, what God has prepared for those who love him" (1 Cor 2:9) is inaccessible.

The unprecedented appreciation of Rick Warren's books, which have sold some forty million copies, is surely related to the word "purpose" in his *Purpose Driven Life* and *Purpose Driven Church*. People in a Sadducean age are ravenously hungry for that which gives them meaning, identity,

---

14. The lesser known Frankl's *logo therapy* is an exception as it brought to therapy a synthesis factor of meaning that could include purpose. Based on his study of concentration camp survivors he said that humans can endure almost any "how" if they have a "why."

and direction. Warren is supplying a great need so it is no surprise that his books are eagerly sought.

Another of the base-born fruit of Locke and the spinning jenny is the identity of persons founded on the statistical average. What is normal about a person? In his popular work on sexuality, Alfred Kinsey never assumed what was intended, purposed to be, or could be. Kinsey, writing unwittingly out of the Sadducean world view, reduced all ethical questions to what is reported (by a radically faulted polling) to be the average behavior of society. If the average person has a cold, is depressed, or is selfish then it is normal to have a cold, be depressed or selfish. Purpose gives us a different sense of normal. Kinsey claimed that there are only three kinds of sexual abnormalities: abstinence, celibacy, and delayed marriage.[15] (What does this say about rape, beastiality, necrophilia, pederasty, etc.?) The idolatry of autonomy, in this instance, is a logic that becomes moralistic and condemning to anyone not copulating. Even Don Quixote's advice is forgotten: "Never let the *is* take final precedent over what is *to be*" (italics mine).[16]

The playwright Eugene Ionesco, in his essay on Kafka, shows how anything "without a goal is absurd . . . when man is cut off from his religious or metaphysical roots, he is lost; all his struggles become senseless, futile and oppressive."[17] This wonder and mystery about the end of man is lost in our age.

WHAT THE SADDUCEE YEAST DOES TO THE ARTS

> What I affirm is the intuition that where God's presence is no longer a tenable supposition and where His absence is no longer a felt, indeed overwhelming weight, certain dimensions of thought and creativity are no longer attainable.[18]

These are the words of the Cambridge professor George Steiner, whose book, *Real Presences*, produced an explosion among his skeptical and secular academic colleagues. In much of the scholarly world the term, God, is like the terms, sunrise and sunset, which seem to survive in spite

15. Crain, "Dr. Strangelove."

16. Wasserman, "Man of La Mancha," 1965.

17. Vos, *Eugene Ionesco and Edward Albee: A Critical Essay*, 6.

18. Steiner, *Real Presences*, 229.

of the Copernican revolution (the earth orbits the sun) having completely replaced the Ptolemaic assumption (the sun orbits the earth). We now know that the sun neither rises nor sets. But even scientists still use those terms. In the ascendant secularism of the West, God is spoken of as a residual term that used to apply to a presumed reality, but is no more than an antiquated relic referring to something we now know not to be true.

Steiner's book argues the reverse. Great works of art cannot be produced, he claims, within a secularized culture. Without transcendence, human creativity is truncated. Steiner insists that "poetry, art and music ... put us in sane touch with that which transcends, with matters 'undreamt of' in our materiality."[19] Immersed as he is among secular colleagues, Steiner has done a courageous deed in bearing witness to a transcendent essence in art and music. Aware of the negative response that such an affirmation would evoke in a secular academic world, he nevertheless asserts: "the attempt at testimony must be made and the ridicule incurred."[20]

An earlier book that also evoked the ire of the secular establishment was H. R. Rookmaaker's *Modern Art and the Death of a Culture*. His disclosure of the romantic rebellion in art against eighteenth-century rationalism, and the later anarchic rebellion against what was seen as repressive institutional and freedom-denying boundaries, was a symptom of a decaying culture. Rookmaaker was no amateur. He was an acknowledged critic and historian of art. He wrote a definitive work on Paul Gauguin and was a personal friend of Pablo Picasso.

His criticism did not stop at modern art but extended with characteristic candor to the art of Catholic scholasticism. Its dualism of a world of revelation and a world of reason gave birth to Renaissance humanism that left no difference between "Christian and non-Christian art."[21] He was equally disdainful of much Protestant art:

> Could it be that the false ideas many people, non-Christians as well as Christians, have of Christ as a sentimental, rather effeminate man, soft and "loving," never really of this world, are the result of the preaching inherent in the pictures given to children or hanging on the wall? Their theology, their message, is not that of the Bible but of nineteenth-century liberalism.[22]

19. Ibid., 226–27.

20. Brown, "Startling Testimony of George Steiner," 420.

21. Rookmaaker, *Modern Art and the Death of a Culture*, 35.

22. Ibid., 75.

These all-important influences of "this world-is-all-there-is-ism" on the arts are further underlined by Ingmar Bergman, the non-Christian producer of numerous widely acclaimed films:

> Regardless of my own beliefs and my own doubts, which are completely without importance in this connection, it is my opinion that art lost its creative urge the moment it was separated from worship. It severed the umbilical cord and lives its own sterile life, generating and degenerating itself.[23]

THE LAMENT OF THE SADDUCEE

That strange but brilliant poet, Ezra Pound, sums up the bankruptcy of a secular age in four lines. It could have been entitled "The Lament of the Sadducee":

> Faun's flesh is not to us
> Nor the Saints' vision
> We have press for the wafer
> Franchise for circumcision.[24]

"Faun's flesh is not to us": faun is the Latin term for the Greek satyr, the symbol of sexual fecundity and lechery. A popular songwriter, Leonard Cohen, expressed this discovery of faun-hood's empty promise: Please remove your lovely body and let me consider something worth investing my passion in. The compulsive character of contemporary sexual search is an illustration of the impotence of sex, of itself, to provide identity and meaning. Andrew Jackson is said to have observed how strange it is that men value themselves by an activity in which a jackass is their infinite superior.

"Nor the Saints' vision" is the perception of this world through the lens of faith in the justice and mercy of God's transcendent grace, a lens so clouded and smeared by the Saducean yeast as to have become opaque and the vision lost.

"We have press for the wafer": the wafer is the host of the Eucharist by which we have been nurtured in the resurrected Word ("they knew him in the breaking of the bread," Luke 24:31). We were fed the confident hope and thankful humility to live amidst the imperfections and ambigui-

---

23. Bergman, *Horizon*, 4–9.
24. Pound, "Hugh Selwyn Mauberley," 731.

ties of all worldly hopes. But this is no longer viable for us as secularists. In its place we have press for wafer: we have the newspaper, the media. The press will edify, inspire, recreate, and reassure. The news will establish us in reality. The editorials will instruct and inform, comics and sports will entertain us, and the financial pages and horoscope will provide (or deprive?) our foundation of safety. "We have press for the wafer."

"Franchise for circumcision": Professor Moelwyn Merchant, who opened these lines to me when I had no idea of their meaning, claimed that we can read baptism for circumcision (Col 2:11, 12). It was only that circumcision rhymed with vision but both terms carry the meaning of identity (in contrast to the truncated identities consequent upon idolatry). In baptism we are made "a member of Christ, the child of God, and an inheritor of the Kingdom of Heaven"—all inaccessible to the Sadducee. For the latter, one's identity lies in being a Democrat, a Republican, or a National Socialist, a grocer, a salesperson, a doctor, or a carpenter. My identity as a secularist is based on my function like a machine with no known purpose. On the other hand, as a Christian I am a forgiven sinner with a God-given purpose that "no eye has seen, nor ear heard, nor the heart of man conceived" (1 Cor 2:9). The others are peripheral expressions of political and transient functions, inadequate foundations for human identity. Professor Clifford Stanley used to refer to the pathetic epitaph on an English tombstone: "John Jones, born a man. Died a greengrocer." His identity as a man is lost. His identity is reduced to a function, like a mere tool.

What is the attraction of the Sadducee yeast that it could so easily seduce us? How could this yeast induce us to relinquish a heavenly vision, a eucharistic (i.e., grateful) nurture, and a God-given identity for a fragile and transient hope founded on a functional or political identity? There are at least four reasons.

Accommodation to the Age

St. Paul warns us, "Do not be conformed to this world but be transformed by the renewal of your mind" (Rom 12:2). Throughout Scripture the world (i.e., the age) is always over against us. By definition the world is bereft of revelation and depends on mere speculation regarding original and final things. From the beginning, Israel's unfaithfulness in accommodating to the surrounding culture was condemned by God through the prophets.

The sociologist Peter Berger continues in this prophetic tradition by rebuking the Protestant world for reflecting the age rather than witnessing to it. From his speech to the Consultation on Church Unity in Denver in 1971 to a more recent book, *A Far Glory: The Quest for Faith in an Age of Credulity*, he has diagnosed and criticized the church's acquiescence in the spirit of the age.

Paul Van Buren's *Secular Meaning of the Gospel* was among the early serious attempts to accommodate Christianity to the secular world. His approach began, not with the assumptions of Christian revelation but with the mind of modern man as a filter through which one pours the Christian faith, accepting only that "which is honest and loyal to the way we think today."[25] This assumption left him with a merely human Jesus bereft of divinity. If he had used the mind of modern man of the fourth century as a filter, he would have lost the humanity and accepted only the divinity, reflecting the climate of the early centuries, as in the popular heresies of Apollinarius and Eutyches that accepted the divinity but denied the full humanity of Jesus.

A popular and less scholarly reflection of Van Buren's approach is that of Bishop John Spong, whose accommodation to secularism leads him to deny theism, the deity of Christ, the bodily resurrection, and the God who hears and answers prayer. He demands assent to vows by those he confirms and ordains that he himself has publicly renounced.[26] The difference between Van Buren and Spong is that Van Buren's sense of honor would not allow him to pose as a Christian.

Sloth

The second is sloth, a spiritual fatigue that makes us desire some sort of sleep, some nirvana, some nothingness, some state that removes anxiety, and banishes pain and fear. A whole school of psychology has insisted that there is a death wish in each of us. In the seventeenth century Bishop Jeremy Taylor acknowledged in a litany: "I . . . was in love with death, and was dead in sin, . . . and loved to have it so."[27] The prodigious, and exorbitantly expensive, civil necessity to keep us from using drugs, the widespread use of alcohol to deaden the frontal brain lobes to enable us

25. Van Buren, *Secular Meaning of the Gospel*, 170.

26. Spong, "12 Theses," 1998.

27. Taylor, *Works*, 292.

to feel better by feeling less, and the alarming rate of suicide, all indicate this desire for a peace that militates against any desire for a hope of resurrection. Instead, sloth desires a hope for final and peaceful oblivion, not redemption.

Fear of Tests

The third factor in human susceptibility to the yeast of the Sadducee is the fear of tests. Anyone who has faced an examination after years of scholarly work is painfully aware of the truth in W. H. Auden's observation that acquiring knowledge is like climbing a glassy mountain with no footholds for logic where knowledge but increases vertigo.[28]

The more one knows the dizzier one gets. The more one knows about a subject the more one knows how much one does not know and how, quite possibly, and even justly, one could fail. I can recall by own examination at Oxford. Years of study had opened to me a much wider vision of all I yet did not know. If the examiners knew as much as I did about what I didn't know I would surely fail. But the examination I must take in the resurrection life is one in which the Examiner knows all, "unto whom all hearts are open, all desires known and from whom no secrets are hid."[29]

The fear of tests has a deep spiritual dimension. The saints testify that the deeper into sanctification one goes the clearer one sees one's sins. The more majestic the vision of God the more unworthy sinners see themselves in his reflection. Confidence is rare in the face of the text: "For we must all appear before the judgment seat of Christ; so that each one may receive good or evil according to what he has done in the body" (2 Cor 5:10). Confidence before such a test may be a mere product of limited self-knowledge or a small god. Freud is said to have remarked: I did that, says my memory. I could not have done that, says my pride . . . Eventually memory yields.

Confidence, therefore, might be a mere function of having a poor memory, a small god, and an inept conscience. For those with better memories, a larger god, and some residual keenness of conscience, sleep could seem more desirable than facing such a test. The Sadducean yeast appears as a welcome drug, a final oblivion, with no accountability. It is a strong motive in all unbelievers. For Christian believers the operative

---

28. Auden, *For the Time Being*, 89.

29. *Book of Common Prayer*, 67.

phrase in the text is "before the judgment seat of Christ" that provides the promise of mercy and the ground on which we are given the courage to face and confess our inexcusable shortcomings (sins), repent, and be forgiven.

The Justice of God

A fourth factor why this yeast is seductive is the haunting absence in the secular mind of the justice of God. We live in a climate that has, to a considerable extent, lost its hope for justice. Anyone with a modicum of realism knows that complete justice is never achieved in history. It can only be approximated. A great deal of injustice goes to the grave with each of us. I recall the following memorable words from a now forgotten play: a young man whines that he is "just asking for justice." An older man replies, "Just asking for justice? . . . which no one has ever had? . . . And you couldn't stand it if you got it."

Church bodies that tend to accommodate faith to the culture when speaking of the afterlife, tend also to universalize salvation. Everyone is saved regardless of either works or faith. God's justice is reduced. Thus, this age believes that no one needs to be saved from one's just desserts by any divine mercy. It's a catch-22 situation. If our hope for justice is so reduced that we need no mercy, we will never know the mercy that enables us to hope for justice. Unfortunately, this in turn affects our hope. The absence of mercy leaves us emotionally unable to hope for justice because it would amount to a hope for condemnation.

There are few more reliable tools for diagnosing the condition of our culture than works of art reflecting a contemporary version of some classical tale and to compare the two versions. Such a work is Archibald MacLeish's *J. B.*, a modern version of the Bible's Book of Job. MacLeish approaches the great classic with commendable humility. He likens his effort to tell the story of Job for our time to the kind of rusted corrugated iron shacks Arabs erected in the magnificent ruins of the great city of Babylon. The prognosis for the play's success was dismal because it is largely a "talking show" and most of the action occurs off stage. Such Broadway shows are rarely successful.

Much to the surprise of critics, *J. B.* elicited enthusiastic appreciation. The modern Job, called J. B. in the play, has lost his oldest son, who was killed while serving in the army because of the stupidity of an officer. His two middle children are killed by a drunken driver. A daughter is crushed by stones when J. B.'s bank disappears in an explosion. His youngest child is raped and murdered by a village idiot. J. B. is afflicted with painful sores and is deprived of all his wealth. He chokes out, "The Lord gave. The Lord taketh away. Blessed is the name of the Lord." Sarah, his wife, responds in anger, saying that she will not let him sacrifice their children to make injustice justice and God good! "Curse God and die," she screams and leaves him. At the end of the play as J.B's health is being restored Sarah returns to him. J. B. then asks, "Why did you leave me alone?" Sarah replied, "I loved you. I couldn't help you any more. You wanted justice and there was none—only love"[30] Nowhere is the sadness of Sadducees better stated. Bereft of heaven there is no justice. Nothing will ever be fair. No justice, only love.

Love without justice, love that is not right, loses itself in abuse, seduction, pederasty, adultery, gluttony, avarice, and selfishness. The contrast between the hope of this secular age expressed by MacLeish in *J. B.* and Job's hope in the original book of Job speaks volumes. "For I know that my Redeemer lives and at last he will stand upon the earth; and after my skin has been destroyed, then without my flesh I shall see God; whom I shall see on my side and my eyes shall behold, and not another" (Job 19:25–27). MacLeish's J. B., in contrast to the Bible's Job, never thinks of usurping God's place because for MacLeish there is no transcendent God. God is reduced to nothing but human love.

Whoever thinks that history will provide complete justice is naïve indeed. And here McLeish is right. Much in this world will never be put right nor will true justice ever prevail. Injustice and betrayal, a slapped face and a slammed door, genocide and ethnic cleansing are irreversible facts in this world. The desperate hopes of Marxist Communism and liberal Protestantism project justice, not for individuals, but for the collective future of impersonal humanity.

MacLeish himself is beyond that naïve hope in the doctrine of progress. His treatment of innocent suffering and injustice in life is both deeply moving and singularly significant. The language is telling, the words visually concrete, the frustration, pain, anger, despair are all too real, touching the reader deeply and capable of producing tears. This poetry is no straw target but a ruthlessly unsentimental vision into our common and uni-

---

30. *J. B.: A Play in Verse*, 151.

versal condition, no matter how varied, of each of us. But the ending and resolution is the personal sacrifice, the giving up of hope for justice.

The universal cry of adolescence, "But it's not fair!" becomes the epitaph on the grave of secular humanity. To breathe the air of despair that justice will never prevail is deeply depressing. An old joke has a psychiatrist reassuring his patient that he doesn't really have an inferiority complex because he is in fact inferior. A contemporary version in our culture's epidemic of depression has the psychiatrist telling his patient, "You're not neurotically depressed—your depression is merely an appropriate response to contemporary reality. Any who are not depressed are living in cloud coo-coo land."

When finally there is no justice, when ultimately nothing is fair, when goodness to which our aims strive is never to be reached, when sin, selfishness, tears, loneliness, cruelty, and death are at last unresolved, unhealed, unredeemed, and unloving realities, it is indeed truly depressing. No Zoloft or Prozac can cure this malignancy.

Because humans will not long endure this cultural condition of Sadducean truncated hope, we may expect the idol factory of the human heart to devise new hopes through transcendent windows. Ancient hopes of Gnostic and cultic religions are already punching holes in the Sadducee self-contained bubble. The danger in this opportunity is that these windows can provide flights into distorted and counterfeit forms of Christianity and into other faiths. Emboldened by the decline of Christianity in the West, Islam is rapidly becoming an alternative to secularism in much of the world. The urgent task at hand is to make sure authentic Christianity is again proclaimed. The justice, mercy, and love promised by Christian faith is largely unknown to many, even in churches, because it has been badly distorted and fatally misrepresented by both the Sadducean and Pharisaic yeast warned against by Jesus: "Take heed, beware," but this time we will treat the yeast of the Pharisees.

5

The Pharisee Yeast

"There are only two kinds of men: the righteous who think themselves sinners and sinners who think themselves righteous."[1]

—Blaise Pascal

PHARISAIC TEACHINGS, UNLIKE THOSE of the Sadducee, represent a
tradition more complex than conventionally appreciated.[2] Pharisees
must not be too easily dismissed. Unless they are duly appreciated we will
miss a deeper understanding of Christianity.

The Pharisees warned Jesus of a plot by Herod against his life (Luke
13:31). They invited Jesus to meals in spite of their dietary scruples
(Luke 11:37; 14:1). Some of them even believed in Jesus (John 3:1;
7:45–52; 9:13–16). Also, they were instrumental in ensuring the survival
of Jesus's followers (Acts 5:34; 23:6–9). Both Nicodemus and Gamaliel
were Pharisees. Each is remembered by Christians with deep and abiding respect.

Even the harsh description of the Pharisees recorded in St. Luke's
gospel needs to be seen in perspective. ("Beware the yeast of the Pharisees,
which is hypocrisy," Luke 12:1.) Hypocrisy itself has some virtuous di-
mensions, especially in the light of its alternatives. La Rochefoucauld,
the seventeenth-century aphorist, has pointed out that "Hypocrisy is the
tribute that vice pays to virtue." In other words, virtuous people do not
pretend to be viceful. Viceful people pretend to be virtuous. And what
would we prefer viceful people to do? Hypocrisy would seem to be one

1. Pascal, *Pensees*, 144.

2. Neusner, *Method and Meaning in Ancient Judaism*, 185–213 and Neusner, *Judaism
in the Beginning of Christianity*. For an excellent study that helps us see ourselves in the
Pharisees, see Hovestol, *Extreme Righteousness*.

of the pillars of civilization. If we never pretended to a virtue above our vices and never covered up our true selves, what would happen to society? Hypocrisy would seem to be one of the essentials of civilized society. If we did not pretend to values, behavior, and standards that exceed our actual desires and behavior, civilization would be in bad shape.

The way we dress and speak in society covers a lot that deserves to be covered. Pretending to standards higher than our inclinations often moves us away from base desires to loftier concerns. I can recall a psychiatrist at St. Elizabeths mental hospital saying that the beauticians who washed and set women's hair did more for their morale than all other therapists. To have one's natural looks improved tends to make one feel better and become better. An adolescent fantasy is that everyone should be naked. Humans without clothes are not so much a moral problem as an aesthetic one. Part of being civilized is to have manners to mask, cover, and control basic human self-centeredness, aggression, and greed. Winchester, the famous English school, has as its motto, "Manners makyth Man."

The epistle of James warns us to "bridle" our tongues (Jas 1:26). Is this not an exhortation to refrain from honest expressions of our feelings? If our thoughts and emotions were sanctified with no residue of sin, we would not usually need to bridle our tongues. Surely James's advice, hypocritical as it is, is salutary and necessary for civilized society. This includes Christians who continually struggle with impatience, anger, lust, and envy and who, unfortunately, still find in themselves some delight in a rival's misfortune. Am I the only one who has to repent the failure to be hypocritical when my unbridled tongue blurted out, "He's just an idiot!"? It may be true that he is an idiot, but idiot is too close to the word fool in Matthew's Sermon on the Mount (Matt 5:22) for me not to repent my failure to be hypocritical.

William Raspberry, columnist for the *The Washington Post*, gave a commencement address at the University of Alabama exhorting his listeners to appreciate the value of hypocrisy in the face of such cultural phenomena as primal scream therapy, the book *Open Marriage*, the appearance of the let-it-all-hang-out view, along with, if it feels good do it.

> We are still paying the price for our abandonment of hypocrisy—in everything from family breakdown to drug spawned crime to the short-sighted selfishness and incivility that threaten to erode our institutions, wreck our economy and topple the pillars of our society. What, you ask, does hypocrisy have to do with it? Just this:

the let it all hang out morality that crashed in upon us in the 1970's accepts no standard, no morality, no code of behavior outside the minds of those engaging in the behavior. The idea is that it's ok to do whatever crosses your mind, as long as you don't hurt anybody. Hypocrisy recognizes that the erosion of standards hurts everybody. It accepts the sanctity of societal standards, even while violating them.[3]

St. Luke is right, the Pharisees were hypocrites. They held to the law and accepted responsibility when it was broken. The law had its integrity because of accountability in the resurrection. What does it matter to a dead man whether the law was obeyed or disobeyed if there is no life beyond the grave?

Sadducean yeast leaves law and custom with no ground of integrity—no accountability. Sadducees cause the kind of societal disintegration Raspberry describes. They become the threat to society while the Pharisees appear to be its pillars.

It would seem therefore that our culture desperately needs more Pharisees. Certainly they were not perfect, but they were indeed among the most dutiful and upright of all citizens in biblical times and so are some today. They would not likely have been part of the outrageous sleaze, pork-barrel bills, and corruption that marks the administration of both of our political parties. Pharisees would have set clear boundaries and limits for the media, TV, movies, and publications. They may have been attracted by pornography, but they would have legislated against it, or fought for family values while having an affair. Yes, they may be hypocrites who are not living up to their own public commitments, but they would not have lowered the standards of the culture to depraved behavior, nor have held that lowered standards were acceptable.

Why then was Jesus much harder on the Pharisees, with whom he agreed on such crucial matters as spirits, angels, and the resurrection, than on the Sadducees? Why would he have more negative things to say to those who would seem to be the very pillars of Jewish society than to the Sadducees, who denied his clear teaching on essential subjects and were vandals destroying the fabric of civilization?

3. Raspberry, *Tuscaloosa News.*

THE BURDEN OF THE PHARISEE

The most significant picture of the Pharisee in Scripture is the story of the Pharisee and the tax collector in the temple (Luke 18:9–14). The Pharisee thanks God that he is not like other men, extortionists, unjust, and adulterers. He fasts twice a week and gives tithes of all that he receives. That is surely commendable and it would seem to be a view to be encouraged. Any society without such Pharisees who know the importance of the law is in deep trouble. Yet here Jesus is saying that the one who is justified is the tax collector, the very illustration of what today would be called a masochist, beating his chest, not even lifting up his eyes and calling himself—God forbid—a sinner. Does not the climate of today applaud the Pharisee and infer that Jesus is backing the wrong man and teaching some singularly bad hygiene? Why then is Jesus particularly critical of the Pharisees?

The object of Pharisee teaching is that by good works one can justify oneself before God and man. Using William Temple's picture of our human nature, we see that the Pharisee is trying to establish and retain his own center. The parable itself shows how such self-centeredness results in contempt for others (e.g., the publican). With his confession the publican acknowledges God, not himself, as center. For those of us who still maintain our self-centeredness it is a hard parable.

SELF-ESTEEM

Biblical Pharisees who attempted to retain their own center by good works and righteous deeds are different from modern Pharisees who seek to retain their centers by self-esteem. It would seem that without a sense of self-worth it would be difficult to succeed or excel at anything. Students, soldiers, athletes, and patients all tend to do better in proportion to their self-esteem.

The most pervasive dogma of the secular world is the religion of self-esteem. It seems to be the very aim of pedagogy, psychology, and religiosity. A recent accounting placed American students over all those of other industrial nations in feeling good about themselves, but way down the list in actual competence in math, sciences, languages, and verbal skills. Richard Erickson, a psychologist in Seattle, has shown that self-esteem is not promise but peril. He is not unaware of the value of self-esteem in effective living and learning, but the basic difficulty with the cult of self-esteem is that it attempts to substitute "disclosure and acceptance" for "repentance and forgiveness." He insists that:

> the popularizers lack a psychology or theology to encompass unremitting or irreversible failure, pain loss, or suffering . . . One cannot function better until one feels better. One cannot show love to others until one loves oneself. One cannot love oneself until one is sufficiently loved by others. At this point responsibility for one's feelings and actions is shifted to others.[4]

Charles Sykes, in his book *A Nation of Victims: The Decay of the American Character*, quotes a sociologist:

> If you add up all the groups—women, blacks, youth, Native Americans,the unemployed, the poor, etc.—that consider themselves oppressed minorities, Aaron Wildavsky calculates their number adds up to 374 percent of the population.[5]

The loss of responsibility consequent upon the self-esteem cult and the current victimology provides the yeast to justify anyone who can claim victimhood. Justification by faith has been replaced by justification by victimization.

The sad price paid for this escape from condemnation is that when one is not held responsible, one begins to be unable to respond. One's very dignity and identity is infected by this yeast. The Pharisee yeast, in its attempt to self-justify, can, therefore, take different forms. A culture, deeply committed to the law revealed by God to Moses, produces very active, upright (if self-righteous) citizens. To a culture already infected with Sadducee yeast, a system that justifies the indolence of victimhood, produces self-indulgent, compulsive seekers after self-esteem. The heavy price paid for this current form of Pharisaism is the irrelevance of forgiveness, the loss of justice, and the nurture of self-indulgent attempts to feel good about oneself.

This compulsion to escape responsibility and to justify oneself, whether it be in the more commendable form of biblical Pharisaism or in the current form of shifting responsibility to others, is a heavy burden to bear. Jesus did not say "Come unto me and I will make you feel good about yourself." Jesus's invitation to all Pharisees, then and now, is:

---

4. Erickson, *Journal of Pastoral Care*.

5. Sykes, *A Nation of Victims*, 12–13. See also the section "Abolition of Sin," 142–47.

> Come to me, all who labor and are heavy laden, and I will give you
> rest. Take my yoke upon you, and learn from me; for I am gentle
> and lowly in heart, and you will find rest for your souls, For my
> yoke is easy and my burden is light. (Matt 11:28–30)

This is an exceedingly strange and incongruous thing for Jesus to
say, since he has just finished the Sermon on the Mount, arguably the
heaviest burden and tightest yoke of any religion anywhere at any time.
The psychologists Theodor Reik, Eric Fromm, and Sigmund Freud each
is said to have pointed to Jesus's Sermon on the Mount as the reason they
could not be Christians. The demands there, in terms of super-ego, could
produce more guilt than any ego could bear.

> You have heard that it was said . . . "You shall not kill . . ." But I say
> to you that everyone who is angry with his brother shall be liable
> to judgment . . . whoever says "You fool!" shall be liable to the hell
> of fire . . . You have heard that it was said, "You shall not commit
> adultery." But I say to you that every one who looks at a woman
> lustfully has already committed adultery with her in his heart. If
> your eye causes you to sin pluck it out and throw it away; it is
> better to lose one of your members than that your whole body be
> thrown into hell. (Matt 5:21–30)

It would take no more than a few yards on a beach paved with bi-
kinis for a healthy young man to run out of eyes. And Jesus tells us, "My
yoke is easy and my burden is light"? The only way we can understand
this apparently appalling contradiction is to look at one of the functions
of the Sermon on the Mount. Martin Kahler put it simply: "To state the
matter somewhat provocatively, one could call the Gospels, *passion nar-
ratives with extended introductions*" (italics mine).[6] The Sermon on the
Mount is not a blue print for society or an individual's rule of life. It is an
introduction to the passion, an invitation to Good Friday.

The Sermon is not some elevated ideal that we are to stretch and
strive for but a window through which to see God's kingdom. It is not a set
of rules by which to live but a vision which enables us to die to self. This
vision empties us of any confidence or trust in our own center. Humility
is the only appropriate posture before the cost of God's love at the crucifixion. Only before the cross are we enabled to want and receive the true
Center in place of our own.

6. Kahler, *So-Called Historical Jesus*, 80.

Clergy often make the mistake of thinking, when they preach from one of the Gospels, that they are preaching good news. Most of the gospel material is not gospel but what leads up to the good news of Good Friday and Easter. A large part of the Gospels is conviction of sinners, rebuke of Israel's unfaithfulness, disappointments of expectation, and declaring salvation as a human impossibility. In contrast, the Epistles are on this side of Good Friday and Easter and are invariably good news.

Much of Easter must be brought to passages in the Gospels for them to be Gospel, for so many of them involve the demand of God's law that prepares us for the crucifixion and resurrection. A visiting lecturer in my parish once tried to squeeze the gospel out of the Sermon on the Mount by claiming that in the text, "You, therefore, must be perfect, as your heavenly Father is perfect," the word perfect simply means complete. "It just means that we are to have all our buttons." He was correct about the word *teleios* (perfect) but seemed to overlook, as a parishioner pointed out, that the demand is to be complete as our heavenly Father is complete. His kind motive was to keep the Sermon from condemning us, but convicting us is one of the very purposes of the Sermon.

Nothing in Scripture is as misunderstood as the Sermon on the Mount. What is often said about it makes one wonder if the speaker has actually read it. It would seem to disallow insurance, lawyers, retirement plans, police, military service, and to counsel perfection and mutilation. No mention is made of atonement or comforting words for the weak and sinful, as in Isaiah 53 and 54. No word says a divine Savior has come to die for our sins or that we are in need of such an act. Regeneration is not alluded to. No repentance is requested or grace promised to confer the power to obey.

The Sermon on the Mount is the necessary, rigorous, and devastating purging of Pharisee yeast. It's chemotherapy for the Pharisee cancer. Any confidence in one's own righteousness before God has no authentic way to wiggle through chapters 5–7 of Matthew. Any genuine pilgrimage through this Sermon leaves us bereft of self-righteousness, with no pedestals from which to judge other sinners. Jesus, in these passages, leaves us in the only posture legitimately possible on Good Friday: on our knees with empty hands to receive the incomparable and desperately needed mercy of God.

I once asked a fellow Episcopal bishop why we couldn't get a simple affirmation of traditional sex ethics out of the committee in the House of Bishops. His reply was, "Oh, it's so condemnatory." I replied that such a position regarding law was going to make forgiveness unnecessary. His response was that he'd never thought of that. I should have pointed out the passage in Romans 11: 32, "For God has consigned all men to disobedience, that he may have mercy upon all." One of the purposes of the law and the Sermon on the Mount is to consign us all to condemnation. We Pharisees need to let down the heavy burden of establishing our own self-righteousness. Our righteousness is simply God's gift of the mercy we have received. The enduring dignity of Christians is found in the triumphant passage in Romans. "Who is to condemn? It is Christ Jesus who died, yes, who was raised from the dead" (Rom 8:34). The Sermon on the Mount is a deeper unfolding of the law of Moses. It leaves no hope that human goodness can replace (or make a waste of) the costly betrayal, rejection, passion, suffering, death, and resurrection of God's action in Jesus Christ.

JOHN AND CHARLES WESLEY

The best way to understand the paralyzing effect of Pharisee yeast, and the power that results when it is purged, is to look at two remarkable eighteenth-century brothers. The lives of Charles and John Wesley clearly illustrate two recovering Pharisees. John was the fifteenth child and Charles the eighteenth of Samuel and Susanna Wesley, and they grew up in a sternly ordered eighteenth-century rectory. Their mother was a remarkable woman, a severe disciplinarian, and gifted musician and linguist. The boys were well educated before they went to Christ Church, Oxford, where they received the best education available at the time.

At Oxford they formed a small religious community that was ridiculed by their contemporaries as the "Holy Club" (or the "Bible Moths" or "Methodists") because of their methodical devotion to Bible study, prayer, and good works. In 1735, after receiving ordination in the Church of England, they both left as missionaries to the colony in Georgia. On the way their ship encountered a terrific storm in which they shared the desperate fears of captain and crew:

> The sea broke over, split the mainsail in pieces, covered the ship
> and poured between the decks, as if the great deep had already

swallowed us up. A terrible screaming began among the English.[7]
(From John Wesley's Journal)

However, a small band of Moravians who manifested a trust and serenity while singing songs and hymns during the storm made a deep impression on both brothers.

While in Georgia, John's preaching against gin and the slave trade made him few friends. He was nursed through a sickness by a young woman, Sophia Hopkey. On his recovery, he found that she had married William Williamson. When Sophia next attended a service of Holy Communion, John skipped her at the rail. Such excommunication implies that one is "an open and notorious evil liver."[8] Mr. Williamson took great offense at this excommunication and charged Wesley with defamation of character. John had to post bail to escape jail.

He subsequently took a row boat across the Savannah River, walked to Bluffton, took a carriage to Charleston, and a ship back to England. He landed at Plymouth and found his old friend of the "Holy Club" days at Oxford, George Whitefield, boarding a ship bound for Georgia. John tried to persuade George to abandon the trip on the scriptural grounds of "pearls before swine." Fortunately, Whitefield persisted and his ministry in the colonies was marked as one of the most popular and effective in their history. During a subsequent visit in 1739–1740, he journeyed up and down the east coast from Georgia to Massachusetts preaching to unprecedented enthusiastic crowds, evoking support and admiration from such a figure as Benjamin Franklin.

Whitefield's preaching, however, was not welcomed by the Anglican establishment. Alexander Garden, the Bishop of London's Commissary (agent) in South Carolina, brought Whitefield to trial at St. Philip's Church in Charleston on the charge of "itinerating" (crossing canonical parish boundaries). When Anglican churches were closed to Whitefield, Franklin helped build an edifice for him in Philadelphia, which became the home of the University of Pennsylvania.

On his return to England, John Wesley was no more effective in his ministry than he had been in Georgia. Discouraged and in despair, he attended a Moravian service in London where Peter Boehler was expounding on Martin Luther's preface to the *Epistle to the Romans*.

7. Heitzenrater, "The Tale of Two Brothers," 13.

8. *Book of Common Prayer*, 84.

There John discovered the wonder of the easy yoke and the light burden (Matt 11:28–30). He laid down his compulsive striving to preserve his self-as-center by his obedience to the law. Recognizing before God his spiritual bankruptcy, he accepted the mercy of Christ as the center of his life, something he neither earned nor deserved. Wesley then (in a now famous expression) "found his heart strangely warmed." The effectiveness of his ministry thereafter is almost beyond comprehension. His visits to prisons, a habit continued from his Oxford days, now, without the pedestal of his own goodness, were greeted by the inmates with a warmth and reception he had never before received or imagined. Prior to Wesley's religious transformation they were required to attend his presentations and exhibited a mixture of apathy and hostility. Now he began to be greeted warmly and the prisoners urged others to attend. Sometimes in parish churches he was forced to preach through a window rather than from the pulpit in order to reach more people outside than could be accommodated inside the church.

Wesley's preaching journeys took him all over England. He made forty-two trips to Ireland and twenty-two to Scotland. He traveled some 250,000 miles often writing in his journal while on horseback. (This is the equivalent of 41 round trips on horseback from Washington to San Francisco over 56 years.) He preached more than 40,000 sermons. A supreme gift was his genius for organization. Wesley's overseeing societies, orphanages, publications, distributions to the poor, doctrinal discipline, while working to abolish the slave trade (he was a considerable influence on William Wilberforce), all amid controversies with Moravians, Calvinists, and Anglican critics would have involved the complete attention of a score of lifetimes. Wesley's account in his journal of his activities has been called "the most amazing record of human exertion ever penned by man."[9] Perhaps the greatest tribute to John Wesley is given by his clerical colleague, and sometimes rival, George Whitefield. "My brother Wesley acted wisely. The souls that were awakened under his ministry he joined in a class, and this preserved the fruits of his labor. This I neglected and my people is a rope of sand."[10]

Whitefield traveled around the countryside, stopping at a village, a town, or even a farm, preaching to people who often responded in dra-

9. Telford, "John Wesley," *Encyclopedia Britannica*, 518.

10. Wakeley, *Prince of Pulpit Orators*, 219–20.

matic ways. He would then get on his horse and leave for another harvest in another place. Wesley, on the other hand, would only accept an invitation if he could preach four times and leave disciples to nurture the new converts.

Three days before John's heartwarming experience, his brother Charles had an astonishingly similar experience. He was depressed and sick having failed as secretary to General James Oglethorpe, Governor of Georgia. Peter Boehler visited Charles during the latter's sickness and asked Charles, "On what account do you expect to be saved?" To which Charles replied, "That I have used my best endeavors to serve God." By Peter's disappointed expression, Charles realized that he had not given the right reply and he was deeply troubled. Peter Boehler left Charles with a copy of Luther's *Commentary on the Epistle to the Galatians.* Four days later (May 21, 1738), Charles confessed that he trusted not in his endeavors or his goodness but in Christ alone. "I now found myself at peace with God and rejoice in hope of loving Him." (We might ask ourselves what would we reply to Boehler's question?)

Before this date Charles had written only a few poems or hymns and none with the power that now flowed from an unburdened heart. Isaac Watts, then the greatest of hymn writers, had produced some 400. To be precise about the number of Charles' hymns is difficult but between 7,300 (Rattenbury) and 8,989 (Townsend) were produced in the fifty years following the deepening of his faith in Christ. Some of them are:

> And can it be
> Lo He comes with clouds descending
> O for a thousand tongues to sing
> Love divine all loves excelling
> Jesus lover of my soul
> Jesus Christ is risen today
> Rejoice the Lord is King
> Hark the herald angels sing
> Come thou almighty King.

Charles Wesley's hymns are sung all over the world and by virtually every denomination. He has more hymns in the Episcopal hymnbook than any other composer or author. One can hardly imagine how we could fully worship without the contribution of Charles Wesley.

How can we account for this astonishing transformation of two singularly inept and unsuccessful clergy into such remarkable, creative, and historically significant figures? To what can we attribute Charles's sudden deluge of creative hymn writing at the age of 31? Or his brother's enormous evangelistic and organizational creativity beginning at age 35? Did their IQ change? Or their DNA? Were they suddenly relieved of having dysfunctional parents? Did they abruptly receive an insight of great self-esteem that their inadequacies were not their fault? No. After being reared in a Church of England vicarage, educated at Oxford, ordained to the priesthood, only now did they understand that by their endeavors they could never fulfill God's demands or be the people God intended them to be. Only by relinquishing their trust in their own goodness and replacing it with trust in Christ's loving sacrifice for them did they have peace with God and the freedom of incomparable achievement (Rom 5:1).

What do the examples of Charles and John Wesley mean for us today? We are living in quite different times with quite different assumptions. In the eighteenth century, the influence of the Sadducean yeast was not as overwhelming as it is in our times. Also, the symptoms of the Pharisaic yeast have changed radically in the last century. John and Charles Wesley breathed an atmosphere of God's justice and transcendence that is exceedingly rare today. Hence, the eighteenth-century Pharisees were closer to the biblical ones who attempted to uphold the law than to modern self-esteem Pharisees who lower the law to the level of their behavior. One can hardly imagine either John or Charles Wesley declaring, prior to their conversions, "I feel good about myself." The same principle was there but the Wesley's were far more rigorous about the works that they thought would make them righteous before God.

In our own arrogant age, self-esteem Pharisaism is more likely to produce depression than repentance. Contemplating the awesome holiness, majesty, and transcendence of God that characterized the time of Amos, Hosea, Jeremiah, Isaiah, and the disciples is now far more difficult than in previous ages. In our own day, grace does not teach "my heart to fear." As a child of this age, celebrating Holy Communion for the first time, I had none of the frightening anxiety before my righteous God that made Luther tremble at celebrating his first Mass. I was merely nervous about making some mistake and incurring criticism from my fellow clergy. The age had robbed me of anything like the humble awe before almighty God that is the mark of Scripture. It has caused serious limitations in my ministry and that of my contemporaries.

The Pharisee Yeast

If grace does not teach "my heart to fear," grace will not "my fears relieve." An accessible fatherly God is the blessing consequent on God's action in Christ who taught us to pray "Our father . . ." (a blasphemous assumption for an Islamist). This access was duly bloody and dearly bought because almighty God is just and of purer eyes than to behold iniquity. God is the implacable enemy and punisher of sin and evil. In his presence the prophets justly trembled. Dietrich Bonhoeffer, the martyr under Hitler, warned us about "cheap grace . . . without price; grace without cost" through which "the world finds a cheap covering for its sins, no contrition is required still less any real desire to be delivered from sin."[11] Heaven is seen in our culture as never having to say no to oneself.

The benevolence and facile accessibility of God is so taken for granted in modern Christendom that the miraculous (there is no other word) transformation of Charles and John Wesley is almost inaccessible for us, inaccessible, that is, as long as we remain sentimental in our domestication of God. If Hitler, Stalin, Pol Pot, and Mao are not held accountable for the millions they killed, if terrorists who kill thousands of innocent men, women, and children for a political or religious point, if the perpetrators of genocide do not have to face God's justice, then God is not just and God is not God and there is no justice.

The trust that there will be justice for them is a Christian trust. But it includes justice for us as well, which none of us can endure. As long as I trust that my relative goodness needs less mercy than that of the murderous Idi Amin (genocidal dictator of Uganda), I am where Charles Wesley was prior to his conversion. This is not to say that there are no significant differences between Amin's atrocities and my sins. But when the gold medal Olympic swimmer, Josh Davis, and I are in a boat together, fishing in the middle of the Pacific Ocean and the boat sinks, it is ultimately unimportant that Josh can swim a great deal better and longer than I can. We both drown. God's justice is bigger than the Pacific Ocean.

My goodness might be related to that of Idi Amin as Josh Davis's swimming ability is to mine. However, there is but one mercy for us both, Jesus Christ, and I need him as much as Idi Amin does. My dignity based on "I'm not as bad as _____ (fill in the blank) is the persistent and tenacious symptom of deadly Pharisaism. It fuels the love of ugly, lascivious, and evil news about other people in the media. It is the cause of

11. Bonhoeffer, *Cost of Discipleship*, 45–46.

gossip, which is no more than the Pharisee's wistful hope that God grades on the curve—that God's standard is not absolute but is relative to average goodness. This hope puts a premium on listening to and spreading bad news about other people. If God grades on the curve I must find as many people as I can who are greater sinners than I am. Then I will pass. If this were true, there would always be room for boasting and pride and an insatiable need to know, and to find glee in, how bad others are. Such a view will never bring us in abject emptiness before God. The emptying of self as center made room in John and Charles Wesley to receive and show God's love and grace and power.

"It is very hard to transcend the idiocy of your own century" is the wise observation of Professor Rod Rosenblatt. The idiocy of our times that has emptied God of his awesomeness leaves us with no laxative for our arrogant constipation. Soaking ourselves in Scripture can show us the holy and wholly transcendent majesty of God that the Sadducee yeast has removed. At the same time the Gospel story cures the malignant confidence that our goodness is enough before God. This latter confidence stands in the way of our experiencing the same power that transformed the lives of John and Charles Wesley.

6

Anglican Pharisees

". . . fear worketh no man's inclination to repentance, til somewhat else have wrought in us love also."[1]

—Richard Hooker (1554–1600)

PHARISAISM, A PERVASIVE COUNTERFEIT of the Christian faith, panders to our universal thirst for self-righteousness. The initial stages of the ministries of Charles and John Wesley are excellent examples of this distorted teaching. Both were Anglican, affirmed the creeds, councils, and articles of faith, but before their religious transformations, their faith consisted mostly of law with little grace. To them Christianity was duty, demands to be obeyed, and sin to be controlled. The gospel they preached was neither good news to them nor to those to whom they ministered. After John's conversion he described his previous preaching in Savannah as "beating the air" and his spiritual state as "one under the law," "in bondage to sin," and "fighting continually but not conquering."[2] John's spiritual guide had been the celebrated devotional writer, William Law, author of *On Christian Perfection* (1726) and the classic *A Serious Call to a Devout and Holy Life* (1728). After John's encounter with the Moravians he wrote to Law asking why he had not taught him the good news of the gospel and suggested that perhaps Law himself had not heard it. John came to see that William Law, along with the "mystic writers" (Michael Molinas, Francois Fenelon, and Madame Guyon), was among "the most dangerous of its [Christianity's] enemies."[3]

1. Hooker, *Works of Mr. Richard Hooker*, VI, iii, 3.
2. Tyson, "John Wesley and William Law," 60.
3. Outler, *John Wesley*, 47.

William Law was an important influence on many eighteenth-century figures who became evangelical leaders. His *Serious Call* and *Christian Perfection* were seen by many as exactly what was needed in a world of rampant depravity. Hogarth (1697–1764) graphically showed this in his popular paintings. The difficulty, however, lay in the very perfection called for by Law's teaching: that sanctification precedes the graciousness of free justification and thus Christ is presented as more of an example to follow than as a merciful forgiver of sinners.

One must admit an unfathomable mystery about salvation. Both Charles and John Wesley realized that William Law's teaching lacked the full dimension of grace; nevertheless, he exemplified the law as a schoolmaster that led them to Christ. Without the serious call to unattainable perfection in Law, would they ever have emptied themselves as completely and accepted their deliverance as deeply as they did, not by works but by Christ as Savior?

Yet it must also be acknowledged that Christianity, presented without the grace of God's action for and in us "while we were yet helpless" (Rom 5:6), often shuts the door to faith for those who would prefer deism or nonbelief to a Christianity that is infected with the legalism of Pharisaism. William Law was a household member and tutor in the Gibbon family for the first twenty-four years of Edward Gibbon's life (1737–1794). Gibbon became one of the greatest English historians but his negative view of the Christian faith led him to attribute the fall of Rome to Christianity. Ample evidence indicates that the young Edward Gibbon had great respect for his tutor, William Law, seeing him as a man of great courage and self-sacrifice but he shared little of Law's faith.[4] The question needs to be asked: Was Edward Gibbon's repudiation of Christianity a rejection of authentic faith or a rejection of William Law's version of it?

Unlike Gibbon, Wesley thoroughly embraced the teaching of Law until his experience of justification by grace through faith. No wonder he looked back with scorn on Law's call to holiness and perfection without the means to fulfill them. Law's teaching that "our salvation depends upon the sincerity and perfection of our endeavors to obtain it" is quite different, according to John Tyson, "from that of Wesley, who insists that works are consequent to our salvation but do not contribute to it."[5] The yeast

---

4. Lowe, *Edward Gibbon*, 10–16.

5. Tyson, "John Wesley and William Law," 60.

that insists on our works as a means of justification gives us something of which we can boast against others who do lesser works. This pride is always a barrier to acceptance of undeserved grace that assures peace with God (Rom 5: 1) and works of thanksgiving. An astonishing number of scholars attribute Wesley's hurtful criticism of his old mentor to Wesley's psychological state, while, at the same time, minimizing the seriousness of their differences in doctrine.

William Law was not alone in presenting Christianity without the indispensable theme of grace. Classical Anglicanism's profound grasp of grace, as seen in Cranmer's Prayer Books, as well as in the Anglican figures, Richard Hooker (c. 1554–1600), Lancelot Andrewes (1555–1626), John Donne (c. 1571–1631), George Herbert (1593–1633), and John Davenant (1572–1641), characterized Anglicanism from the Reformation through the first half of the seventeenth century. A radical departure from this understanding of law and grace occurred at the time of the Civil War, leading to a period in which the message of the gospel was often distorted, legalistic, and moralistic.

The Wesleys grew up at the end of almost a century of this drought, but they were vital factors in bringing the drought to an end. The writings of John Bunyan (1628–1688), *Grace Abounding* (1666) and *Pilgrim's Progress* (1678 and 1684), were outstanding exceptions to this drought, but Bunyan had to suffer twelve years in prison for the proclamation of his faith.

During and following the English Civil War, fear of antinomianism (i.e., the belief that, without the threat of God's condemnation of sinners, people would become ungovernable) was widespread and influenced much that was written during that time. The most popular devotional writing, an anonymous work called *The Whole Duty of Man* (1657), was influential in giving rise to the so-called Holy Living School. One could scarcely find a better example of Pharisaism: earning by works one's own salvation.

Little in *The Whole Duty of Man* would lead one to suppose that the gospel contains good news. The gospel is described predominantly as threats. The purpose of preaching is merely "to remind us of our duties."[6] Sin is overcome by first considering the guilt of it and then fearing the danger of damnation that would no doubt follow. "And sure, if this were

6. *Whole Duty of Man*, 4.

but thoroughly laid to heart, it would restrain this sin."[7] In striking contrast is Richard Hooker's claim that we cannot "possibly forsake sin, unless we first begin again to love . . . I therefore conclude, that fear worketh no man's inclination to repentance, till somewhat else have wrought in us love also."[8] The problem, as set forth in *The Whole Duty of Man*, is that "men do either not heartily believe that this sin will damn them, or if they do, they look on it as a thing way off, and so are not much moved with it." The solution, therefore is to help "sinners to apprehend their damnation and to grasp its nearness."[9]

The famous philosopher David Hume abandoned Christianity altogether by the time he was twenty. He had been made to read *The Whole Duty of Man* and he found it depressing, without hope, and with no good news. He wrote, "Upon the whole I desire to take my Catalogue of Virtues from Cicero's *Offices* and not from *The Whole Duty of Man*." Alasdair MacIntyre, who quotes this exchange, does not notice the gospel distortions in *The Whole Duty of Man* but attributes Hume's dismissal to philosophical reasons.[10] Hume regretted on his death bed that he was dying before he could extirpate Christianity from Scotland. Professor Leonard Hodgson was very wise when he taught us to ask a non-believer what it was he did not believe. Almost invariably it was such a distortion of Christianity that Hodgson could say that neither did he believe it. That approach can open up meaningful opportunities. Would that someone had asked David Hume this question and shared his disbelief in *The Whole Duty of Man*. William Cowper (1731–1800) called *The Whole Duty of Man* the "repository of self-righteousness and pharisaical lumber."[11] One cannot help but conjecture what difference it would have made had Hume been given the works of Hooker, Andrewes, Donne, and Herbert, which were free from the Pharisaic yeast of self-righteousness.

Charles Simeon (1759–1836), one of the most influential of Anglican evangelicals, was similarly inhibited and frustrated by being fed the yeast of infected writings of William Law and *The Whole Duty of Man*. As a student at Cambridge, Simeon was required to attend Holy Communion

---

7. Ibid., 70.

8. Hooker, *Ecclesiastical Polity*, 3.

9. *Whole Duty of Man*, 70.

10. MacIntyre, *Whose Justice? Which Rationality*, 282.

11. Southey, *Life of William Cowper*, 81.

twice a year. He carefully studied *The Whole Duty of Man* to prepare, but "I made myself quite ill with reading, fasting, and prayer" as he attempted to fulfill the sinless conditions demanded by *The Whole Duty of Man*. Fortunately, he came across a book by Bishop Thomas Wilson (1663–1755), *Instruction for the Lord's Supper*. Here he first saw that God's redemption for sinners by Christ lay at the heart of the gospel: "Has God provided an offering for me, that I may lay my sins on his head? Then, God Willing, I will not bear them on my own soul one moment longer."[12]

When seeing Jesus only as an example to follow was replaced by the assurance of undeserved forgiveness by the sacrifice of Christ, Simeon's life was remarkably changed. His experience of Holy Communion after hearing the good news from Thomas Wilson was a life-changing event, and he came to have a far greater influence "than that of any primate (archbishop)," in the words of the great historian Thomas Babington Macaulay.

Another influential figure who had to go through the crucible of the teachings of William Law and *The Whole Duty of Man* before finding the freedom of the gospel was Henry Venn (1725–1797), the father of John Venn, Vicar of Clapham and pastor to William Wilberforce. Henry, who had been deeply convicted by the requirements of sinlessness before coming to Communion, was driven back to Scripture to find relief and comfort. He wrote:

> Since Christ the lawgiver will always speak in vain unless Christ the Saviour be first known . . . All treatises therefore written to promote holiness of living must be deplorably defective, in which the cross of Christ is not laid as the foundation . . . This is the apostolic method of inculcating Christian obedience; and all other obedience is Pharisaical, a mere refined species of self-righteousness.[13]

Venn was persuaded by friends to write a corrective in reply to *The Whole Duty of Man* that he titled *The Complete Duty of Man or a System of Doctrinal and Practical Christianity* (1763). It became a widespread antidote to the legalisms being substituted for the Christian faith.

The climate of rationalism in eighteenth-century England following the upheavals of the Civil War in the seventeenth century saw the rise of what would be called Latitudinarianism. John Tillotson (1630–1694),

---

12. Carus, *Life of Charles Simeon*, 5.
13. Venn, *Complete Duty of Man*, xxxiii.

Archbishop of Canterbury and a famous advocate of tolerance, produced fourteen volumes of sermons that became unrivaled homiletic resources in both England and the American colonies. In Tillotson there is none of the serious call for holiness and perfection that is found in Law and *The Whole Duty of Man* but also nothing of grace, the cross, or justification. Tillotson's teachings were singularly relevant and accommodating to an age confident in human reason's ability to establish morals and to rely on human will to fulfill them. This confidence led him to present Christianity as a rational system without need of justification by faith or any atonement by Christ. George Whitefield observed that Tillotson "knows no more of Christ than Mohamet."[14] It was in some sense true, but it was also a rather impolitic observation. Tillotson was a symbol of the enormously influential school of Latitudinarianism that sought to mediate between Puritans and High Anglicans on the basis of reason. Among them were the Cambridge Platonists, whose gifts and undoubted talent were marred by a confidence in unconverted human nature. Benjamin Wichcote (1609–1683) expressed the grandeur but little of the misery of which humans are capable: "The spirit of man is the candle of the Lord."

Following the Civil War these two traditions, the Holy Living School and the Latitudinarians, helped to squeeze out of English-speaking Christianity any biblical teaching regarding how sinners are saved. They replaced it with repackaged Pelagianism, the idea that God's favor is deserved through good works. This was the case until the Methodist and Anglican evangelical revivals began in the late 1730s. (John Bunyan, as noted, was a remarkable exception.)

A less critical yet significant view of this era of history is that of the eminent historian, Norman Sykes:

> Perhaps the key to true religion *as understood by the age* (italics mine) may best be found in its favourite manual of devotion, *The Whole Duty of Man*, published in 1658 and enjoying an extraordinary vogue for the ensuing century . . . If William Cowper stigmatized it as "a repository of self-righteousness," and George Whitefield classed its author with Tillotson as one who knew "no more about true Christianity than Mahomet," it nevertheless constituted an abiding monument to the sober, rational piety of an age which believed firmly, in accordance with its title, in the

---

14. Henry, *Wayfaring Witness*, 107.

injunction, "Fear God and keep his commandments; for this is the whole duty of Man."[15]

This whole duty is bereft of any clear description of how God enables us to fulfill these duties. It is empty of any news of what God has done in Christ for those of us who have failed in this whole duty. Quite unlike *The Whole Duty of Man*, a congruent and cogent consensus existed among the classical Anglicans, from Cranmer and the Prayer Books of the sixteenth century until the Civil War in the next century that proclaimed the gracious and prevenient action regarding the gospel. The legacy of the Holy Living School and Latitudinarian distortions of the Gospel, born at the time of the Civil War, is best shown in the public writings (as distinct from the prayers) of Bishop Jeremy Taylor (1613–1667).

Few Anglicans have been more uncritically praised and recommended than Taylor, the seventeenth-century prose genius, Chaplain to Charles I, and author of *Holy Living* and *Holy Dying*. The overwhelming acceptance of Taylor's teaching by the academic elite over the last three centuries is conclusive evidence that the Christian gospel has been misrepresented and obscured. One of the few scholars whose judgment was not distorted by this Pharisaic yeast was Samuel Taylor Coleridge. He described Taylor's writing in the following terms:

> If ever a book was calculated to drive men to despair, it is Bishop Jeremy Taylor's on *Repentance*.[16]

> Now the necessary consequences of Taylor's scheme is a conscience worrying, casuistical monkish work-holiness.[17]

The fundamentally cruel thing about Taylor is his denial that God loves sinners:

> He that commits any one sin by choice and deliberation is an enemy to God, and under the dominion of the flesh.[18]

> In short he is not a child of God that knowingly and deliberately chooses anything that God hates.[19]

---

15. Sykes, *From Sheldon to Secker*, 187.

16. Coleridge, *Notes on English Divines*, II, 38.

17. Ibid., I, 268.

18. Heber, *Whole Works of the The Rt. Rev Jeremy Taylor*, VI, 258.

19. Ibid., IV, 259.

[When] the will loves it [lust], and so long as it does, God cannot love the man; for God is the prince of purities, and the Son of God is the king of virgins . . .[20]

He that is in the affection, or in the habit, or in the state of any one sin whatsoever, is at such distance from and contrariety to God, that he provokes God to anger in every prayer he makes . . .[21]

These texts are not isolated or exceptional. They constitute a theme that runs through almost everything he wrote except his prayers. Once in the New Covenant Taylor insists that if we fail to be like Christ, there is no longer any dealing with us in "the method of his kindness" and here the wicked hope in vain for pardon "because God accepts no breakers of their vows."[22] One is forgiven after baptism on the condition of repentance but "true repentance must reduce to act all its holy purposes . . . For to resolve to do it and yet not to do it is to break our resolution and our faith . . . and to make our pardon hopeless and our hope fruitless."[23] According to Taylor our holy life is the only ground for hope for God's love and forgiveness:

a holy life is the only perfection of repentance, and the firm ground upon which we can cast the anchor of hope in the mercies of God through Jesus Christ.[24]

Because forgiveness is impossible on grounds other than a holy life any deathbed absolution is impossible. (The thief on the cross example is dismissed by Taylor as one of "the first access" and not applicable to a baptized person in the covenant.) Taylor frequently uses the phrase "justification by faith" but claims that "by faith in Christ we are admitted to the pardon of our sins, if we repent and forsake them utterly."[25] In *Holy Living* it is made quite plain that he:

that resolves to live well . . . just when the temptation comes again, sins again, and then is sorrowful, and resolves once more against it, and yet falls when the temptation returns, is a vain man . . . no true

20. Ibid., V, 64.
21. Ibid., V, 65.
22. Ibid., XV, 87.
23. Ibid., IV, 260.
24. Ibid., IV, 260.
25. Ibid., XV, 418.

penitent, nor in the state of grace, and if he chance to die in one of these good moods, is very far from salvation; for if it be necessary, that we resolve to live well, it is necessary we should do so.[26]

Another serious departure from classical Anglicanism is Taylor's novel doctrine of the new covenant. It differs from the old covenant in that it is a "more lenient" one:

Under the first covenant, the covenant of works no endeavour was sufficient because there was no allowance made for infirmities, no abatements for ignorance, no deductions of exact measures, no consideration of surprises, passions, folly and inadvertency; but under the new covenant, our hearty endeavour is accepted . . .[27]

Although such a view cannot be found in the preceding generation of Anglicans (Hooker, Andrewes, Donne, et al.), this novel teaching is echoed by Taylor's contemporary, Henry Hammond (1605–1660), when the latter quaintly describes Christ as having "brought down the market."[28]

Taylor was not altogether consistent in the matter of how much sin was allowable in the regenerate, but he was certain that Romans 7:19–25 ("The good that I would I do not and the evil that I would not, that I do . . .") could not possibly be consistent with a state of regeneration ("how if this be a state of regeneration, I wonder what is, or can be, a state of reprobation!"). [29] He even suggested, at one point, that sins committed after baptism and confirmation are what is meant by the "sin against the Holy Ghost."[30] Also:

We are but once to change our whole state of life, from the power of the devil . . . After this change if ever we fall into the contrary state . . . God hath made no more covenant of restitution to us; there is no place left for any more repentance . . . or new birth: a man can be regenerated but once . . .[31]

Another despairing thing about Taylor's theology is his insistence on man's, not God's, initiative:

26. Ibid., IV, 260.

27. Ibid., VIII, 292.

28. "Hammond's Sermons," *Library of Anglo-Catholic Theology*, 113–14.

29. Heber, *Whole Works of The Rt. Rev. Jeremy Taylor*, IV, 247.

30. Ibid., II, 398–99.

31. Ibid., IV, 256.

For a holy life being the condition of the covenant on our part, as we return to God, so God returns to us, and our state returns to the probabilities of pardon.[32]

Yet even that forgiveness or pardon obtained by sinlessness is only partial, problematic, and conditional:

For because the body of sin dies divisibly, and fights perpetually, and disputes with hopes of victory, and may also prevail, all this life is a condition of suspense; our sin is rather covered, than *properly pardoned*; God's wrath is suspended, not satisfied; the sin is not to all purposes of anger imputed, but yet is in some sense remanent, or at least lies ready at the door[33] (italics mine).

[The church] can by sermons, declare all the necessary parts of repentance and the conditions of pardon, and can pronounce limited and hypothetical or conditional pardons; concerning which, the penitent must take care that they belong to him.[34]

Jeremy Taylor insists that one must earn the pardon, grace, and love of God and that the rewards of heaven are so great that it is shameful to expect them "at a lower rate than a holy life":[35]

Charity with its twin daughters, alms and forgiveness, is especially effectual for procuring God's mercies in the day and the manner of our death.[36]

Every deadly sin destroys the rewards of seven years' piety.[37]

A hearty endeavour, and an effectual general change shall get the pardon . . .[38]

Considering Holy Communion for example, Taylor's requirements for forgiveness are in stark contrast to the Anglican *Book of Common Prayer*, and especially the absolutions in Morning and Evening Prayer which recognize that worship and absolution are means of power and grace to sinful people by praying for true repentance after the declara-

32. Ibid., IV, 261.
33. Ibid., II, 411.
34. Ibid., XV, 637.
35. Ibid., IV, 636.
36. Ibid., IV, 382.
37. Ibid., VI, 50.
38. Ibid., IV, 256.

tion of absolution. True repentance is possible only by the grace of absolution.

Taylor reminds his readers of the necessity of having on the "wedding garment" (Matt 22:1–14). Hooker, Andrewes, and John Donne had seen the wedding garment as the righteousness of Christ by which we sinners are clothed before the presence of God. John Donne has a particularly apt use of the Jacob-Esau story claiming that as Jacob received the blessing of his father by wearing the garments of Esau we, like Jacob, receive God's blessing clothed with the garments of our elder brother, Christ. Taylor insists outrageously that the wedding garment is the whole conjugation of our own works of charity by which "we are fitted to this heavenly supper of the king."[39] Nor must we presume to come to the Lord's table except we be "clothed with white garments, the righteousness and justification of the saints."[40] It would seem that only sociopaths, paranoids, and iatrogenic[41] theologians could come to Communion on Taylor's terms.

All who are unable of themselves to help themselves, who are consciously aware of their sin, who are not confident that they have the righteousness of the saints, who are not free from all uncleanness or sinful desires will only anger God by prayer, come to Holy Communion to be damned, be hated by God, and until they become sinless by their repentance cannot hope for any pardon or forgiveness. Here is a gospel that helps only those who have been able to help themselves. It is not authentic Christian faith but the self-righteousness of malignant Pharisaism.

In his prayers Taylor manifests a gospel that is different in no way from that of his Anglican predecessors. These prayers explicitly contradict what he had said in his theological, devotional, and homiletical works. In his prayers he insists on the necessity for God's action before ours. Romans 7 is a description of us all even those in a state of grace. The deathbed confessor is reassured by the example of the thief on the cross. People who have tied themselves up with vows and little by little have willingly and knowingly broken God's commandments can petition for forgiveness that is assured as true pardon. Coleridge, almost alone among moderns, saw Taylor's Pelagianism but failed to see the contradiction

---

39. Ibid., XV, 518.

40. Ibid., XV, 586.

41. Iatrogenic is a term used in medicine for physician-caused maladies.

in his prayers in which there is not the slightest hint of such teachings.[42] Coleridge instructs us further here with his statement, which not only describes Taylor's theology accurately (except in his prayers), but also outlines in one sentence the drift of theology since the middle of the seventeenth century. "In short, Socinianism is as inevitable a deduction from Taylor's scheme as Deism or Atheism is from Socinianism."[43]

Socinianism is the quintessential Pharisaic doctrine and has had widespread and baleful influence in the last three centuries. Both Adolph von Harnack and Paul Tillich agreed that it dissolves the classical and creedal teaching concerning Christ and the Trinity:[44]

1. Socinianism begins with the Pelagian assumption that humans are born free and have the power to overcome sin and self-centeredness.

2. Justification by grace is not needed as we are able to produce behavior which is acceptable to God.

3. Jesus is no longer a sacrifice for sin who makes us one with God but merely an example for us to follow.

4. Jesus himself is only a model of what we should and can be.

The result is a Unitarian deity with no "at-one-ment" with God through Christ. He fulfilled the law, became perfect, and was rewarded by God with a delegated divinity. What is lost is the good news of what God did in Christ so that we undeserving sinners in bondage to our self-as-center might receive justice and mercy. To Socinians, Jesus is not the personal human expression of our gracious God but a heroic figure we are to emulate. For spiritually drowning people he is not a savior but a swimming coach. We lose not only his mercy and forgiveness but the comfort of his present Holy Spirit (whose very name is comforter, *parakletos*, cf. John 14:16, 26; 15:26; 16:7).

Coleridge's genius compresses too much into one sentence for it to have the needed historical effect. That Taylor's life of Christ was titled *The Great Exemplar* comes as no surprise. Taylor's contemporaries were far

42. To my knowledge no other authorities on Taylor have noticed this. The whole matter is fully discussed in Allison, *Rise of Moralism: Proclamation of the Gospel from Hooker to Baxter.*

43. Coleridge, *Notes on English Divines*, I, 278.

44. Tillich, *History of Christian Thought*, 267.

more aware of the danger of Socinianism than are contemporary scholars, many of whom themselves are blinded by this Socinian form of the Pharisaic yeast.

What is of special importance is not merely one figure, Jeremy Taylor, who departed radically from the gospel, but the pervasiveness of the malignant yeast in the teaching of the modern elite of academic Anglicanism. At least twelve contemporary scholars who have published works or lectured as authorities on Jeremy Taylor show no objection to Taylor's distortion of the Gospel. Nor have these scholars shown any indication that they were aware of his being accused of Pelagianism by four of his contemporary bishops in an age that still took doctrine seriously.[45] His works continue to be recommended without caution by scholars who themselves need to heed the warnings of Jesus regarding the yeast of the Pharisees.

The historical context in which Jeremy Taylor and others were writing is important to acknowledge. The Civil War raged intermittently for ten years, from 1642 to 1652. King Charles I had been beheaded in 1649. The monarchy was not restored until 1660. Thus, Taylor lived twelve of his most productive years in the most chaotic and unstable of times. He was a loyalist, imprisoned, then sequestered during events of upheavals in society. One can understand his caution in telling of God's unmerited mercy, forgiveness and love, lest people get the impression that it is unnecessary to behave. This reaction to the gospel has been with us since the beginning, "Are we to continue in sin that grace may abound?" (Rom 6:1). Fear of antinomianism seems always to be a justification for Pharisaism.

A good example of the effect of the fear of antinomianism is that of Archbishop James Ussher. In 1656 amidst the troubling times, an anonymous writer entreated the Archbishop to explain his views on justification and sanctification. At an earlier time the writer had heard him preach on these issues and it seemed to make these doctrines more clearly intelligible than anything he had heard before. Ussher had indeed been deeply concerned in the 1630s to explicate such matters with evangelical lucidity, but in the perilous times of 1656 concern withered for biblical teaching as to how we are saved. He barely mentioned the matter about which he was asked, but launched immediately into dire

---

45. See the writings of McAdoo, Stranks, Thornton, Huntley, Every, Hughes, Carroll, Williamson, Elmen, Dewar, Scott, and Greer. All have lectured or published material on Taylor and they recommend Taylor's works uncritically.

predictions of an imminent apocalypse as the certain consequence of disturbing contemporary events.[46]

The seventeenth century cared a great deal more about theology than later times. In spite of Taylor's close connections with both Archbishop Laud and Charles I, his faithful loyalty to the Crown during the Commonwealth, and his unquestionable prose genius (on this issue Coleridge ranks him with Shakespeare, Bacon, and Milton), he is not given an English episcopate, in spite of his desires, but one beyond the pale in Ireland. Nor was Taylor allowed to take part in the revision of the Prayer Book in 1662. Four of his contemporary bishops explicitly cited him for Pelagianism.

Fear of disorder and immorality is the context in which the Pharisaic yeast grew. Jeremy Taylor and William Law deeply influenced many early evangelicals: George Whitefield, Charles and John Wesley, Henry Venn, Thomas Scott, and Henry Martyn. They changed but others did not. Law's theology, as well as that of *The Whole Duty of Man*, Jeremy Taylor, and Richard Baxter played a major role in molding how Christianity was taught and believed in much of the eighteenth century.

Taylor's views are not to be found in the early seventeenth century but are quite widespread in the second half following the Civil War in the writings of Henry Hammond, Richard Baxter, and George Bull. The Pelagianism in these writers, that human will power alone can enable us to obey God's law, is counterfeit Christianity. Sadly, the rejection of the unattainable, Pharisaic counterfeit has not always brought about a renewed reliance on grace. Like David Hume's case, this doctrine has often been the reason people repudiate what they believe to be Christianity. Within Anglicanism, Jeremy Taylor placed the banana peel of Pelagianism on the cliff of Unitarianism.

46. Unsigned manuscript.

7

Roman Catholicism and the Council of Trent

"I confess to almighty God . . . that I have sinned exceedingly in thought, word and deed by my fault, my fault, my very grievous fault."

—Roman Catholic Mass

R EFORM OF THE CHURCH in the sixteenth century was by no means an exclusive concern of Protestants. The need for moral, educational, and administrative reform was everywhere acknowledged. The calling and intermittent meeting of the Council of Trent from 1545 to 1563 is a complex story but considerable needed reform was accomplished in training clergy, discipline, renewal of spiritual life, and administration. However, our focus will be on the 5th Session, which dealt with original sin (1546) and the 6th Session, which dealt with justification (1547).

No tradition (or generation of believers) is without the need to hear our Lord's warning concerning the self-righteous yeast of the Pharisees. The decrees of the Council of Trent about sin and justification are to Pharisaism as cigarettes are to cancer. Some issues at these two sessions evoked special criticism from Anglicans and Protestants and dismay among many Catholics as well. Among the latter were Cardinal Seripando, head of the Augustinian order, and Reginald Pole, later the Catholic Archbishop of Canterbury under Queen Mary. Pole was so distressed by the decisions at the 6th Session concerning justification that he left the Council in a state of depression from which it took him many months to recover.[1]

What was the decision that distressed these two Roman Catholic leaders? The simple issue lay beneath a layer of scholastic terms: What

1. See Fenlon, *Heresy and Obedience in Tridentine Italy*.

is it that makes us justified or acceptable before God? The answer given at Trent was: righteousness of our own, infused into us at baptism.[2] The technical language was: the "single formal cause" of our justification is the "infusion of inherent righteousness." (Formal cause simply means that which makes a thing to be what it is.)

The dismay among many Roman Catholics and most Protestants was caused by the teaching that denied any recognition of sin in Christians who are in a state of grace, that is, in favor with God. Session 5 had already asserted that venial sins do not have the formal nature of sin. Thus, the righteousness of Christians in a state of grace would satisfy God's justice, notwithstanding the presence of venial sins.[3]

The claim that this righteousness is "infused" wards off the charge of Pelagianism, or that we have established this righteousness by our wills. However, the claim that infusion of righteousness at baptism is the *single formal cause* means that nothing but our own righteousness, though infused (given), is necessary for us to be justified before God. Cardinals Seripando, Pole, and Contarini (who died in 1542 before the Council of Trent) each saw that no one's righteousness, however infused and given, was adequate to meet God's justice without being joined with the righteousness of Christ that is reckoned (imputed) to us.

Criticism of Trent by Anglicans ran along similar lines. Richard Hooker (1554–1600) called this statement concerning the formal cause of justification, "that grand question which hangeth yet in controversy between us and the Church of Rome about the matter of justifying Righteousness."[4] The Anglican alternative to Trent is clearly expressed by Hooker: "The righteousness whereby we shall be clothed in the world to come is both perfect and inherent. That whereby here we are justified is perfect, but not inherent. That whereby we are sanctified is inherent, but not perfect."[5]

2. Council of Trent .6. Decre. 1.7 Alberigo-Jedin, 673–74.

3. A mortal sin is sin committed with full knowledge and consent of the will in a grave matter. A venial sin is sin committed with less than full knowledge and consent of the will in a slight or peripheral matter. Venial sins not having the formal nature of sin can exist in a regenerate person and do not destroy one's state of grace. Mortal sin, on the other hand, does destroy one's state of grace and requires the sacrament of penance to recover the favor of God.

4. Hooker, "A Learned Discourse of Justification," par. 3, 512.

5. Ibid., 512.

This understanding of salvation acknowledges that it is only by God's perfect action in Jesus Christ that we are either forgivable or forgiven. Because no one, not even Christians in a state of grace (being in a right relationship with God), is without sin, so our righteousness in the process of sanctification is ours but in this life is imperfect. The righteousness of our final consummation is both ours and perfect.

Trent claimed that our present infused righteousness is in itself enough to satisfy God's almighty justice. This mistake was a breach in the air lock that guards the faith from resting on one's own goodness (which in this life remains imperfect).[6]

SUPEREROGATION AND INDULGENCIES

Let us examine three reasons why this issue is important. First is the claim that our righteousness, given at baptism, satisfies the justice of God. This reduces that righteousness to include venial sins and it can be improved by doing good deeds over and above what is required by the Church. These works are called "works of supererogation." For instance, a layperson can become a nun or priest, which is more than the minimum required of a Christian, and be rewarded accordingly. St. Augustine and other saints of antiquity, on the contrary, insisted that "what is not of love is sin" and that no Christian has yet fulfilled the complete love in response to the love God shows to sinners. Jesus tells his disciples, "So you also, when you have done all that is commanded you, say 'We are unworthy servants; we have only done our duty'" (Luke 17:10).

The Anglican Article XIV of the 39 Articles explicitly denies the possibility of works of supererogation. Article XI deals with our chronic unworthiness before the majesty of God. We are accounted righteous before God because of the righteousness of Christ being reckoned or worded to us.

---

6. Non-Roman Catholics must take care in casting stones at the Communion representing a majority of Christians in the world. And especially is this so since there is no greater bulwark to the accelerating Sadducee yeast of secularism, along with militant Islam, the most serious threat to Christianity in the world. These, however, are not "stones" being cast but a humble plea not merely from non-Roman Catholics but from Catholic antiquity as well as from some within that Communion who are not as free as is someone outside to raise these questions. It is in this spirit that these criticisms of Trent are offered.

While attending the Council of Trent, Cardinal Seripando and Reginald Pole objected to the claim that our infused righteousness *alone* is the formal cause of justification because no one's righteousness, whether infused or not, is equal to God's justice and must be supplemented by Christ's righteousness. They were put down by the General of the Jesuit Order, Diego Lainez, as holding a "novelty" invented by Luther. Lainez claimed that the position of Pole and Seripando "would undercut the structure of *satisfactions, indulgencies, and purgatory*"[7](italics mine).

LOGIDZOMAI: IMPUTE OR RECKON

The word in Scripture, denoting the event that makes us worthy to stand before almighty God, is *logidzomai*. "In the beginning was the Word (*Logos*) and the Word was with God and the Word was God" (John 1:1). And the Word became verb, *logidzomai*. It is inadequately translated as: account, regard, treat as, reckon, deem, or impute. Impute (a word scarcely used today except by accountants) is an exceedingly weak translation of *logidzomai*. But it is crucially important to understand this term in order to see that *logidzomai* (impute) is the verb form of *Logos*—the word by whom the worlds were made and by whom we are saved. "Imputation" of the righteousness of Christ is a term that has been used since the Reformation by the Lutheran, Reformed, and Anglican traditions in contrast to Trent's "infused" as that which makes us worthy before God. Imputation is the righteousness of Christ worded to us, although we were yet sinners and knowing this we may begin to become righteous. The Tridentine term, infusion of righteousness, establishes our favor before God on the basis of our own righteousness alone. On the other hand, when sinners realize by faith that they have been *worded* as righteous by God, in their gratitude they begin to become truly righteous, not self-righteous. The trust (faith) evoked by God's sacrifice in Christ changes our hearts so that we begin to love what he commands.

Works of supererogation and indulgences, in contrast, are the logical and historical result of the claim that we are worthy before God by virtue of the righteousness within us, a righteousness we can add to for merit. Henry VIII (1491–1547) believed and acted on these unreformed teachings and died in these beliefs:

7. Pelikan, *Reformation of Church and Dogma*, 284.

> By his will . . . money was left for a great number of masses to be
> said for the repose of his soul . . . and that until the Revolution in
> 1792 Mass was said annually for him . . . at the Cathedral of Notre
> Dame in Paris.[8]

So-called chantry masses are financed by endowments. A priest, in consecrating the host, can offer the sacrifice of Christ to God in the name of others whose time in purgatory might be shortened. These transactions, called indulgences, were not permission to commit sins but were reductions of time in purgatory because of the need for restitution. If John steals ten dollars from Jack and is forgiven he still must pay back the ten dollars to make restitution. Restitution not made in this life is accomplished by time in purgatory. Pre-Reformation teaching regarding merit and indulgences were not reformed at Trent or by the 2nd Vatican Council (1962–1965). Roman Catholic scholar Gregory Baum asked in an issue of "The Ecumenist" following the 2nd Vatican Council, "Why silence on indulgences?" The distinguished Roman Catholic scholar, Karl Rahner, is obviously embarrassed by the teaching concerning indulgences but is relieved "that the interest in indulgences is largely diminishing in the church."[9]

NO SIN IN A STATE OF GRACE

Second, denying sin in the regenerate (*simul justus et peccator*: at the same time righteous and a sinner) has a debilitating effect on social and political responsibilities. Since the Council of Trent if a person is a sinner he cannot be in a state of grace or in favor with God. Consequently, definitions of sin must be carefully defined so that one can be considered sinless. The article on "Grace" in the *Catholic Encyclopedia* indicates the results of the Tridentine mistake:

> For since sin and grace are diametrically opposed to each other the
> mere advent of grace is sufficient to drive sin away . . . immediately
> brings about holiness, kinship with God, and a renovation of spirit
> . . . and therefore a remission of sin without a simultaneous inte-
> rior sanctification is theologically impossible. As to the interesting
> controversy whether the incompatibility of grace and sin rests on

8. Ollard and Crosse, *Dictionary of English History*, 264.
9. Rahner, *Encyclopedia of Theology*, 702–10.

merely moral, or physical, or metaphysical contrariety, refer Pohl (1909), Scheeben (1898).[10]

This claim by Trent in regard to denying *simul justus et peccator*, or sin in the regenerate (those in a state of grace), precludes any acknowledgment of corporate or collective guilt. For example, an article entitled "Collective Responsibility" in the *New Catholic Encyclopedia* deals with collective guilt as a legitimate Old Testament phenomenon and teaching, but not one appropriate to the New Testament or to church history. If sin to be sin must have full knowledge and consent of the will, citizens of a country where torture is practiced have no culpable responsibility so long as they themselves neither perpetrate nor assent to the torture. They are justified in their passivity. This teaching seriously diminishes the quality of social duties. On the other hand, if Christians are taught to share complicity in society's sins they are likely to be led to correct them. However, that very complicity carries the nature of sin. For example:

> Then they also will answer, "Lord when did we see thee hungry or thirsty or a stranger or naked or sick or in prison, and did not minister to thee?" Then he will answer them "Truly I say to you, as you did it not to one of the least of these, you did it not to me." And they will go away into eternal punishment. (Matt 25:44–46)

The refusal to acknowledge collective responsibility is a consequence of Trent's denial of sin in the regenerate. Only those who have full knowledge and consent to bribery or tyranny can be held accountable for social and corporate wrongs. This fact has had a debilitating effect on Roman Catholic cultures and countries. Without a sense of corporate accountability democracies do not flourish; tyranny and corruption do.

The nineteenth-century English jurist, Lord Moulton, accurately observed that "the greatness of a nation, its true civilization is measured by the extent of its obedience to the unenforceable."[11] This requires a keen sense of social and corporate responsibility, what has been called a Protestant conscience. *The New Catholic Encyclopedia* acknowledges that throughout the Old Testament God holds Israel corporately responsible for justice and faithfulness. Is this corporate responsibility not also ascribed under the New Covenant? Are not responsibility and accountabil-

---

10. *Catholic Encyclopedia*, 704.

11. "Laws and Manners," 1–5.

ity even loftier and more arduous in the New than the Old? The Old is not abrogated but fulfilled.

For Christians to share responsibility for the Holocaust and other horrors that they as individuals had no willful part in is an unbearable burden for one whose state of grace depends on the absence of any culpability. William Wilberforce owned no slaves and gave no consent of his individual will to the institution of slavery, but his sense of corporate responsibility drove him and others to work successfully for the abolition of the slave trade. Surely it can be shown in both St. Augustine and St. Bernard that similar responsibilities, and acknowledgment of corporate complicity, were on the shoulders of Christians in regard to the Empire, Donatists, or papal schisms. St. Bernard insisted that "not to sin is God's justice; but the justice of man is the pardon of God."[12] At that time this was a bearable responsibility because such acknowledgment of culpability was not tantamount to the loss of grace as was later claimed at the Council of Trent. Sin was a much deeper and wider phenomenon in Patristic and Medieval theology than in its post-Tridentine definition. Christians are enabled to accept complicity and corporate responsibility in actions of a family, tribe, company, church, city, or nation when they know their acceptance by God is not based on their own worthiness but on that of Christ, which is worded, imputed, and reckoned to them.

Since the decree of Trent in 1547 it seems to be assumed that any statements by St. Thomas Aquinas, St. Anselm, St. Bernard, or others concerning unconscious, unknown, non-deliberate, or corporate sin must be understood as venial sin, because "full knowledge and consent of the will" is not involved. If one regarded unconscious fault or corporate guilt as sin, it would be virtually impossible to maintain the interpretation that sin and grace are mutually exclusive or that Christians, in a state of grace, cannot be sinners. The result of these teachings at Trent is the claim that regenerate Christians in a state of grace are not sinners.

The fact of sin among Christians is obvious from the most general reading of Scripture. More than half of the Epistles would be irrelevant if Christians were not sinners. The situations addressed in Galatians, I and II Corinthians, and the book of Acts make it abundantly clear that the early Christians, and even the disciples, were not devoid of sin. (See the quarrel among Paul, Barnabas, Mark, and Silas in Acts 15: 39–40.)

---

12. Hall, *Works*, IX, 47.

Teaching people that they are of themselves righteous, if they have not committed a mortal sin with full knowledge and consent, can quarantine them from grace and appropriate responsibility. Being in a state of grace is to be no longer under condemnation because of what has been done for us by Christ, not because we are no longer sinful.

DENIAL OF UNCONSCIOUS SIN

Third, this denial at Trent that sin can be present in a state of grace has unfortunate implications for our spiritual lives and for therapeutic endeavors. Ancient pastoral wisdom and contemporary depth psychology testify to the reality that many intractable patterns and compulsions are symptoms of unconscious roots. These need to be exposed and acknowledged in order that the damaging patterns no longer will have sway over a person's actions.

Dom Victor White, the English Roman Catholic Dominican, saw this serious limitation of Trent's teaching:

> This idea of "unconscious sin" is often a difficult one for the moral theologian to grasp. Especially if he has been brought up in the traditions of Post-Reformation Catholicism [after the Council of Trent] he may find it particularly hard to square with his correct notions that mortal sin must be voluntary, performed with full knowledge and consent. But it is a fact that the psyche is much less indulgent to unconscious breaches of its own laws and demands . . . and will revenge itself for their disregard . . .[13]

He appends a valuable observation:

> The exclusive emphasis of later theologians on "full knowledge and consent" can have the unfortunate result of putting a certain premium on unconsciousness, irresponsibility and infantilism.[14]

As an obedient Roman Catholic, White must put unconscious sin in quotation marks because it seems to conflict with the correct notions that, since Trent, mortal sins must have full knowledge and consent. But clearly he feels quite unhappy with this restraint under which spiritual directors and psychiatrists must work to stay in accord with the church's teachings after Trent.

13. Mairet, ed., *Christian Essays in Psychiatry*, 165.
14. Ibid.

The article on "The Psychology of Guilt" in the *New Catholic Encyclopedia* indicates the same direction but with new and even more awkward problems. Although it recognizes unconscious guilt to be a pervasively destructive phenomenon, it does not relate such guilt to one's spiritual condition and distinguishes it from moral guilt by terming it material guilt.

> The issue of material guilt has no meaning to it other than its producing a feeling of excessive fear of retaliation in interpersonal relationships about wrongdoing (due to ignorance, misconceptions, immaturity, or to repression, displacement, and substitution), which loses its significance at death since it vanishes then, or before death as one learns from experience. Moral guilt, however, binds one to an accounting for wrongdoing in the relationship with God, to be resolved by His judgment at death; therefore one must consciously seek to do good and avoid evil.[15]

This solution puts a premium on keeping material guilt unconscious, thus rewarding irrationality, ignorance, "repression, displacement, and substitution," as Dom Victor White pointed out. The article insists that unconscious aspects of guilt "must be considered, for they are recognized as disruptive in personality function," but when they are *"once realized"* (italics mine) they become sin (VI, 854). If true, this would mean all therapy and counseling jeopardizes one's state of grace at precisely those points where it successfully brings into consciousness the hitherto unrecognized roots of one's sinful behavior.

It follows that separating material guilt from moral guilt, and claiming that material guilt is neither sinful nor something for which we are held accountable, might be necessary to maintain Trent's teaching. However, it results in what Dom Victor White warns against: repression and endeavors to keep such matters unconscious, where it is claimed that they do not endanger one's soul but merely infect one's psyche. Separating matters of the psyche from matters of the soul has no theological or philological rationale. Both words are translations of the single word in Greek, *psuke*.

Bruno Bettelheim has argued convincingly that translators have made spurious use of Freud to make scientific what was essentially humane.[16] Translating the German to read psyche instead of soul is one

---

15. *New Catholic Encylopedia.*
16. Bettelheim, *Freud and Man's Soul*, 32.

such case. It would be a shame for Christians to continue this distortion by making separate arenas for psyche (material guilt) and soul (moral guilt) for which there is absolutely no biblical or theological justification. In fact, it has become a secular sleight-of-hand to reduce much of religion to mere psychology. The word soul in Scripture is always the translation of *psuke*, never psyche.

Treating material guilt as having "no meaning to it" in relation to our souls' health is pastorally irresponsible, and echoes the seventeenth-century Jesuit teaching that excuses sins done in ignorance. As Blaise Pascal (1623–1662) has pointed out, this rewards ignorance. Surely the traditional recourse to distinguish between vincible and invincible ignorance, can serve certain practical purposes in avoiding administrative and penal injustices that would punish people for what they were unable to alter. (Invincible ignorance excuses one from culpability because it does not involve the will to sin. Vincible ignorance, however, is culpable for it involves neglect to acquire information necessary to avoid sin.) Nevertheless, it falls short of approaching positively those areas of darkness in a person's soul (psyche) that need the light of grace for one to grow toward the perfect image that is Christ.

I recall counseling a married couple at a theological seminary. In a role reversal each was asked to pretend to be the other partner in extended conversations. When it was over the husband said, "I knew she cried easily but I thought I was just a big tease. I had no idea how much I was hurting her!" Surely his ignorance of how he had hurt her was no mere "material sin" needing no accountability.

A more serious problem results from this teaching of the Roman Catholic Church since the Council of Trent that for sin to be sin it must have full knowledge and consent of the will. Such teaching renders irrelevant Jesus's cry to us from the cross, "Father forgive them; for they know not what they do" (Luke 23:34).

Worth noting is the way the Roman Catholic theologian Hans Kung handles this question of sin and culpability that remains in Christians. He claims that *simul justus et peccator* (at the same time just and a sinner) is itself a Catholic teaching in spite of traditional understandings of the Council of Trent. He justifies this by showing that the revision of the Mass is replete with illustrations of confession of sin by priests and people who are clearly assumed to be in a state of grace, and therefore it is Catholic doctrine that those in a state of grace are yet sinners. This text of the Mass was established in the sixteenth century as the official liturgy, a higher claim than traditional interpretations of Trent.[17] A quotation from it is used to introduce this chapter: "I have sinned in thought, word, and deed by my fault, my fault, my very grievous fault."

The best illustration of Trent's lasting mistake can be seen in John H. Newman's republication of his 1838 *Lectures on Justification*, which he had written as an Anglican. Later, writing as a Roman Catholic, he spent six pages of the introduction and sixty-one pages in an index trying unsuccessfully to include something like "the cognate[18] presence of Christ in our souls" as a part of the *formal cause* of justification. Finally, he relinquished the task and submitted to Trent's single formal cause. If he had been successful Roman Catholics would be relying not on their own infused righteousness but on Christ's presence with them, recalling the position taken in the sixteenth century by Cardinal Contarini, Cardinal Seripando, and Reginald Pole. It would have been a good antidote to the Pharisee yeast, as the faithful would be taught to rely not on their own goodness (righteousness) but on Christ's.

In Scripture, St. Augustine, St. Chrysostom, and St. Bernard ample evidence exists to regard unconscious sin as no invariable cause for condemnation to them that are in Christ Jesus (Rom 8:1). Unless one can at least consider the possibility that sin can be consonant with a state of grace, any suggestion of unconscious sin or corporate guilt will sound to one nurtured in what Dom Victor White called post-Reformation moral theology as pastorally cruel, claiming everyone to be in sin. This is in fact true but, in the light of the teaching of the Mass (in contrast to Trent), being a sinner does not mean that one has lost one's favor with God.

On the contrary, acknowledging the discrepancy between a regenerate person's righteousness and the righteousness that is to be in complete

---

17. Kung, *Justification*, 237–39. Kung writes: "Perhaps the most impressive example of the Catholic 'simul justus et peccator' is the *Roman Mass*. We have to allow these texts to speak for themselves and to remember that the Church is severely strict in demanding of the celebrating priest the 'state' of grace. Hence it is presupposed that the one who prays these texts, at least the priest, stands before God as just. In spite of this we find throughout—especially at decisive points in the Mass—a declaration of a state of sin and a prayer for forgiveness of sin put in the most outspoken terms. It should be noted, too, that the reform of the Mass was instigated by the very Council which issued the decree on justification, and that consequently the Catholicity of these texts is precisely the Catholicity of this Council."

18. Cognate: allied by having the same source.

sanctification (following St. Augustine's dictum that "what is not of love is of sin") can become an antidote to self-righteousness and encourage compassion for other sinners. Knowing and admitting we are sinners is a gracious matter of staking out areas for grace to do its work until we all attain "to the measure of the stature of the fullness of Christ" (Eph 4:13).

This criticism of Roman Catholicism needs to be set in context. Criticism of Anglicanism, and in the subsequent chapters concerning the Reformed (Presbyterian), Lutheran, and Methodist traditions, is meant to help each tradition be more faithful to our Common Founder and avoid the Pharisaism of which Jesus warned us. The Christian witness of the Church of Rome is exceedingly important because she represents approximately half of all Christians in the world, dwarfing all other denominations. How the Catholic Church makes its Christian witness to contemporary alternatives, such as Islam and secularism, is of far-reaching significance for all Christians.

The Anglican poet, T. S. Eliot, made the following prophetic statement in 1930:

> The World is trying the experiment of attempting to form a civilized but non-Christian mentality. The experiment will fail; but we must be very patient in awaiting its collapse; meanwhile redeeming the time: so that the Faith may be preserved alive through the dark ages before us; to renew and rebuild civilization, and save the World from suicide.[19]

Since Eliot made that comment almost a century ago, we are seeing the Anglican Church, and much of mainline Protestantism, increasingly accommodate to the culture, while the Catholic Church is losing much of its influence in its most historic Catholic countries: Ireland, Quebec, Spain, Italy, and Poland. It might be said that of all the traditions Roman Catholicism is among the most unfriendly to self-criticism (although true to some extent in all traditions). Those to whom it is not given to love the Roman Catholic Church should be angry at none other than Martin Luther. Historian Roland Bainton writes:

> Luther saved the papacy. Such was the judgment of Jacob Burckhardt in his famous study of the Renaissance. He pointed out with great sagacity that the See of Peter in the age of the Renaissance was on the way toward becoming a secularized city-

19. Eliot, "Thoughts After Lambeth," 332.

state. If that process had not been arrested the result for the papacy would have been far more drastic than anything which did happen. A secularized Italian city-state would not have continued to command the obedience of the nations, nor even of the other Italian city-states. Luther revived the religious consciousness of Europe. Luther was responsible for the calling of the Council of Trent. The popes persistently opposed the calling of a council lest their wings be clipped. The Lutheran peril at last compelled them to acquiesce in the demands of the emperor that a general council be summoned. These statements are, of course, not meant to imply that the positive contributions of Luther extended no further than the reform of Catholicism, but only to point out that in addition to the beneficial results in the Protestant world There were also beneficial results in the Catholic world.[20]

Recalling that all Christians are but branches grafted onto the tree root of Israel (Rom 11:17), the history of Israel can be an example for repentance and a new spirit today. As Luther triggered significant reform within the Catholic Church, so the challenges to all Christians today are the occasions of new opportunities. If we do not heed Christ's warning about the yeast of the Pharisees and repent, the consequences will be dire. As St. Paul warns us: "For if God did not spare the natural branches neither will he spare you" (Rom 11:21).

Is it possible that God is using secularism and Islam, as he used Assyria in the eighth century BC as the "rod of my anger" (Isa 10:5) to punish Christendom for our faithlessness and denominational idolatry?

20. Bainton, *Erasmus of Christendom*, 280–81. Tuchman vividly describes the condition of the Papacy from 1470–1530, which provoked the Reformation. *March of Folly*, 51–126.

8

Protestant Pharisaism

So then it is not of him that willeth nor of him that runneth, but of God that showeth mercy.

Romans 9:16

THE DEVIL IS AN equal opportunity deceiver. He kneads the Pharisaic yeast in the bread of all traditions. The very Protestantism that recovered the teachings (justification, etc.) designed to release people from bondage to the law produced its own versions of Pharisaism. We have seen how the Church of England was affected during the seventeenth century when it departed from the teachings of Cranmer, Hooker, Andrewes, Donne, and Herbert and embraced the moralism of Jeremy Taylor and *The Whole Duty of Man*. This chapter will seek to highlight a critical moment of theological importance within several of the Reformation traditions. This is not to suggest that mainline churches are the only ones that yield to the Pharisaic temptation but simply to affirm William Temple's earlier point, that our reluctance to acknowledge any center other than self, renders all of us susceptible to any teaching that might encourage us to rely on our own goodness.

LUTHERANS

Lutheran tradition gave birth to one of the outstanding scholars in the church's history. Adolph von Harnack (1851–1930), an enduring source for understanding the early church, is known today as a fair-minded scholar, whose treatment of positions he does not himself hold, is largely reliable. He also possessed a simple piety, rare among academicians. He attempted to simplify the complexities of theology and doctrine to make them understandable to all. The motive was commendable but the result was catastrophic.

Harnack believed that much of the doctrine and dogma of Christianity was unnecessary. Accretions derived from Greek philosophy created unnecessary complexities. In an enormously influential book, *What is Christianity?* (English translation in 1901), he replaced the creedal affirmations concerning Christ and the Trinity with the "brotherhood of man" and "fatherhood of God." His strong emphasis on morals overshadowed the traditional teachings of grace. Biblical themes of sacrifice for sin, expiation, and the atoning death of Christ were replaced by the exhortation to follow the life and example of Jesus.

I can remember being asked as a seminary student to preach on the phrase, sacrifice for sin, taken from a prayer: "Almighty God, who hast given thine only Son to be unto us both a sacrifice for sin, and also an example of godly life . . ." As a child of the age and an unknowing victim of Harnack's teaching I was struck dumb. The concept of sacrifice for sin was like something emanating from the dark side of the moon. I could have easily done many sermons on an example of godly life.

Jesus, as an example for the brotherhood of man and a teacher of fatherhood of God, became a new law to be obeyed and followed. When Christianity is reduced to be like Jesus, it loses its grace and becomes a mere law that can be obeyed only by inflated confidence in human nature's ability to fulfill all obligations and/or by lowering the law to levels that one can obey.

As we have seen before, this confidence in human will to effect brotherhood makes Pharisees blind to the intractable self-centeredness in our nature. Harnack denied that we are in such bondage.[1] Reinhold Niebuhr illustrates this Pharisaic blindness even in the writings of this historian:

> Harnack's criticisms must of course be discounted, as those of other Christian moralists, because he is as unable to understand the doctrine of original sin, when stripped of its literalistic errors, as when stated in its crude form. His assertion that "turn as he will, Augustine affirms an evil nature and thereby a diabolical creator of the world" *is simply not true* (italics mine).[2]

---

1. Harnack, *History of Dogma*, V, 217.
2. Niebuhr, *Nature and Destiny of Man*, 262.

This teaching of Harnack (and he was not alone) became a wave that washed over Western Christianity until it broke on the rocks of World Wars I and II. The twentieth century disclosed a deep and desperate need for something more than Harnack's naïve confidence to keep us from destroying each other, and from exchanging the fatherhood of God for the brotherhood of Hitler and Stalin. The Swiss theologian Karl Barth (1886–1968) preached in a parish where he could almost hear the actual guns of World War I and he could no longer sustain the liberal naiveté regarding human nature. He became a decisive and convincing critic of Harnack's Pharisaism. His return to the doctrine found in classical creeds was termed Neo-Orthodoxy. This school included such figures as Reinhold Niebuhr, Paul Tillich, Emil Brunner, and Helmut Thielicke, among others. Barth claimed Scripture as the source and justification for the recovery of orthodox doctrine. His role in opposing Hitler and especially his support of the Barmen Declaration of 1934 (a statement of the Synod of the German church against the tendencies of accommodation by the church to Nazi teachings) gave him a later prestige that, combined with his massive theology, accorded him a reputation in the eyes of many as the outstanding theologian of his age.

But the victory of Neo-Orthodoxy over Harnack's renewal of the Pharisaic yeast was only temporary. Diogenes Allen of Princeton claimed that the great question for our day is "Whatever happened to Neo-Orthodoxy?"[3] Pharisaism flourished in spite of and within Neo-Orthodoxy largely because Scripture was left to the skepticism of biblical critics who had removed confidence in the Bible as the foundation for the creeds and councils.

In 2005, Carl Braaten, an outstanding Lutheran scholar and author of dozens of excellent books, wrote a serious challenge to Mark Hansen, the Presiding Bishop of the Evangelical Lutheran Church of America. Braaten claimed that the classical Lutheranism of Gustav Aulen, Dietrich Bonhoeffer, and Wolfgang Pannenberg had been replaced by a different Lutheran witness of today. Harnack's dismissal of dogma, creedal affirmations concerning Christ and the Trinity, left only the option of accommodation to a secular age that undermined traditional and classical Lutheranism. Braaten declared that "what is happening is nothing less than a tragedy. The ELCA is driving out the best and brightest theolo-

3. Allen, "Theology Today," 34.

gians of our day, not because it is too Lutheran, but because it has become putatively just another protestant denomination."[4]

The Roman Catholic scholar Father Harry McSorley showed extensive evidence that contemporary Lutherans had abandoned Luther's position especially in regard to the doctrine of justification by faith. This does indeed seem to be true of such influential scholars as William Wrede, Albert Schweitzer, Karl Paul Donfried, and Krister Stendahl. The Lutheran scholar, James A. Nestingen, agreed with McSorley's charge:

> Lutheran theologians, including many leading Luther scholars, have backed away. And what is true in the scholarly community is even more so popularly. In the corrosive reduction worked by the American melting pot, with few exceptions, Lutherans have become indistinguishable from their generic Protestant counterparts for whom free choice, the decision of the will, is the hallmark of true faith.[5]

PRESBYTERIANS

John Calvin was thirty-seven-years old when Martin Luther died in 1547. Calvin's teaching and influence spread from Switzerland through Germany, Romania, and Hungary to Holland, England, Scotland, and through the diaspora of the Huguenots to Ireland, South Africa, and the American colonies. Calvin's treatment of predestination has been a bone in the throat for many in subsequent centuries. Calvin and Presbyterians are unfairly accused of inventing the doctrine. It is in fact affirmed by Scripture (Rom 8:20, 30; Eph 1:5, 11), as well as Augustine, Bernard, Aquinas, Luther, Cranmer, and Roman Catholics.

The simple, undeniable, and unavoidable fact is that predestination is not a denial of freedom but its veritable foundation. There are few biblical teachings that are as countercultural or more shocking to human presumption than the Christian claim of predestination and the fact that it is our only hope of true freedom. A full explanation for this seemingly unpalatable fact will be treated in the next chapter.

The following warning about a development within Presbyterian tradition like that within Anglicanism is not a criticism of the biblical affirmation of predestination. Predestination was for Calvin an irreducible

4. Adams, "The Layman," 2.
5. Forde, *Captivity of the Will*, 19–20.

mystery. He denounced the curiosity that pushed some to the presumption of knowing the secrets of God. History is full of examples of how predestination has been twisted to justify the self-righteousness of the Pharisee, but it must be noted that in the final edition of Calvin's *Institutes*, predestination and election are put in the section on salvation, humbly reflecting the initiative of God and not man. As salvation is God's action no one can boast. We have no merit in choosing God. He has chosen us.

Basil Hall, a Cambridge scholar of Calvin studies, has shown how Calvin's successors lifted predestination out of the section of how we are saved and placed it in the section on the nature of God[6] and how he orders things instead of humbly leaving it in the section on how God's action, not ours, saves us. Here the great unexplained mystery in Scripture is replaced by speculation. Many of Calvin's successors attempt to resolve the issues of freedom and election, responsibility and predestination, by theories of limited atonement, sublapsarianism (God's decree concerning election came after the Fall), or supralapsarianism (God's decree came before the Fall). Calvin himself regarded predestination as an inscrutable mystery even though he himself indulged in some measure of rational intrusion into the mystery. But his successors speculated, where Scripture is silent, in ways that opened the tradition of Calvinism to the malignant yeast of the Pharisee.

Thedore Beza (1519–1605), successor to Calvin at Geneva, established for the seventeenth century much of what became known as Calvinism. Beza's emphasis on the "elect" explained how God manages things rather than simply expressing how we are saved. When anxiety arose as to whether one was of the elect, Beza's reassurance was to urge one to look at one's life to see if the fruits of good works are sufficient to demonstrate that one's election is true.

Thus, we are justified by the righteousness of Christ that is we are received by faith, but we are assured of our salvation by our works in sanctification.[7] Calvin had clearly shown that in this life "believers are

6. Hall, "Calvin against the Calvinists," *John Calvin*, 19–37. Hall was followed on this point by Brian Armstrong's *Calvinism and the Amyraut Heresy*. These works would seem to be lasting contributions to understanding Calvin and Calvinism on the issue of assurance even if they do not succeed in exonerating Calvin himself from some "overcurious" speculations and human logic for which we have no biblical warrant.

7. It is interesting that there is a contemporary example of this in Sanders, pointed out in Carson, *Justification and Variegated Nomism*, 544. By putting covenant theology, not grace, over against merit theology, Sanders has managed to have a structure that

in perpetual conflict with their own unbelief,"[8] and that assurance is not to be based on anything in ourselves. Calvinism, as taught by Beza and the English Puritan William Perkins (1558–1602), tended to resolve the anxiety and doubt regarding one's election by having the doubter look at the works in his life for assurance. The result was that if the doubter succeeded in assuring himself of his election because of his goodness he was hardly different from the Pharisee in our Lord's parable. If he is not reassured by the quality of his life he is thrown into despair.

The focus here, in this context, concerning this very complex argument[9] is a simple one. The issue is not to settle the argument but to see how the claims regarding sanctification function pastorally in later Calvinism. Looking toward our own life as grounds for assurance of salvation is an open invitation to the Pharisaic yeast. Although Beza believed that we are justified freely by Christ and not by our own merit, this pervasive malignancy of looking to our own worthiness in sanctification, aided by natural arrogance in human nature, Pharisaism reenters our lives by pointing our concerns toward our own goodness. Believing that we are assured of our election by our works is a double-edged sword. It comforts the self-righteous who are confident of their goodness and discourages the humble who are aware of how sinful they are. This tradition brings good news to non-Christians in justification but can become bad news for Christians in sanctification.

---

preserves grace in the "getting in" while preserving works (and frequently some form or other of merit theology) in the "staying in."

8. Calvin, *Institutes* 3. 2. 4.

9. There has been an extensive argument among Hall, Kendall, Armstrong, Beeke, Carson, Helm, et al., on this matter. For criticism of Hall and Armstrong's position, see Beeke, *Quest for Full Assurance: Legacy of Calvin and His Successor* (Carlisle, PA.: Banner of Truth Trust, 1982) and Helm, *Calvin and the Calvinists* (Carlisle, PA.: Banner of Truth Trust, 1982). One of the best judgments of this contentious issue can be found in Collinson's review of Kendall's book in the *Times Literary Supplement*, 561. Beeke believes that the difference between Calvin and the Calvinists is "substantial but not antithetical," Beeke, 17. It is commendable of Beeke to list 21 scholars whose convictions are similar to one or more of Hall's and Kendall's thesis. Among them are Barth and Moltmann, Beeke, p. 3. A more recent work on Calvin and Calvinists is by Muller, "Calvin and the 'Calvinists': Part 1 and 2" in *After Calvin Studies in the Development of a Theological Tradition*, 63–102, and in his *Post Reformation Reformed Dogmatics*, 1. Muller is dismissively critical of Hall, Armstrong, Barth, McGrath, Althaus, Torrance, and Parker on their respective criticisms of "Calvinism."

Honesty about the remaining sin in born-again converts has led a whole stream of conservative Christians, with perfectionist interpretations of Scripture, to repudiate the evangelical tradition. The young man who shot and killed members of the Christian church in Colorado in 2007 wrote that his fury toward Christians was because he was not able to "obey the rules." He could not live up to the sinless behavior he thought they had demanded.

Reliance on our own goodness is a serious departure from Calvin's insistence that assurance should never be based on anything in us but only by looking on the sacrifice of Christ.[10] Beeke quotes Beza: "Seeing that good works are for us the certain evidence of our faith, they also bring to us afterwards the certainty of our eternal election."[11] This begs the question: Would one rather go on a ten-day vacation with those who were certain that they were of the elect of God because of their own goodness or with those who, knowing their own unworthiness, gratefully rely on their acceptance by Christ?

A conscientious and honest believer would be devastated to hear that, "If your so-called grace, which you say you have received, does not make you keep the law, you have not received grace."[12] When we reflect honestly on the two Great Commandments, "You shall love the Lord your God with all your heart and with all your soul and with all your mind . . . you shall love your neighbor as yourself," it would seem obvious that all of us are yet sinners and have not kept the law. If we believe we have fulfilled this law our confidence is of sociopathic proportions and our witness to others singularly unbecoming. If we believe we can of ourselves fulfill these two commandments we will soon know condemnation and despair. Pharisaic strategies will only increase the despair.

Calvin himself showed far more pastoral awareness of the persistence of sin in converted Christians and the reassurance that comes not

---

10. Beeke, *Quest for Full Assurance,* 76. Beeke shows that Beza differed from Calvin by "upgrading the external testimony of sanctification and the internal testimony of the Spirit as two pillars upon which rests [our assurance] as *firmly as on the applied promise of God in Christ*"(italics mine). This seems to contradict the Westminster Confession (1647): "But the principal acts of saving faith are accepting, receiving, and resting upon Christ *alone* for justification, *sanctification* and eternal life, by virtue of the covenant of grace" (Chap. XIV) (italics mine).

11. Ibid., 19.

12. Murray, *David Martin Lloyd-Jones,* 726.

from our sanctification but from faith in Christ's freeing us from the condemnation of the law:

> Emancipated by grace, believers need not fear the remnants of sin.
> . . . they might object that they still bore with them their flesh, full
> of lusts, and that sin dwelt in them. Paul adds this consolation, in
> freedom from the law. It is as if he said: "Even though they do not
> yet clearly feel that sin has been destroyed or that righteousness
> dwells in them, there is still no reason to be afraid and cast down in
> mind as if God were continually offended by the remnants of sin,
> seeing that they have been emancipated from the law by grace, so
> that their works are not to be measured according to its rules.[13]

Fortunately, not all of Calvin's followers made the mistake of looking to their own works for reassurance. John Owen (1616–1683) saw the danger of this Pharisaic influence in some of his Puritan colleagues. Owen insisted that the Christian's "great temptation is to turn in upon himself and his own degree of sanctification" and insists that "to be holy is necessary; to know it sometimes a temptation."[14] While the Christian is concentrating on Christ's merciful righteousness, he will be little preoccupied with, or confident of, his own holiness.

The Pharisaic yeast that crept into the Presbyterian system was particularly virulent in Scotland. The needs of our self-righteous malignancy always drive us to concentrate on minutiae or external matters that seem more amenable to self control: dancing, card playing, the externals of proper behavior, and the suspicion of ornaments and vestments. This certainly happened in Scotland and within Puritanism in general. A certain lack of joy characterizes Pharisaic malignancy.

The battle continued into eighteenth-century Scotland with Thomas Boston (1676–1732) and the "Marrow Men" fighting the moralism of the Presbyterian Assembly.[15] Boston, a Scottish minister, found a book in 1704 that had been brought into Scotland by an unknown Commonwealth soldier. *The Marrow of Modern Divinity*, written in the seventeenth century, eloquently proclaimed the evangelical doctrine of grace. In spite of its being condemned by the General Assembly that book became a force for

13. Calvin, *Institutes*, 838.
14. Fergusen, *John Owen on the Christian Life*, 115.
15. Elwell, ed., *Evangelical Dictionary of Theology*, 179.

revival in Scotland through the sermons and writings of Boston and his followers.

The Pharisaic corruption within the Presbyterian tradition is especially ironic as few traditions have been as careful about how precisely to fashion the doctrine of grace and justification. The devil is indeed an equal opportunity deceiver.

METHODISTS

The insidious thing about the Pharisaic yeast is that it is a counterfeit of the Christian faith. We have seen how the Anglican tradition of Cranmer, Hooker, and Herbert was infected in the latter part of the seventeenth century by the teachings of Jeremy Taylor and *The Whole Duty of Man*. We have seen the difficulty for Roman Catholics in the Council of Trent's claim that *our* infused righteousness is enough *Coram Deo* (face to face with God) and the Council's denial of sin remaining in a person in the state of grace. We have seen in Presbyterians the departure from Calvin and the temptation to look to our own worthiness rather than to Christ for assurance of salvation.

A virtual gospel drought for almost a century before Charles and John Wesley's conversions has been noted. They marked not only a graceful break in that pervasive moralism but they were incomparably significant in regaining the power and joy of the Gospel even beyond the limits of the English-speaking world.

It is, therefore, all the more surprising that even the great John Wesley was not immune to the yeast of the Pharisees. In spite of his stringent criticism of the rigorist and perfectionist tradition of William Law and others, this same yeast reappears in his later ministry.

John had accused his mentor, William Law, the author of *On Christian Perfection* and the classic *A Serious Call to a Devout and Holy Life*, of not teaching the gospel. However, later in his ministry, Wesley reprinted and recommended the works of Richard Baxter (1615–1691), which were very similar to those of William Law on this subject. In *Aphorisms on Justification*, Baxter taught that Christ himself fulfilled the conditions of the old covenant and thereby purchased for us easier terms within the new covenant. (This recalls the similar claim by the Anglican Henry Hammond that "Christ has brought down the market," which makes easier conditions in the new covenant. See chapter 6.) On account of Christ's righteousness our own righteousness, is reckoned or imputed as acceptable righteousness. For Baxter, the focus is not on Christ's righteousness mercifully reckoned and worded to us but on our righteousness. In other words, we are justified by our own righteousness on account of the righteousness of Christ.[16] For Baxter, the formal cause (that which makes something to be what it is) of our justification was not the perfect righteousness of Christ imputed to us but *our* righteousness now acceptable because of the righteousness of Christ. Wesley later followed this teaching, but it was explicitly condemned by the Westminster Confession (1647): "But the principal acts of saving faith are, accepting, receiving, and resting upon Christ *alone* for justification, *sanctification*, and eternal life, by virtue of the covenant of grace" (italics mine).[17]

Baxter taught that it is not God's will "that any man should be justified . . . who hath not some ground in himself of personal and particular right and claim thereto . . ."[18] Faith is described in ways similar to those of Jeremy Taylor to include works. Faith is "the understanding's assenting trust, the will's consenting trust, and the executive power's practical, venturing, obeying trust."[19]

Baxter was criticized by some nine divines and excused himself as having written *Aphorisms*—while in the army and without libraries—but William Orme's judgment is that he "adhered to the substance of its (*Aphorisms . . .*) sentiments to the last."[20]

Baxter's life was marked by a courageous independence and dedication to his ministry. He is properly famous for the memorable comment on preaching: I have preached as never sure to preach again, as a dying man to dying men. He fought for Parliament against the king but was critical of many of Oliver Cromwell's policies. His *The Saints' Everlasting Rest* (1650) was an influential Puritan classic. He is one of many examples of someone who combined a commendable character with serious doctrinal flaws. Wesley's admiration of Baxter is understandable with their similar difficulties with the leadership of the Church of England. This might at first have led him to overlook Baxter's departure from Reformation teaching.

16. Allison, *The Rise of Moralism*, 156–57.
17. Smith and Schaff, eds., *Creeds of the Evangelical Protestant Church*, 598–673.
18. Baxter, *Aphorisms of Justification*, 60.
19. Baxter, 448.
20. Orme, ed., *Practical Works of Richard Baxter*, 503.

However, Wesley was growing in congeniality with Baxter's teachings, thus opening the way for Pharisaic yeast to enter into Methodism. A glaring example of this yeast in later Methodism is in the *Minutes* of 1770 Annual Conference held in London:

> We have received it as a maxim that a man is to do nothing in order to justification. Nothing can be more false. Whoever desires to find favor with God should 'cease to do evil and learn to do well.' Whoever repents should do 'works meet for repentance.' And if this is not in order to find favor, what does he do them for?

1. Who of us is now accepted of God? He that now believes in Christ with a loving and obedient heart.

2. But who among those that never heard of Christ? He that feareth God and worketh righteousness, according to the light he has.

3. Is this the same with 'he that is sincere'? Nearly, if not quite.

4. Is not this salvation by works? Not by the *merit* of works, but by works as a *condition*.

5. What have we, then been disputing about for these thirty years? I am afraid about words.

6. As to *merit* itself, of which we have been so dreadfully afraid we are rewarded 'according to our works'—yea, 'because of our works.' How does this differ from 'for the *sake of our works*'? And how differed this from *secundum merita operum*, as our Works deserve? Can you split this hair? I doubt I cannot.[21]

The contents of these *Minutes* brought down on Wesley's head a barrage of criticism. He was reducing to a matter of words careful distinctions by Christians since the days of the Reformation. He seemed to assume that good works, truly good, were accomplished without a prior grace but by one's natural will thereby denying the necessity of prevenient grace. Adding to this he began to claim that "a Christian may be so far perfect as not to commit sin and be freed from evil thoughts . . . and from evil tempers."[22]

The key rallying word for the Reformation was "imputation" (cf. Chapters 6 and 7). Wesley was against the necessity of affirming this term on the grounds that "He that feareth God and worketh righteousness is

---

21 Tyerman, *Life and Times of Rev. John Wesley*, 169–70.

22. Wesley, *Sermons on Several Occasions*, 579–80.

accepted with him."[23] Does this not mean that those who fear God and produce righteousness are justified without Christ? If this is possible we need only to do what is required in the Old Testament. We do not need what Christ has done for us.

The upsetting issue, among his close friends, was Wesley's insistence on perfection. Both his brother Charles and his friend George Whitefield remonstrated with him on this issue as well as his dear colleague, the remarkable Selina Hastings, Countess of Huntingdon. She was at first completely taken in by this later teaching of John on perfection, but her "subsequent repudiation of the teaching sprang from an increasing understanding of the biblical teaching coupled with her own experience of repeated failure. She knew she fell far short of what she ought to be."[24]

This woman's remarkable ministry was an invaluable part of the Methodist success. She used her considerable influence in court and society to pave the way for chapels and congregations to have legal rights for John Wesley's clergy to preach the life-changing gospel in Britain. At the Countess's own expense, she established a college in South Wales to train evangelical clergy because she steadfastly hoped to keep the revival within the Church of England. She was not only a benefactor, warm friend, and supporter of both John Wesley and Whitefield, but she was, on the whole, a singularly wise and perceptive theologian.

The Countess's influence on Henry Venn (1725–1797) was the turning point in his life that led to his enormously influential ministry. George Whitefield had brought Venn, who was in a state of deep spiritual frustration and lethargy, for a visit to the Countess. Venn had been laboring under the burden of William Law's standards of Christian perfection. The Countess shrewdly detected the heavy Pharisaic burden Venn was carrying, because she too had struggled under the weight of such teaching. Hoping to help relieve her new young friend's burden she wrote to him the following letter:

> Christ, and Christ alone, must be the only Mediator between God and sinful men—no miserable performances can be placed between the sinner and the Saviour. Let the eye of faith ever be direct to the Lord Jesus Christ . . . And now, my dear friend, no longer let false doctrine disgrace your pulpit. Preach Christ crucified as the only foundation of the sinner's hope. Preach him as the Author

23. Wesley, *Journal 5*, 243–44.

24. Cook, *Selina, Countess of Huntington*, 208.

and Finisher, as well as the sole object of faith—that faith which is the gift of God.[25]

George Whitefield was soon able to report to the Countess:

> Your exertions in bringing him to a clearer knowledge of the everlasting gospel have indeed been blessed. He owes your Ladyship much, under God, and I believe his whole soul is gratitude to the divine author of his mercies and to you, the honoured instrument in leading him to the fountain of truth.[26]

Henry Venn was the author of *The Complete Duty of Man* that corrected the unfortunate teaching we have seen in *The Whole Duty of Man*. He was the father of John Venn (1759–1813), the Rector of the Anglican parish at Clapham and spiritual leader of the famous Clapham Sect. William Wilberforce, Zachary Macaulay, Charles Grant, James Stephen, and other affluent and influential lay leaders of that parish were instrumental in getting the slave trade abolished, legislation passed relieving squalid conditions of labor and the poor, as well as sponsoring missionary endeavors in India and Africa. Lady Huntingdon's influence is difficult to exaggerate.

In spite of the close friendship and love among the leaders of this remarkable movement called Methodism, differences among them persisted. The division of views that occurred labeled on one side as Calvinism (Whitefield, Augustus Toplady [1740–1778], author of the hymn "Rock of Ages," and the Countess of Huntingdon) and the other as Arminian (John Wesley and John Fletcher [1729–1785]). These disputes divided the Methodists internally and externally, rendering their witness less effective.

Calvinism tended to become the term applied to Evangelicals who insisted that sinners are not free until grace sets us free. But some were Calvinists in the most pejorative legalistic sense of that term and they gave the doctrines of grace and free justification a bad name. John Walker (1768–1833), an early Methodist leader, was just such a figure. He attacked Methodism with a virulent claim "that the Arminian John Wesley was in hell."[27] Walker evoked a significant following, but he managed to alien-

---

25. Seymour, *Life and Times of Selina Countess of Huntingdon*, I, 225–26.

26. Ibid., 225.

27. Carter, *Anglican Evangelicals*, 74.

ate not only the Methodists but also Anglican evangelicals, the Roman Catholic Church, and he divided his own followers.[28]

Wesley, too, had to deal with the opposite lawless distortion in one of his early followers, Thomas Maxfield. Albert Outler gives a paraphrased summary of Maxfield's distortion of the Reformation doctrine:

> Christ had *done* as well as suffered *all*; that *his righteousness* being imputed to *us*, we need none of *our own*; that seeing there was so much righteousness and holiness *in him*, there needs none more *in us*; that to think we have any, or to desire or seek any, is to renounce Christ; that from the beginning to the end of salvation, all is *in Christ*; nothing is *in man*; and that those who teach otherwise are "legal preachers" and know nothing of the gospel.[29]

Against such extremes as the claim that Christ's righteousness meant we needed none of our own and the claim that we are to seek none, Wesley attempted to work out parameters for the gospel. He wished to be both loyal to the Reformation tradition of grace and to human responsibilities for Christian holiness. He was not the first to struggle with this dilemma. The issue, later described as Calvinism vs. Arminianism, predates the Synod of Dort in 1619. The mystery beneath God's initiative and election and man's freedom and responsibility is a pervasive one throughout history and it crosses all traditional lines.

Roman Catholics were not immune from the struggle. A little known but important controversy, *de Auxiliis,* broke out in 1597 between the Jesuits and the Dominicans. Three attempts by the commission appointed by Pope Clement VIII to censure the Jesuit theologian, L. deMolina, finally failed in 1607. Pope Paul V decreed, in spite of the commission's recommendation favoring the Dominicans, that the Dominicans could no longer call the Jesuits Pelagian and the Jesuits could no longer call the Domincans Calvinists. The Jesuits had much in common with the later Arminians and the Dominicans with Calvin.

Recent scholarship has been divided over the question of whether Arminius was actual an Arminian.[30] Dr. William G. Witt shows that Arminius held a careful view similar to that of Richard Hooker in which

28. Ibid., 77–102.

29. Outler, *John Wesley*, 380.

30. Witt, *Creation, Redemption, and Grace in the Theology of Jacob Arminius*, PhD dissertation.

we are justified by God's gracious reckoning by which he imputes to us the righteousness of Christ. Faith is not a work but a gift by God, an act by which we apprehend the "other" (not our) righteousness of Christ and are begun to be made righteous in sanctification. Roger Olson builds on this recovery of Arminius's teaching to salvage and embrace (as did Wesley) the very term "Arminian," but he fails to acknowledge the subsequent and widespread semi-Pelagianism that deserved the pejorative term "Arminianism."[31] The term took on a life of its own. Arminius, himself, denied the very proposition affirmed by Baxter and Wesley that faith and works occur together or that our faith is the formal cause of justification.[32] When Charles H. Spurgeon (1834–1892) claimed: "The doctrine of justification itself as preached by an Arminian, is nothing but the doctrine of salvation by works,"[33] he was not pointing to the doctrine of Arminius as described by Olson but the teaching that sinners by their wills are free (able) to accept or reject the gospel as if rejecting Christ is an example of what it means to be free. This assumption results in replacing the grace-bearing gospel story with exhortations to use their freedom to do what is right.

This controversy appeared among the Roman Catholics between 1597–1607, among the Dutch Reformed Church and others, at the Synod of Dort in 1619, among the Anglicans in the seventeenth century, and among the followers and critics of Methodists in the eighteenth century. As we have seen, some of these later critics were indeed antinomian (Thomas Maxfield) or the irresponsible extremist on the legalist side (John Walker). Yet none of the critics of Wesley's perfectionism and Arminianism (he embraced the terms) were either extreme Calvinists or antinomian. No doubt some Arminians inferred from Wesley's teachings a semi-Pelagian assumption concerning the power of the human will to initiate our salvation if sufficiently exhorted. This led to the popular belief that human

31. Olson, *Arminian Theology: Myths and Realities*.

32. *Writings of James Arminius*, 2:119. "I. That faith and works concur together to justification, is a thing impossible. II. Faith is not correctly denominated *the formal cause* of justification; and when it receives that appellation from some divines of our profession, it is then [abusive] improperly so called. III. Christ has not [*promeritum*] obtained by his merits that we should be justified by the worthiness and merit of faith, and much less that we should be justified by the merit of works: But the merit of Christ is opposed to justification by works; and, in the Scriptures, faith and merit are placed in opposition to each other."

33. Quoted in "Modern Reformation," 30.

self-centeredness would begin to become God-centered when commanded or when the threat of hell was adequately shown.

The window through which the Pharisaic yeast came to Methodism
was Wesley's following Richard Baxter on justification. We have noted
the serious flaws in Baxter's teaching, especially in his *Aphorisms of
Justification*, for which he himself had apologized but never repudiated.
But Wesley chooses this very book in the 2nd Annual Conference, August
1, 1745, to be *the* guide for Methodists.[34]

As we have seen, Wesley followed Baxter in departing from
Reformation teaching by substituting the "imputation of our faith" for
the "imputation of Christ's righteousness" as that which brings us into
favor with God. To say that our faith is regarded (treated) as our justification before God, who has lowered the standard of righteousness for us by
Christ, is to give merit to us and to our faith rather than to Christ. This
confidence that our righteousness is the cause of justification in Christ's
new lowered covenant reserves to us Pharisees a righteousness of our own
that cooperates together with Christ for our salvation. This view of faith
can produce one of the least attractive aspects of some Christians, which
is the temptation to regard our faith not as a gift but as an accomplishment that others have not achieved.

William Temple's insight regarding our role in God's saving action is
that we contribute nothing to our salvation except "the sin from which we
need to be redeemed."[35] Bishop John Rodgers says: "Our part in securing
our salvation is that we brought two pieces of wood and some nails."

This claim that we have contributed something other than our sin to
deserve and secure the favor of God is pregnant with the capacity of com-
parisons with others who have not done as much as we have, "like the tax
collector" (Luke 18:11). This later Methodism shares with the other traditions a rebirth of the Pharisaic yeast, especially when that same conference in 1745 officially claimed that "fruits or works meet for repentance"
precede faith.[36]

The underlying assumption here is the unspoken confidence that
people are free and able to produce good works before either faith or
grace. If this were true we would need no New Testament, no Messiah,

34. Outler, *John Wesley*, 148–49.
35. Wells, *By Faith Alone*, eds. Johnson and Waters, 15.
36. Outler, *John Wesley*, 148.

and no Christ, except as an example. We would only need to fulfill the requirements of Psalm 15: "O Lord who shall sojourn in thy tent? Who shall dwell on thy holy hill? He who walks blamelessly, and does what is right, and speaks truth from his heart."

This confidence in our human self-centered will leads in preaching to exhortation, scolding, and threats rather than telling the "old, old story." That story alone begins to enable us to do with humility what God commands because only that story inspires the love that adopts us and begins to change us. Exhortation has its place, but its place and role are best indicated by where it appears in Paul's Epistle to the Romans. Romans is the only letter that is not responding to specific matters. Rather it describes faith in its wholeness for those, for the most part, he did not know in a city he had not visited.

The whole story Paul tells is virtually absent of any exhortation until chapter 12:1: "I appeal to you therefore, brethren, by the mercy of God, to present your bodies as a living sacrifice, holy and acceptable to God, which is your spiritual worship." This entire chapter is one of a score of specific exhortations, but it comes after the word "therefore." He has taken eleven chapters to describe God's judgment, his mercy, his promise, the function of faith, the source of peace, the purpose of the law, the power of grace, the lifting of condemnation, and the place of Israel and the Gentiles.

All of this is the story of grace, the power to enable us to respond to the urgently necessary injunctions, advice, demands, requests, and exhortations:

> Let love be genuine; hate what is evil, hold fast to what is good; love one another with brotherly affection; outdo one another in showing honor. Never flag in zeal, be aglow with the Spirit, serve the Lord. Rejoice in your hope, be patient in tribulation, be constant in prayer. Contribute to the needs of the saints, practice hospitality. (Rom 12: 9–13)

It would be a mark of Pharisaism to put chapter 12, with its forty exhortations in twenty-one verses, before chapters 1–11. This reversal is to turn the gospel upside down and the results are counterproductive. Such a reversal is not an academic mistake, but a mistake that stems from sin. Given our original condition that we believe we are the center of the world, we are unable to do what we ought. Only by a change of heart, a new birth, inspired by God's contagious love for us, can we begin to want to do what we should: to love what God commands.

To begin with the wise and wonderful demands, without first establishing the means of grace for enabling us to respond to them as shown in Romans 1–11, is a mark of Pharisaic malignancy. We tell ourselves the lie that we are free to fulfill these marvelous exhortations in chapter 12, but this lie denies our bondage to self as center as we will see in the next chapter.

9

Why Did They Lie?

Since Adam, being free to choose,
Chose to imagine he was free
To choose his own necessity . . .[1]

—W. H. Auden

Jesus then said to the Jews who had believed in him, "If you continue in my word you are my disciples, and you will know the truth,
and the truth will make you free." They answered him, "We are
descendents of Abraham and have never been in bondage to anyone. How is it that you say, 'You will be made free'?" Jesus answered
them, "Truly, truly, I say to you, everyone who commits sin is a
slave to sin . . . if the Son makes you free, you will be free indeed."

—John 8:30–36

"WE HAVE NEVER BEEN in bondage to any man." What an extraordinary lie! Had they forgotten their bondage in Egypt, the bricks
without straw, the plagues, the Passover, the parting of the Red Sea, and
the celebration each year to remind them of their redemption from bondage? Interestingly, Jesus did not remind them of their history of slavery in
Egypt and Babylon. He simply pointed out that whoever sins is a slave to
sin; but if the Son makes you free, you will be free indeed.

NOT BORN FREE BUT BORN TO BE FREE

The important question is: Why did they lie? They lied about their freedom for the same reason we lie about our freedom. One meaning of freedom simply implies that no external restraint, coercion, or force binds or

1. Auden, *For the Time Being*, 78.

inhibits a person. Auden uses it in that sense in the quotation above. But being free in this sense merely means that our natural instincts and drives are without external controls. We are left adrift in anarchy and chaos, a most unfree condition. Inasmuch as we are sinners, we see ourselves as the center of all we survey. We hope, we wish, we want to have whatever we desire. And we believe that being able to have or to do what we want is freedom. We tell such lies as "we are born free," "he's free to choose to take revenge or to forgive," "he's free to get drunk or to stay sober," "she's free to commit suicide or to renew her hope," "terrorists are free to kill innocent people or to refrain from doing so." Each destructive choice is made from bondage. Drunkenness, suicide, vengeance, and mass murder are instances of bondage, not freedom. Having no restraints is not freedom but license, a state of hazardous slavery.

The bondage of others is easier to see than our own. We never have to teach children to misbehave. They can figure that out on their own. Restraints, even necessary ones, are almost always perceived as bondage: "Put up your bicycle!" "Have you done your homework?" These requests seem like impositions on one's freedom even though the bicycle is saved from rust or theft, and homework done opens us to greater opportunities. Rules, restraints, laws, and obligations are inevitably seen at first as inhibitions and barriers to our freedom, when they are merely restraints on our unfree wills.

I recall being consulted by a couple with enormous wealth about when to give and how much to give to their son. They wisely perceived that a great deal of money early in life might give him the license (what the immature would call freedom) to avoid the discipline and restraint necessary for maturity, responsibility, and a truer freedom. An Oxford don observed that he had never known an independently wealthy scholar to finish work for a doctorate in the time required. Wealth seemed to give one choices to delay, procrastinate, and put off work that needed to be done. Students, whose financial circumstances did not allow them the choice of continuing delay, tended to finish their work on schedule. Money confers the power of wider choices, but that very power can reinforce bondage.

Lord Acton's dictum, "power tends to corrupt and absolute power corrupts absolutely," is an insight not only about power but about the nature of freedom. This easily documented wisdom is based on the unacknowledged fact that our wills are not free unless they desire to do what they should. Professor Leonard Hodgson used to object to Acton's statement on the grounds that God is absolute power but not corrupted. This is true because God is not sinful and centered in a false center as we are. Too often Acton's quote is cited without the word, tends. "Power tends to corrupt . . ." because humans tend to self-centeredness. Yet there are many examples of the use of power without corruption.

The great countercultural wisdom advanced by Dante's *Divine Comedy* is that no one gets dragged into hell, or barred from heaven, by anything external. People get what they desire in the circles of hell. Cowards flee and haters hate for all eternity. That is what their wills choose because that is where their hearts are. Some with an invitation to heaven willfully decline because they do not wish to relinquish the self-destructive commitments that cannot live in heaven. C. S. Lewis's *Great Divorce* describes this beautifully. His stories and illustrations of human hearts committed to lust, self-pity, or revenge prevent them from desiring eternal bliss in heaven. With God's forgiveness and love, and our repentance (a change of heart), our wrongful desires are gradually replaced, our wills are changed as expressions of a changed heart, and we begin to desire what God desires for us.

The fact that our wills are in bondage can be learned from non-Christians as well as Christians. Few have illustrated the true nature of human captivity of the will more dramatically than Jean Paul Sartre in his play *No Exit*. People choose to be in a room from which nothing physical prevents their leaving, but they have no desire to do so. All of them are miserable and they encourage further misery in each other. Their wills imprison them and they are left among others who are similarly committed to self-willfulness. Here Sartre, a non-Christian, teaches us the seriousness of the bondage we mistakenly call freedom: "You remember all we were told about torture-chambers, the fire and brimstone, the 'burning marl.' Old wives tales! There is no need for red-hot pokers. Hell is—other people."[2]

Our wills are the agents of our hearts. Appeals to will power are limited without a change of heart. Scripture teaches that "the heart is deceitful above all things and desperately wicked" (Jer 17:9). Until our hearts begin to be changed we will continue to desire those things that lead to conflict and destruction. The German Lutheran theologian Philip Melanchthon (1497–1560) is credited with the observation: "What the heart desires, the

2. Sartre, *No Exit*, 5.

will chooses, and the mind justifies." The power for good or ill is in our hearts; our wills are mere agents of our hearts' desires.

Desire can be every bit as incarcerating as being in jail if the object of our desires is inappropriate or pathological. Such desires can consume enormous emotional energy and produce great frustration. It is said that, if one marries for money only, one earns every penny. Getting what we want can be very expensive in the long haul and be anything but true freedom. Finishing a whole pizza while struggling with obesity is getting what we want, but this is bondage not freedom. As a procrastinator, I think I am free if I can put off a duty until another day and it merely increases the bondage of that day. The overwhelming tide of these secular times panders to our Pharisaic inclination that we are free when we get what we want. "You deserve it," the advertisement says. This is only true if what we want corresponds with what is true and appropriate. Children, who are always given what they want, tend to become disagreeable. When given what they need and is best for them there is a greater possibility for their health and joy. This is true of adults as well. Self-indulgence is every bit as binding in an adult as in a child with a gross of Hershey bars. True freedom is true joy.

This issue of freedom is confusing. Not everyone is completely self-centered. Our hearts are complex and ambivalent. The natural graces of family, friendship, and communal loyalty, as well as empathy in suffering and care for nature, give us some modicum restraints on our self-centeredness and produce some genuine desire for the good of others. But the lingering and persistent self-as-center inevitably limits, threatens, and too often destroys these natural expressions of loyalty and love. Only trust in Christ's Easter triumph over sin and death as a final reality can keep us on track for a life of greater freedom.

Although freedom is an unfathomable mystery, we are able to say some clear things about it. There seems to be a mystery about why our stomachs don't digest themselves, but that mystery does not mean we should give up eating or that we cannot learn a great deal about what we should eat. Childbirth is a profound mystery but that should not put obstetricians out of work. Several things need to be said about freedom without assuming one can dispel its mystery.

First, we need to be reminded of what our Lord emphatically told us: that when we sin we are the slaves of sin. Jesus was not arguing about some academic mistake the Jews were making. He was confronting their hearts. They naturally believed that having their way was freedom; but only when their way becomes Jesus's way could they be truly free. Sinning and freedom will always appear to sinners as synonymous. But according to Jesus sin is slavery: "He who sins is a slave to sin." We object to what Jesus tells us on the grounds that we have free will, that our wills are free to sin. This objection is merely a mask to hide our desire to keep ourselves as the center. It is Satan again whispering that we can be as gods. W. H. Auden says it as only a poet can:

> Poor cheated Mephistopheles
> Who think you're doing as you please
> In telling us by doing ill
> To prove that we possess free will.[3]

Second, freedom is not to be equated with having choices. Some choices will lead to freedom and some will lead to bondage. Making right choices is an expression of freedom. Destructive and damaging choices are expressions of slavery. When Charles Wesley was enabled by the story in Galatians to choose to lay down the heavy burden of confidence in his best endeavors and instead trust in Christ's easy yoke (Matt 11:30), the result was an astonishing freedom and productivity (as shown in chapter Five).

A hostage chained in a locked room has few external choices. He is not physically free. A person in a rewarding job has no choice to change jobs, not because he cannot but because the choice does not occur to him. One's loyalty to a friend or a spouse can be so ingrained in the heart that it eliminates any decision or option to betray, not because of any physical impediment to such a choice, but the heart simply can't engage the will to do something contrary to its desire. An alcoholic has the choice of rum, gin, vodka, bourbon, or scotch before breakfast. But having such choices is sadly and demonstratively a form of bondage. Sometimes freedom from choices is true freedom. Liberation from the choices of addiction can be a most wonderful freedom. The person, whose character has been so molded that deception and lying are not choices to be made each day, enjoys a greater freedom than one hounded constantly with choices to deceive and frantic attempts to recollect what lies were told that need to be covered.

3. Auden, *Collected Poetry*, 277.

Sir Walter Scott saw the bondage that results in the choice to lie: "Oh, what a tangled web we weave, when first we practice to deceive!" A tangled web is a veritable straight jacket in comparison with the freedom stemming from an honest heart. Deceit and lying are not acceptable choices to one whose commitment is to truth.

Third, we need to see that freedom and salvation are one. The New Testament scholar C. K. Barrett teaches us that freedom, according to Scripture, "is nothing other than a synonym for salvation."[4] Nowhere in Scripture is freedom or salvation assumed in humanity's natural condition: "you who were once slaves of sin have become obedient *from the heart* to the standard of teaching to which you were committed and having been set free from sin, have become slaves of righteousness" (italics mine) (Rom 6:17, 18); "For freedom Christ has set us free" (Gal 5:1); "and the truth will make you free" (John 8:32); "where the Spirit of the Lord is, there is freedom" (2 Cor 3:17). When we are being set free we are being saved. When we are completely free that is our salvation.

FREEDOM AND RESPONSIBILITY

We object to the claim that we are in bondage and not initially or naturally free because it seems to deny responsibility. How can we be held responsible for believing and acting as if we are the center of the world when this is how God made us? This is how we came into the world. It would seem to be unfair to be held responsible for a condition we did not choose but was given in our human nature. But responsibility does not depend on being free: "Now we know that whatever the law says it speaks to those who are under the law that every mouth be stopped and all the world may be held accountable before God" (Rom 3:19). We are held accountable and are guilty not because we are free but that we might become free. Being held responsible while not being free is no injustice. This bondage, this sin, St. Augustine called "original" because it began with Adam and human rebellion against the center, God, "and you will be like God" (Gen 3:5) says the serpent. Being held responsible is the only way we are enabled to respond. This is as true in rearing children as it is in God's holding us accountable.

4. Barrett, *Gospel According to St. John*, 285.

FREEDOM AND BEING CHOSEN

Children do not naturally take turns and share toys. We choose to hold children to such responsibilities. They are chosen so that they may begin to become responsible by themselves. Jesus reminds us, "You did not choose me, but I chose you" (John 15:16). Philip Rieff shows us how choice and responsibility are related to freedom.

> There is no feeling more desperate than that of being free to choose, and yet without the specific compulsion of being chosen. After all, one does not really choose; one is chosen. This is one way of stating the difference between gods and men. Gods choose; men are chosen. What men lose when they become as free as gods is precisely that sense of being chosen, which encourages them, in their gratitude, to take their subsequent choices seriously. Put in another way, this means: Freedom does not exist without responsibility.[5]

I once heard a scurrilous rumor about a colleague that I immediately denied was true. I knew he was incapable of treating someone with the cruelty that was alleged and the charge was shown to be false. He was certainly not perfect but, in this instance, I knew that his character was such that he was unable to do what he was accused of having done. He was certainly much freer than someone who by great effort managed to control himself and not commit what was alleged. If he had been of that sort I would not have been so sure he was wrongly accused.

William Temple tells us:

> There is a popular notion, miscalled Free Will—philosophically foolish and theologically heretical—which suggests that the Will is essentially a Jack in the Box that crops up when least expected . . .[6]

True freedom often reveals itself "in certain splendid incapacities, as when it is said of a man accused of taking bribes—'He could not do it.'"[7]

When Hurricane Hugo hit Charleston, South Carolina in 1989, the power lines were down and trees were strewn across the streets. I rode a bicycle from home to the Diocesan headquarters and went immediately to check the archives in a large closet on the second floor. The door closed

---

5. Rieff, *Triumph of the Therapeutic*, 93.

6. Temple, *Nature of Personality*, 44.

7. Ibid.

behind me and I heard the lock click. There was no window and no light. I tried the heavy metal door and could not push it open. No one knew where I was. I wondered how long it would take to be found. I examined the hinges with my hands hoping that I might be able to remove the pin in the hinge. Then I realized that it opened in and not out. I was in terrible bondage because I did not recognize the necessity that the door simply needed to be pulled and not pushed. When I recognized this reality, this necessity, I was free.

A simple story, perhaps, but in the long run God's unseen spiritual realities are in this sense no different from material and physical ones. In pushing on that door I was reminded of the account of Paul's conversion. "It hurts to kick against the goads" (Acts 26:14). Kicking against God's spiritual realities is as frustrating as kicking against the steel door. Any who have experienced addictions know what this is like. The central question is whether my will, or God's will, will prevail. Our kicking will not avail against God's gracious will.

The poet Robert Penn Warren expressed this fundamental point: "For the recognition of *necessity* is the beginning of freedom" (italics mine).[8] Lenin was right in claiming that necessity is the ground of freedom. He was wrong about what that necessity was. When people lost confidence in Communism's inevitability of a worldwide classless victory, Communism began to fall apart. When trust in the final inevitability of God's victory is lost, things begin to fall apart in Western civilization.

In summary, freedom remains a mystery, but some things can and should be said about it: self-centered humans, regardless of intelligence, believe that to sin is an expression of freedom. To sin is not freedom, but slavery. Freedom cannot be equated with merely having choices but the choices made that lead to freedom are those in response to having been chosen. Freedom must be in accord with necessity that is God's will, the final and ineluctable necessity.

PREDESTINATION

A promise was made in the last chapter that we would try to explain the crucial and unavoidable fact that predestination (our destiny is in God's hands) is not a denial of freedom but its true foundation. No other Christian doctrine is as offensive and shocking to human

8. Warren, *Brother to Dragons*, 214.

and cultural sensibilities. The reason for this is simple. As we resent a sibling or colleague, who has a rival center, all the more do we resent God who is *the* center.

This resentment is universal. It infects everyone from children to the intellectual elite. "It's all about me" is too often the persistent but often unconscious posture of adults. That we are not the center of the world is a fact that some only slowly and reluctantly admit while others never do. When we encounter the claim of God's predestination this reluctance can turn to anger and denial. But when we realize that freedom utterly depends on some necessity, some reality, we must ask, what necessity, what reality, is it? Is it not some residual antagonism toward God as center that makes us resent the very idea that God's destiny for us is the ultimate necessity, the only sure ground for our freedom? The title of a Broadway production expresses it well: "My Arms are too Short to Box with God."

Article XVII of the Anglican 39 Articles states:

> As the godly consideration of Predestination, our election in Christ, is full of sweet, pleasant, and unspeakable comfort to godly persons . . . so for curious and carnal persons lacking the Spirit of Christ to have continually before their eyes the sentence of God's Predestination, is a most dangerous downfall . . . doth thrust them either into desperation, or into wretchlessness of most unclean living, no less perilous than desperation.[9]

Curious in the sixteenth century meant: "Desirous of knowing what one has no right to know or what does not concern one, prying" (OED). Carnal is the English word that translates flesh (*sarx*) as opposed to spirit as it is described in Galatians 5:19–21 ("fornication, impurity, . . . enmity, strife, jealousy, anger," etc.). "Flesh," as used by St. Paul, is the natural enmity humans have toward any center other than self.

To see and hope for a destiny centered in God's will is not possible as long as we are looking at the world simply from our own center. No threat, no law, no fear can make us welcome God's destiny for us. But the vulnerable love that God has shown in Jesus gives us a vision of "unspeakable comfort" in the trust that his will, his mercy, his justice, his love will triumph. This destiny is not a perhaps, or problematic, or one that depends on us. It is assured and predetermined, for it is God's final and

---

9. *Book of Common Prayer*, 871.

certain victorious will. For those of us who resent the very idea of predestination, how would we answer the question, "What final destiny or for what purpose do we hope, God's will or ours?" This is why we began this chapter with the quotation from W. H. Auden: "Since Adam, being free to choose, chose to imagine he was free to choose his own necessity." We are not free to choose our own necessity. As with gravity, we can defy it (jump off a roof and flap our arms), but we are much freer when we obey and work within its laws.

In a scene in C. S. Lewis's novel, *Perelandra*, Ransom makes a courageous decision he once believed to be impossible:

> You might say, if you liked, that the power of choice had been simply set aside and an inflexible destiny substituted for it. On the other hand, you might say that he had been delivered from the rhetoric of his passions and had emerged into unassailable freedom. Ransom could not, for the life of him, see any difference between these two statements. *Predestination and freedom were apparently identical* (italics mine). He could no longer see any meaning in the many arguments he had heard on this subject.[10]

Predestination is often misunderstood and rejected as determinism, but it is in fact the very foundation of our freedom. Mystery is still here but this we know: there is no freedom that is not in accord with reality and the ultimate reality is God's will. It is important to explain carefully how God aligns our wills with his in order to understand that predestination is not determinism.

Jesus did not run after the rich young ruler, who went sadly away, asking, "Do you realize you will go to hell if you don't follow me?" He would not impose or coerce. Predestination is not a matter of coercion but the attraction of a loving necessity. He invited but did not draft his disciples. He submitted to the rejection of Caiaphas, Pilate, and the multitude without forcing their compliance. He did not restrain Judas, but allowed the betrayal. He will deal with us in the same way. He will only evoke and elicit the response of faith. This is not because he refuses to violate our freedom, as has too often been expressed, but because force and coercion can never evoke love and create true freedom from bondage. As St. Augustine has taught us, we are not saved *by* our wills, but God will not save us *without* our wills. We are not coerced, we are invited. Thomas

---

10. Lewis, *Perelandra*, 125.

Cranmer's prayer expresses the invitation, "in whose [God's] service is perfect freedom."

The fact is that our freedom lies in God's will and his service. The mystery lies in the final triumph of justice, mercy, and love and how we are, or are not, a part of that victory. Our human nature persists in attempting to abolish the mystery by the lie that in our freedom it is *we* who choose to have the faith that saves. Scripture and the saints have unanimously insisted otherwise: God has chosen us and our faith is his gift, not our accomplishment. How do we account for those to whom faith is not given and those who are not saved? We don't. How God manages these matters remains a mystery. One of the many blessings of not being God is that we can leave the remaining mystery with him.

An early and reoccurring heresy taught that the unity of Jesus's divinity and humanity was accomplished by the replacement of something in Jesus's humanity (his mind or his spirit) with divinity.[11] It was soundly repudiated at the Council of Constantinople in 381 because the grace of God never destroys nature and what God in Christ did not take on, did not assume in his full humanity, he did not redeem. If divinity replaced Jesus's mind or his will, our human minds or wills will not be redeemed. W. H. Auden described this when he put into the angel Gabriel's announcement to the virgin Mary, "Love's will requires your own"[12] and this same love requires our own will. Everything about Jesus's life and witness even unto death was not to destroy our wills but to engage, change, and free them. This is not determinism.

The temptation to replace or destroy our wills with God's will is still with us. The otherwise beautiful words to Hymn no. 707,[13] "Take my will and make it thine; it shall be no longer mine," makes our wills no longer ours. When they are transformed they are not lost but fulfilled. Much better is Charlotte Elliott's hymn, "Renew my will from day to day, Blend it with thine and take away, all that now makes it hard to say Thy will be

11. The heresy is called Apollinarianism. Its teaching regarding the replacement or destruction of human will continues to live on in modern examples such as the enormously popular work by Skinner, *Beyond Freedom and Dignity*, and in certain behavioral therapies that seek to train, educate, or cure people with methods and techniques that circumvent or destroy the will. This is true of all tyranny, political or personal, something markedly absent from the life of Jesus. Burgess's book and movie, *A Clockwork Orange*, is a classic example of the appeal and the horror of this "solution" to human behavior.

12. Auden, *For the Time Being*, 77.

13. Havergal, # 707, *Hymnal of the Protestant Episcopal Church*.

done."[14] Redemption does not replace, take away, or destroy our wills or minds, but harmonizes them with God's will where they remain distinctively ours but now fulfilled. This is redemption not determinism.

The sinful assumption that we are born free has also crept into much of our teaching and devotional material, especially the catechism of the Episcopal Church's present Prayer Book. No catechism before 1979 ever explained freedom this way:

> What does it mean to be created in the image of God?
>
> It means that we are free to make choices: to love, to create, to reason, and to live in harmony with creation and with God.
>
> Why then do we live apart from God and out of harmony with creation?
>
> From the beginning, human beings have misused their freedom and made wrong choices.
>
> Why do we not use our freedom as we should?
>
> Because we rebel against God, and we put ourselves in the place of God.[15]

The truth of earlier catechisms was replaced with a Pharisaic lie. In the 1928 Prayer Book the catechism reads:

> Catechist: My good child know this; that thou art not able to do these things of thyself, nor walk in the commandments of God, to serve him without his special grace; which thou must learn at all times to call for by diligent prayer.[16]

Freedom is not an agency, but rather a condition of not being in prison physically, psychologically, or spiritually. We come into this world unfree. We are not born free to live in harmony with others, "with creation and with God," as the more recent catechism falsely asserts. We are born out of harmony with God and others, and observe everything from our own center's perspective.

But some will say, "Are we not free to reject God's offer of grace and salvation?" We are certainly able to reject God's offer but we are not free to do so. Such rejection is an expression of bondage not freedom. Certainly

14. Elliott, # 420, *The Hymnal of the Protestant Episcopal Church*.

15. *Book of Common Prayer*, 845.

16. Ibid., 580.

TRUST IN AN AGE OF ARROGANCE

some do reject offers of grace and salvation, but only those infected with Pharisaic yeast call that rejection "freedom." Scripture calls such decisions slavery and bondage (John 8:34).

Bishop James Pike was a victim of this Pharisaic yeast. He showed that he was on his path to disbelief on page 80 of his *Time for Christian Candor*,[17] where he assumed the lie of our being *free in the initial situation* (born free): "A necessary corollary is that not only is man free to do good and constructive things but he is also free to do evil and destructive things." Doing evil and destructive things is not freedom but bondage. Repeating the lie about sinners being free excludes the need for grace. It eliminates the need for God's atonement in Christ's sacrifice. By page 124 the logic had led Bishop Pike to relinquish belief in the Trinity, which he observed "is not essential to the Christian faith." If we are already free we need no Trinitarian action of the Father's love, the Son's redemption, and the Spirit's encouragement.

Archbishop William Temple, in contrast, has expressed not only the reality of our bondage but the true nature of our freedom.

> What is quite certain is that the self cannot by any effort of its own lift itself off its own self as centre and resystematise itself about God as its centre. Such radical conversion must be the act of God, and that too by some process other than the gradual self-purification of a self-centered world assisted by the ever-present influence of God diffused through nature including human nature. It cannot be a process only of enlightenment. Nothing can suffice but a *redemptive* act. Something impinging upon the self from without must *deliver it from the freedom which is perfect bondage to the bondage which is its only perfect freedom*[18] (italics mine).

Jesus Christ in his redemptive act impinges on us from without with the invitation, "Come to me all who labor and are heavy laden, and I will give you rest" (Matt 11:28). This does not mean that we are free when we reject his offer. The choice of refusal, that sinners naturally call their free will, is precisely what Temple calls the freedom that is perfect bondage. We need to be reminded that freedom and salvation are synonyms.

---

17. Pike, *Time for Christian Candor*, 80, 124. Bishop Pike (1913–1969) was author of a score of books and was one of the most popularly acclaimed clergymen of his generation. He was censured by the House of Bishops for his "tone and manner" not for the substance of his denial of the creedal affirmations regarding Christ and the Trinity.

18. Temple, *Nature, Man and God*, 397.

Ultimately, the internal trajectory of our human bondage is self-destructive. Jesus tells us quite plainly that we are not free unless the Son makes us free. We have seen that freedom is not freedom unless it fits with necessity, and the final necessity is the will and love of God.

The Roman Catholic Fr. Harry McSorley can teach Protestants what they desperately need to know:

> If the doctrine of justification is the article on which the church stands or falls, then the doctrine of the unfree will is the FOUNDATION of the article on which the church stands or falls, or the article on which Luther's doctrine of justification stands or falls.[19]

A pastorally frustrating result of assuming people are naturally free is that clergy will have little or no compassion for sinners. If their parishioners are not tithing, not attending church regularly, not giving to missions, and not behaving, or if they believe the parishioners are free in this behavior and are able of themselves to do otherwise, their sermons will be scolding, exhorting, rebuking, and fussing. Or more likely in a permissive age, the sermons will skirt most personal moral issues and emphasize tithing and politically correct issues. Their sermons will not tell the story of grace and hope that will set people truly free. If they do not believe that members of their flock are in bondage, but rather are misusing their freedom, they will have little tenderness or sympathy for them. "Why in heaven's name won't they do what they should?" Assuming the lie that sin is freedom is a rationale for frustration and, ultimately, hatred.

This is as true of the laity as it is of clergy. If our attitude toward people, who are damaging themselves and us, is one that assumes they are free in this behavior, we will have no understanding or inclination to forgive and little capacity to love them. Understanding that sin is bondage, and that when the Son makes us free we are free indeed, we can look at unacceptable behavior with sadness rather than having aggressive counterproductive anger and resentment. Understanding is the enabling first step in human forgiveness.

Forgiveness is difficult, sometimes humanly impossible, because the injustice, pain, and suffering seem too great. Yet the necessity to forgive is even greater the more serious and unfair the hurt. When we understand that all sin is an expression of bondage, not freedom, we can begin to see

19. McSorley, *Luther Right or Wrong*, 11.

that as God has forgiven us for our acts and choices in our bondage so we are enabled to forgive others in their destructive bondage. Neither we nor they deserve forgiveness.

A young woman in Rwanda tells of her struggle and agony in confronting her neighbor, Felicien, who had slaughtered her family and stolen their possessions. She heard the killing while hiding and praying that she would not be found. She heard a voice in her head: "Why are you calling on God? Don't you have as much hatred in your heart as the killers do? Aren't you as guilty of hatred as they are? You've wished them all dead; in fact, you wished that you could kill them yourself! You even prayed that God would make them suffer and make them burn in hell."[20]

In returning to her village after the genocide, the authorities brought Felicien, now a prisoner, to be confronted. He was disheveled and pitiful. He would not stand up, and only looked at the floor. The warden jerked him to his feet and forced him to look at the young woman whose mother and brother he had killed and whom he had sought to kill. She writes:

> Felicien was sobbing. I could feel his shame. He looked up at me for only a moment, but our eyes met. I reached out and touched his hands lightly and quietly said what I'd come to say. "I forgive you."[21]

The warden was furious.

> That was the man who murdered your family. I brought him to you to question . . . to spit on him if you wanted to. But you forgave him. How could you do that? Why did you forgive him?[22]

She answers him with the truth: "Forgiveness is all I have to offer."[23] At that moment a great weight was taken off her heart and she was set free from the yoke of hatred. To forgive is not a part of our human nature. When we realize before God that we have deserved no forgiveness, yet are forgiven, the heavy burdens of hatred, resentment, and bitterness are removed from our souls

Acknowledging that we are unable to do what we should leads us to the recourse of the "old, old story" that carries the grace that can break

20. Llibagiza, *Left to Tell*, 92.
21. Ibid. 203–4.
22. Ibid.
23. Ibid.

our bondage. This is not sentimentality but tough love, as we see in Jesus's harsh statements regarding Sadducees, Pharisees, and Scribes. Sin is indeed a serious and destructive reality in everyone's life. God will judge the sins of our enemies but also ours. As we have received undeserved mercy, so we are able to show undeserved mercy to others.

"If you continue in my Word, you are truly my disciples and you will know the truth and the truth will make you free" (John 8:31, 32). The order in this verse is crucial. First must come the Word, the good news of God's love and action in saving sinners. Then we become his disciples, the messengers of his Word. Then we shall know the truth and finally we shall be made free. The Pharisaic yeast reverses the text by beginning with the assumption of freedom to obey God's law before we continue in his word and become his disciples.

The Pharisaic system, so congenial to our basic nature, offers the false hope that we can by our wills do what is necessary to be saved. When we believe that by our wills we can have faith (evangelical Pharisaism), an inevitable condescension and antipathy to those who have not used their wills to accept Jesus as their savior results. Scolding people for not believing in Jesus is a symptom of the lie and is invariably counterproductive.

The belief that by our wills we can gain sufficient knowledge and self-control to attain salvation (high-church Pharisaism) is also a symptom of the lie. An example of the latter can be found in an article on Moral Theology in the first two editions of the *Oxford Dictionary of the Christian Church*. Moral Theology is defined as: "The science of Christian conduct, trusting of God as man's last end, and of *the means by which he may be attained*" (italics mine).[24] This has been mercifully replaced in the third edition by a significant corrective.[25]

Following Jesus as our supreme example, while omitting the story of God's initiating love, is the form of the lie told by many liberal theologians. We are not saved by Jesus's example but by his sacrifice that established his mercy. In turn, in gratitude we begin to follow his example. This tradition, that reduces Jesus to merely an example to follow, has perhaps had more influence on our culture than the evangelical and high church traditions combined. Its father is Desiderius Erasmus (1469–1536), who taught that if what was commanded is not in everyone's power to obey the

24. Cross and Livingstone, eds., *Oxford Dictionary of the Christian Church*, 921.
25. Ibid., 1110.

numerous exhortations in Scripture would be irrelevant. All the promises, threats, reproofs, and expostulations would be useless unless we were able to fulfill them by our free will.

The clear assumption behind this assertion is that we sinners are indeed able to do what is commanded of us. One cannot help but wonder if Erasmus or his followers believed they could fulfill God's commandments: "You shall love the Lord your God with all your heart and with all your soul, and with all your mind, and with all your strength . . . and your neighbor as yourself." We do not fulfill these two commandments but instead they bring us to our knees to purge us of self-righteousness and to receive the grace (power) to begin, and begin again, to love God and neighbor.

Luther, in his reply to Erasmus, pointed out that the exhortations directed to us in our bondage draw us to the promise and grace that alone sets us free.[26] Erasmus's work, *The Freedom of the Will*,[27] is the foundational lie that panders to our natural Pharisaic inclination to believe that we are free before grace. This undergirds the whole liberal tradition from the seventeenth century until now. If Erasmus is right we can see how Christianity would become simply a matter of numberless exhortations, reproofs, threats, and scoldings without the saving story of God's loving and enabling sacrifice. If we were able to love God and our neighbor as ourselves his sacrifice would be unnecessary.

No wonder one of the definitions of preach is: "to give religious or moral instructions and especially in a drawn-out, tiresome manner." A definition of sermon is: "a lengthy and tedious reproof or exhortation."[28] Any dictionary definition, which includes gospel or good news in it, is extremely rare. Because dictionaries merely record how words are used over time, more convincing evidence of Pharisee yeast can scarcely be found. Erasmus's assumption that the exhortations in Scripture are meaningless unless we are able to obey them leads to this corruption: that we are naturally free and not in bondage. Luther's reply to Erasmus in *The Bondage of the Will* is the abiding antidote to this lie.[29]

26. See especially pp. 197–200 of *Luther and Erasmus*, eds. Rupp and Watson, 2006.

27. Winter, ed., *De Libero Arbitrio*.

28. *American Heritage Dictionary of the English Language*.

29. See *Martin Luther on the Bondage of the Will: A New Translation* by Packer and Johnston, and *Captivation of the Will* by Forde. Its introduction by James A. Nestingen is especially invaluable as a simple, clear exposition of biblical freedom.

This antidote to the sickness of bondage is not easy to swallow. Professor Gerhard O. Forde warns us:

> Writing a book on Luther's *Bondage of the Will* is a foolhardy business—not because the arguments are so hard to understand but rather because they are so difficult for sinners to take.[30]

When one begins with the false assumption of being free, all concern will be involved with how to keep such freedom in check, how to control sin. The result is the deadly religion of the Pharisee. If one begins with the assumption of bondage, the concern will be how to proclaim the gospel story in kindness, patience, and love so that people are enabled to be set free.

The crucial answer to both the Pharisee, as well as the Sadducee, is the very person of Christ "impinging upon the self from without." Christ's sacrifice gives us access to the only true meeting of mercy and justice, without which humans ultimately can not know the love that begins to set them free to be whole and saved.

Another spiritually pathological result of assuming that we are born free is the so-called "free will theodicy," the attempt to explain innocent suffering on the grounds that such victims have misused their freedom. As with all powerful lies this one, too, has partial truth in it. One can certainly explain some headaches by recalling how much rum one drank the night before or the relation between smoking and cancer, a corollary of the falsehood that he was free to smoke (in contrast to he was in bondage to smoke). But many things happen that have nothing to do with any choice we may have made. Random calamities, personal, genetic, and social, occur from myriad causes having nothing to do with human volition.

Rabbi Kushner's book *When Bad Things Happen to Good People* mentioned in chapter 1 eloquently and justly dismissed the free will explanation for his son's fatal illness (the son had done nothing to deserve his malady), even if his own solution (to forgive God) is vain. However, that self-centered autonomy in each of us often takes inappropriate responsibility and produces neurotic guilt for random calamities. A woman dying of cancer in Chicago is ridden with false guilt, insisting it is her fault. "If I had not left Chillicothe, Ohio, I would not be dying of cancer." Our natural Pharisaism drives us to insist that we are always in control.

---

30. Forde, *The Captivation of the Will*, xvi.

When we lose that control we often neurotically blame ourselves. The very fact that Kushner needed to write this exceedingly popular book to absolve people of false guilt indicates the spiritual pathology that stems from the claim of autonomy. A terrible price is paid for believing we are a law unto ourselves (autonomous). Our self-centeredness naturally tends to resolve issues by control. This idea is so pervasive that control has now become a psychological term of neurosis. A fruit of our self-centeredness is arrogant assumptions about our freedom and, in this case, responsibility for innocent or random calamities, a cruel and heavy burden of false guilt.

Given human nature, this tendency to assign inappropriate responsibility showed itself in Scripture and continues today:

> There were some present at that very time who told him of the Galileans whose blood Pilate had mingled with their sacrifices. And he answered them, "Do you think that these Galileans were worse sinners than all the other Galileans, because they suffered thus? I tell you, No; but unless you repent you will all likewise perish. Or those eighteen upon whom the tower of Siloam fell and killed them, do you think that they were worse offenders than all the others who dwelt in Jerusalem? I tell you, No; but unless you repent you will all likewise perish. (Luke 13:2–5)

Jesus makes it quite clear that all calamities are not punishment for sins. This false theodicy was a large part of the comfort of Job's false friends. I remember calling on a parishioner who had just been diagnosed with a terrible immune-type disease. She asked the universal question, "Why me? What have I done to deserve this?" I responded with Jesus's words about the tower of Siloam to assure her that there are random acts that have no relation to behavior. Multiple sclerosis is bad enough without the added burden of false guilt.

But I didn't finish the text. I didn't tell her what Jesus added, "but unless you repent you will . . . likewise perish." It did not seem to be a gracious thing to do at that time. But I should have told her, at some time, about the good news of what true repentance is—a change of heart that promises joy and abundant life in God's unassailable center.

REPENTANCE: RENEWING THE POWER TO LOVE

All that we have considered in this chapter begs this question: why does Jesus demand repentance of his hearers who, like those upon whom the tower of Siloam fell, are presumably no more sinful than others? The fact is that the need for repentance is universal and points to something deeper than sins committed. Repentance treats something more profound, our commitment to our self-as-center, that which causes us to sin and to believe that we are in control.

The Pharisaic influence in the church's history has soiled the image of the term repentance. What Jesus is asking is something deeper than being sad or remorseful about something we have done. Ashley Null's book on *Cranmer's Doctrine of Repentance: Renewing the Power to Love* is important, not only for its excellent study of Thomas Cranmer but also for its deeper and much needed positive understanding of repentance. Oxford University Press erred badly when they did not include the subtitle on the cover of the first edition. Renewing the power to love conveys a much different spirit from merely feeling bad about something we've done—the superficial and conventional view of repentance. As long as our hearts are unchanged "it's all about me." I must control my desires, hide my self-interest, and pretend to virtues I do not possess. It's a real prison compared to a heart changed to genuinely desire to do, think, and feel as I should.

Change of heart is an exquisite expression of true freedom. It needs to be noted that in this contrast between a religion of control and one of redemption, perfection is not given to us in this life. The list of the fruit of the Spirit in Galatians: love, joy, peace . . . ends with self-control (Gal 5:22–23).

The insight from Philip Melanchthon deserves repeating: "What the heart desires, the will chooses, and the mind justifies." Jesus is demanding not mere sorrow for transgressions, or remorse concerning sins, but a change of heart that enables us to love. All human loves are tainted, whether friendship, romance, or domestic loyalties. They are, in themselves, good, but they are ultimately betrayed by a self-centered heart. As C. S. Lewis shows, natural human loves are good but not good enough.[31] In spite of the literal meaning of repentance (*metanoia*) as a change of

---

31. Lewis, *Four Loves*. The quotation on the title page from John Donne should not be missed: "That our affections kill us not, nor dye."

mind, the overwhelming meaning in Scripture, as we see in the context each time it is used, is a change of heart.[32] On one hand, the expectation that our wills can respond to demands of the law without a change of heart brings frustration, hypocrisy, and depression. On the other hand, to have some measure of loving that which God commands, even in small doses, brings expressions of true freedom, real joy, and growing love.

One of my friends is a Methodist pastor. He ministers not only to his own flock but to the whole town. Whenever a problem, tragedy, or catastrophe occurs, the social workers, police, physicians, and others call him. I have seen him in what most people would regard as singularly awkward and disagreeable situations of drug addiction, suicides, crime, and heartbreak. He is invariably upbeat, tender, reassuring, realistic, and encouraging. He seems to have more energy than anyone since John Wesley. His explanation is that he truly wants to do what he is called to do. He doesn't tell his wife, "Oh, Lori, I'm afraid I have to go back to that dysfunctional, self-destructive family again." He doesn't have to make himself go. He wants to go.

Why? And how? Because he has been given a new heart to do so. What the heart desires, the will chooses, and the mind justifies. How was he given a new heart? Many years ago, like the prodigal son, he found himself in tears on his knees at midnight in the only unlocked church in town. He sobbed out the recognition that his self-as-center was rotten and that it was the source of what was wrong in his life. How did he get a new heart? He asked for it. How was he able to ask for it?

He had been given, but had previously ignored, a picture of true love. This picture of God's vulnerable love in Christ who suffered and died a horrifying death on a cross for him was no longer a mere picture but an experience, an experience that freed him from the destructive escapes of self-indulgent permissiveness. That love broke his heart and reset it in a new center. Only the love that has chosen us can change our hearts and set our wills free to choose him.

Because God will not save or set us free without our wills, he not only gives us this same picture and action of his love, but especially so at those humbling and distressing times, when our self-as-center is not working and we are miserable. On those occasions we are most susceptible to having our hearts changed. When our self-reliance on our ability

32. Kittel, *Theological Dictionary of the New Testament*, IV, 626–29.

to control gives way and we can see and experience that bloody love, as did the Wesleys, Charles Simeon, William Wilberforce, C. S. Lewis, and Charles Colson, then are we blessed with a new heart that is grounded in the joy, certitude and service that is perfect freedom?

George Herbert describes the condition in two short lines:

> Who in heart not ever kneels,
> Neither sin nor savior feels.[33]

How can we receive this experience? Not by wasting the humbling times but by allowing them to become what they were for my Methodist friend.

---

33. Marty, *George Herbert*, 97.

10

Blood of Christ

Just as I am, and waiting not
To rid my soul of one dark blot,
To Thee whose blood can cleanse each spot,
O Lamb of God, I come.

—Charlotte Elliott, "Just as I Am" (1835)

SELF-AS-CENTER IS THE SIMPLE way William Temple accurately described our natural human condition. In this post-Christian age, trust in God rather than ourselves is being increasingly challenged. The Sadducee's creed, devoid of eternal hope, produces today's secularism and chops at the moral and ethical roots of Western civilization. Without trust anchored in reality of a providential God we are left with mere speculation, false hope and hollow wishes that spawn myriad pathologies. We are forced to look to ourselves or some historical power for a source of meaning. In so doing we draw the shade on hope for any ultimate justice and mercy. Arrogance flourishes and spiritual or moral direction is lost. When imperfect man is the measure of all things we are measuring with a flawed standard. Our compass has no magnetic north and gives guidance to nowhere. In the shadows of self-interest we find only the deeper darkness of depression, despair, war, tyranny, terror, and genocide.

Pharisaic trust is the other side of the same coin. No less human-centered than the Sadducee, the Pharisee confronts the world's Sadducean arrogance with a religious arrogance. When Christianity is reduced to a religion of control, an endeavor to keep order by condemning sinners and giving no word that enables us to escape our bondage, it loses all joy and love. People will naturally turn away from such an atmosphere and seek the worldliness of the Sadducee rather than the joylessness of

148

the Pharisee. Or they would prefer the grave as the final word believing oblivion better than eternity with church people. We recovering Pharisees need to remember how David Hume turned against the false faith he was fed in *The Whole Duty of Man*, how Karen Armstrong's atheism was a revolt against a gross distortion of Christianity, how Edward Gibbon's attack on Christianity was doubtless influenced by his view of the faith received through William Law, and how Ayn Rand rejected the joyless distortion of Christianity she received through Immanuel Kant. No wonder Jesus was more severe with the Pharisees than the Sadducees. The former tend to produce the latter.

Pharisee yeast is like cancer. Even after a profession of faith the seeds of Pharisaism remain in us, and like cancer it can reoccur at any time for the rest of our lives. Anyone who has survived cancer knows the diligence of self-examination that is necessary even while in remission. A prayer by Thomas Cranmer, to be said before receiving Communion, can help to save us from trust in our own goodness (which can be as true of Sadducees as Pharisees).

> We do not presume to come to this thy table, O merciful Lord, *trusting in our own righteousness* (italics mine), but in thy manifold and great mercies. We are not worthy so much as to gather up the crumbs under thy Table. But thou art the same Lord whose property is always to have mercy . . . [1]

When a celebrant at a theological seminary used this prayer in a worship service, five seniors walked out in protest. The prayer cuts across the grain of the current religious dogma of self-esteem that substitutes mere acceptance for needed transformation.

We have seen that Roman Catholicism, after the Council of Trent in the sixteenth century, insisted that our own righteousness (even if given) renders us righteous before God. We have seen that some Anglicans in the middle of the seventeenth century began to teach that our faith (defined as our endeavors) was treated as if it were a righteousness that made us acceptable to God. We have seen that some Methodists, after the conversions of the Wesleys in the eighteenth century, began to follow the misleading example of the Anglicans. In the nineteenth century some Lutherans taught us to trust in our ability to unite in the brotherhood of man and the fatherhood of God without trust in God's enabling grace. In

---

1. *Book of Common Prayer*, 337.

the twentieth century, as well as today, we can see that some Presbyterians tended to distort John Calvin's doctrine by asserting that our sanctified goodness is the grounds of our assurance of election. The yeast of trusting in our own righteousness is as pervasive today (and has been throughout history) as it was when Jesus warned against this teaching of the Pharisees and the Sadducees. Nowhere can there be four lines that better encompass faith free of Sadducee and Pharisee corruption:

> Lord, I did not freely choose you
> 'Til by grace you set me free;
>> for my heart would still refuse you
>> had your love not chosen me.[2]

—Josiah Conder (1789–1855)

Much of our present-day distortion of Christianity stems from the big lie—the lie that we are born free, free to do right or wrong, to do as we please, and worship however and whatever we want. The self-centered notion of free will feeds this lie. Although no Christian tradition taught this lie officially, when trust in God gives way to confidence in man the yeast in the loaf is unmistakable. Roman Catholicism, even at the Council of Trent, never claimed that sinners were free to believe but that their bondage could only be broken sacramentally by grace.[3] The classical Anglican prayer books and Martin Luther's *Bondage of the Will* agree with official Roman Catholicism about authentic freedom rather than the lie that we are born free. Through Luther's teachings in Galatians and Romans, Charles and John Wesley were converted and given a freedom and effectiveness they had not previously possessed. Also, in agreement are the faithful followers of John Calvin who taught us to forego curious speculation into God's mystery and to leave election and predestination in the context of how God has saved us, by setting us free, not how God orders the world. Richard Hooker calls the lie that we are born free the heresy of free will: "The heresie of free will was a millstone about the Pelagian's neck . . ."[4]

2. Conder, # 706, *Hymnal*, 1982.

3. Rahner, "Freedom," *Encyclopedia of Theology*, 545. "Freedom is subject to the impulses of concupiscence, and is said to be diminished, weakened, and wounded . . . Furthermore, without the gratuitous grace of God this freedom is absolutely incapable of salutary acts. (and) . . . freedom is a mystery to itself and all others. It is a mystery as the primordial dialogue, as freedom liberated from bondage and called into the absolute mystery."

4. Hooker, *Laws of Ecclesiastical Polity*, 525.

St. Augustine called it the cruel teaching of the Pelagians; cruel not only because the assumption is false but because it deprives us of compassion for sinners and ourselves. The lie is the seed bed for noxious weeds of both Sadducees and Pharisees. It subverts the promise of true freedom (Temple's "bondage that is perfect freedom") and the promise of salvation which, in the New Testament, is the synonym for freedom.

The Jews *who believed on him* heard Jesus give three steps to freedom (John 8:31–32): (1) "If you continue in my word you are truly my disciples"; (2) "you will know the truth" ("I am the way the truth and the life"); and (3) "that truth will make you free." We continue to tell their lie ("we've never been in bondage") precisely because we *are* in bondage. We are only free when the Son makes us free.

The first step to freedom is *to continue in my word*. The lie, that we sinners are free, leads us inexorably to approach Scripture (the story of how we are made free or redeemed) as if we are already free. Like desperately malnourished people, bloated on popcorn and Twinkies, we examine and judge the contents of a magnificent dinner while denying we have any need.

The second step is to follow him as disciples, to be followers and ministers of Christ, to bring his love to a lonely, hurt, and needy world, treating other sinners as God has treated us. In the activity of discipleship our trust is fed and enhanced. As a diocesan bishop, remembering what Jesus had said about prisoners not being visited (Matt 25:44), I tried to thank those involved in Kairos, a ministry to prisoners. The almost unanimous response was, "Don't thank me; I thank you for the opportunity to be a part of this ministry. I had some faith before I went into the prisons in the Kairos program but I was astonished at how powerful a little bit of God's love could be in people's lives. This experience has given me a deeper faith and love than I had known before. I thank you." Here is an example of the servant being served in his serving. Our discipleship opens our eyes and hearts to deeper trust and knowledge of truth, the truth that makes us free.

The third and last step is to know and trust Christ: "And you will know the truth and the truth will make you free." Pontius Pilate asked the universal question, "What is truth?" The answer is none other than Jesus Christ. "I am the way and the truth and the life" (John 14:6). Pilate's question carries the query of humans. Is evil, lying, suffering, hurt, and injustice the final truth? Here is the promise that the final truth, the ultimate fact, the inevitable reality is fairness, justice, and mercy personified in Jesus Christ, the beginning and the end, "I am the Alpha and the Omega, says the Lord God, who is and who was and who is to come, the Almighty" (Rev 1:8).

THE CRISIS OF TRUST REGARDING SCRIPTURE

The malignant influence of the Pharisee and Sadducee are two permanent holes in the church's ark. Scripture is the bailing bucket. Each generation from every tradition must bail as if no one had ever bailed before. These influences naturally spring from our common bondage and we cannot avoid them. Christians cannot produce other Christians by procreation. Each child and each generation must be enabled to trust by the Scripture's story and be set free from self-as-center.

The Bible, unfortunately, has become largely inaccessible, not unlike the situation before the sixteenth century when it was written in a language few could understand. This inaccessibility today is not due to illiteracy, and certainly not to the lack of translations, but to the flawed way we have been taught to study it. We approach Scripture as our arrogant culture approaches God. As C. S. Lewis has shown in his essay, "God in the Dock," we have become the judge of God, so we are also the judge of Scripture and not Scripture of us. Suspicion and skepticism, minus any trust with which studies are begun, leaves us with a book devoid of reliability or power to trust the Lord who sets us free.

The slavish accommodation to skepticism by modern biblical critics deserves the comment of Professor J. V. Langmead Casserley:

> We are confronted with the paradox of a way of studying the Word of God out of which no Word of God ever seems to come, with an imposing modern knowledge of the Bible which seems quite incapable of saying anything biblically or thinking biblically.[5]

Since the middle of the nineteenth century every discipline used to study the Word of God through Scripture uses the term "criticism": higher criticism, lower criticism, form criticism, historical criticism, literary criticism, redactor criticism, and so on. The canonical approach of Professor Brevard Childs of Yale is a rare and valuable exception.[6]

5. Casserley, *Toward a History of Theology*, 116.

6. For an appreciation of Childs's work, see Seitz and Green-McCreight, *Theological Exegesis: Essays in Honor of Brevard S. Childs*.

Modern biblical scholars exhibit an astonishing philosophical naïveté by relying on the skepticism of Rene Descartes and John Locke who taught us that doubting is the way to truth. Descartes' oft quoted "I think therefore I am" was the foundation for truth after he had doubted everything except the fact that he doubted. He *then* could build truth on that foundation by accepting clear and distinct ideas. This widely taught skeptical approach has been devastating to trust in the word of God.

Even the orthodox scholar, Bishop Charles Gore, in his endeavor to establish authority for the Bible, demonstrated his cultural captivity to Cartesian skepticism: "I endeavoured to pursue a purely critical method . . . In result it appeared that the intellectual construction which best satisfied the requirements of reason and criticism *was* substantially the traditional faith of Christendom."[7] That false and fatal confidence in the requirements of reason and criticism soon eroded. This is not to deny *any* role for the critical approach to Scripture. The critical textual studies since 1880 have produced an agreed text of the New Testament "which is as close to the original as we can hope for on the basis of the evidence currently available. This was a major achievement, and can be justly regarded as the one truly assured result of modern criticism."[8] A critical approach can also prevent interpretations from flying off into fantasy and is indispensable in getting behind the difficulties of language and translations, but for many critics it has led to their fatal refusal to recognize that great tradition of Augustine, Bernard, and especially Anselm. The latter taught that revelation is accessible only with the risk of trust:

> I do not seek, O Lord, to search out your depths,
>> but only in some measure to understand your truth, which
>> my heart believes and loves.
> I do not seek to understand so that I may believe,
>> but believe that I may understand.
> For this I know to be true:
>> that unless I first believe I shall not understand.[9]

Trust is an essential ingredient in knowing, not only concerning revelation, but in all the important matters of life. Unfortunately, trust has been overwhelmingly absent in the modern approach to Scripture. If Jack

7. Gore, *Reconstruction of Belief*, xi.
8. Bray, *Biblical Interpretation Past and Present*, 325.
9. *St. Anselm's Proslogian*, 115.

meets Joan, and treats her in the same way we have been taught to treat Scripture, he will doubt her friendship until there is nothing left to doubt and before he can begin to build on what cannot be doubted. Even after some period of observation the most he can know is that she has behaved so far as if she were a friend. In the meantime, she will likely have vanished, like confidence in Scripture among the victims of the hermeneutic of skepticism. The risk of trust is indispensable to friendship, to love, and to hearing God's word in Scripture.

The remarkable scientific achievements of the English Royal Society at the end of the seventeenth century, and the industrial accomplishments of the eighteenth century, could not have occurred without trust in cause and effect (which David Hume correctly denied to be capable of proof). No one *knew* that effects do not exceed their causes and many under the influence of magic denied it. Unless one *trusted* that no effect could exceed its cause, essential truths of modern science would never have been known.[10]

Professor Luke Timothy Johnson, of Emory University, described what happens when the Bible is taught without the eyes of faith. He made these insightful comments to a group of chaplain interns while he was teaching at Yale. He spoke of the study of Scripture as it is taught in most theological schools:

> The result of taking these NT exegesis courses is like getting raped. One is never quite innocent again, but neither is one in love. The student knows that it is old fashioned and wrong to treat the text in the naïve fashion he or she had before. The student knows that critical study of the NT has just given rise to an infinite series of questions about the historicity of this and that. The student knows that he or she *should* use the Scripture . . . but cannot, simply cannot. There is no bridge made available between the literal meaning of the text in the first century and what it might mean today. The result is simply that ministers do not pay any attention to the Scripture at all, regarding it as the arcane playground of specialists, and therefore lose their roots in the normative document of our religion, and become pop theologians and pop psychologists, posing as ministers of the word. Or for some, exposure to NT

---

10. Isaacson, *Einstein*, 324–25. An apparent attack on Albert Einstein's trust in causation evoked his distress over the inferences that Niels Bohr and Werner Heisenberg were making from quantum mechanics. Einstein believed that if trust in causation were not true *it means the end of physics*.

scholarship means nothing. They simply go back to treating the texts as they always have. In which case, there has perhaps been little damage, but certainly not much gain.[11]

Some recovery of trust in Scripture among contemporary scholars is refreshing to see. David Steinmetz, historian at Duke University, wrote a seminal article "The Superiority of Pre-Critical Exegesis" showing how the modern way of reading Scripture, instead of being an improvement, was inferior to that of commentaries before the arrogant loss of trust.[12] Professor Richard Hays, a New Testament scholar at Duke also, states,

> I want to argue that a hermenuetic of trust is both necessary and primary. In order to get our bearings on the question of our fundamental attitude toward Scripture I propose that we take our cue from the Reformation and return to Scripture itself. If we attend carefully to Paul's treatment of trust and distrust in his Letter to the Romans, the apostle may lead us to suspect our own suspicions.[13]

A most important recent work that helps us out of the critical cul de sac is Professor Richard Bauckham's *Jesus and the Eyewitnesses*.[14] He argues for a clean break with the form critics whom he shows to be in error by their overlooking the source of eyewitnesses for the canon of Scripture. The long-standing assumption was that New Testament material circulated for a considerable time as anonymous community traditions. Bauckham shows from internal and contemporary evidence that the four Gospels are closely based on eyewitness testimony of those who personally knew Jesus.

A much simpler and shorter (21 pages) but no less valuable criticism of the way Scripture is being taught can be found in C. S. Lewis's *Fern Seed and Elephants*—"the best thing he ever wrote," according to his friend and fellow Oxford academic, Austin Farrer.[15] Recovery of trust in scriptural

11. First of two unpublished papers delivered to chaplain interns, 8, 9.

12. Steinmetz, "Superiority of Pre-Critical Exegesis," 37.

13. Hays, "Salvation by Trust? Reading the Bible Faithfully," 218–19. This article was based on an address he gave to the Society of Biblical Literature, Nov. 1996. Further reading on this important matter can be found in the writings of Polanyi, *Personal Knowledge*; Packer, *Knowing God*; Minear, *Eyes of Faith*; Napier, *From Faith to Faith*. Brueggemann says: "It was this book that decided for me a life of study in the Old Testament," *Struggling with Scripture*, 29.

14. Bauckham, *Jesus and the Eyewitnesses*, 537.

15. Hooper, ed., *Fern Seed and Elephants*, 9.

authority is essential for our using the biblical bucket to empty the ark of the Pharisaic and Sadducean heresies.

RECTITUDE OF THE HEART

When we speak of heresy we need to be reminded of S. T. Coleridge's correction of popular understandings. He comments on Bishop Jeremy Taylor's insight:

> For heresy is not an error of the understanding but an error of the will. (Taylor, *Liberty of Prophesying* p. 461.) To this Taylor should have adhered and to its converse, Faith is not an accuracy of logic but a rectitude of the heart.[16]

The reality of heresy is shunned and ignored in modern times largely because of its symbiotic relationship to sin. Heresy is not an error of the understanding but an error of the will. Sin and heresy feed on each other. Our self-centered wills, not our minds, produce classical heresy as well as contemporary ones. In the case of the whole family of Gnostic heresies, trust is placed in knowledge and seeks to avoid the risk involved in the messy human arena of political and social responsibilities. It is easier and safer to give intellectual assent than to trust with our hearts.

The difficulty with trust is that it makes us vulnerable. Trust involves the vulnerability of commitment, possibility of disappointment, hurt, betrayal, broken hearts, and suffering. In fact, suffering seems inescapably linked with trust. If we don't trust, don't hope, don't care, it seems that we will be less likely to suffer. The expression "I couldn't care less" is invariably used to insulate us from disappointment and hurt. This universal human reluctance to trust stems from our desire to defend our center. To trust is to put oneself in a dangerous place, with one's own center undefended. Many people believe in Jesus but trusting him, and following him come what may, involves risk that they are unwilling to take. Of course, everything depends upon the reliability of the object of our trust. We cannot live with the loneliness and isolation that result from trusting nothing. The issue for each of us is, what or whom do we trust? If we insulate ourselves from inevitable hurt with cynicism and hopelessness for ultimate peace, mercy and justice, the resulting loneliness and absence of meaning will haunt our waking and sleeping. We are tempted to justify

16. Coleridge, *Notes on English Divines*, 215.

the self-protective cynicism by how unfair our lives seem to be. To avoid further hurt we close down any commitment and final hope of anything ever being fair and right.

Into this very universal condition God sent his only son. He sent him in flesh into the arena of hurt and suffering, to be hurt and to suffer. That which we fear the most— suffering and death, Christ experienced to show us the Father's gracious nature and his power over sin and death. This act, too profound to be comprehended by the word "courageous," nevertheless inspires our courage to trust.

Robert Frost shows this courageous unguarded vulnerability implicit in Christ's incarnation ("substantiation") in these words:

> But God's own descent
> Into flesh was meant
> As a demonstration
> That the supreme merit
> Lay in risking spirit
> In substantiation.[17]

Let us not ignore the fact that God's risk did result in betrayal, suffering, and death but the love embodied in the risk evoked the willingness of the disciples to follow that risk and likewise experience suffering and death. The transformation of these puzzled, uncomprehending, timid, and fearful friends of the historical Jesus into confident, committed, and courageous witnesses and martyrs, who spread the teaching of a despised sect across the civilized world, is nothing short of miraculous. Witnessing Christ's life, death, and resurrection was an experience not merely of their minds but of their hearts. And so it is with us.

"The mind lives on the heart/Like any parasite," writes Emily Dickinson. The will that chooses heresy is but the agent of the heart. Thus, heresy must be met by what will change one's heart, not by force, threat, burning, or ostracism. Coleridge is right. Faith is not the mind's accuracy about doctrine but a "rectitude of the heart." What the heart desires. the will chooses, and the mind justifies. A change of heart is needed and this is the true meaning of repentance, *metanoien,* to renew the heart's power to love. (*Metanoien,* as we have seen, literally means change of mind, but the context in which it is used in Scripture is not change of mind but invariably change of heart.)

---

17 Frost, "Kitty Hawk," *In the Clearing,* 49.

THE PENDULUM AND THE CROSS

Odour of blood when Christ was slain
Made all Platonic tolerance vain
And vain all Doric discipline.[18]

The life-saving, freeing love of Christ is obscured by the malignant teachings of Sadducees and Pharisees without and within the church. Yeats declares the vanity of all human pretensions that cannot smell the "blood when Christ was slain."[19]

On the one hand "Platonic tolerance" can be taken to symbolize the long list of conjugations of the spirit that seek to resolve our human predicament by toleration, acceptance, and mercy. On the other hand, "Doric discipline" can be taken to comprise the virtues of justice, discipline, and responsibility.

Platonic Tolerance	Doric Discipline
Mercy	Justice
Toleration	Judgment
Forgiveness	Accountability
Permissiveness	Responsibility
Compassion	Discipline
Liberalism	Conservatism
Cooperation	Competition
Acceptance	Discrimination
Sadducees	Pharisees
Uncircumcision	Circumcision[20]

18. Yeats, *Collected Plays of W. B. Yeats*, 73.

19. To read and study scholars who cannot "smell the blood" is a fruitless endeavor. One will look in vain for any indication that Schleiermacher, Von Harnack, Macquarrie, members of the "Jesus Seminar," Crossan, Borg, Spong, or Ehrman (perhaps the most influential New Testament teacher in America) can smell the blood.

20. St. Paul faced something of this polarity in the circumcision party stressing the demands of the Torah and the uncircumcision party advocating freedom from the law, hence his claim: "For in Christ Jesus neither circumcision nor uncircumcision is of any avail, but faith working by love." Galatians 5:6.

These are not air-tight compartments. Changes in historical contexts confuse any simplistic application of these polarities. For instance, Alexander Hamilton, the ardent Federalist, would doubtless favor the Democratic party of recent times with its desire to use the offices of the federal government to implement the welfare of its citizens. On the other hand, Thomas Jefferson, the great democrat, would doubtless favor traditional Republicans in their concern that the least government is the best government. In modern France conservatives are ardent advocates of change while liberal socialists wish to have as little change as possible. However, the basic set of polarities is generally true and they represent inescapable tensions in nursery schools, families, Fortune 500 companies, nations, and in the churches today.

Western civilization has reached unprecedented achievement by a strong tradition of Doric discipline, competition, and accomplishment. The tradition of scientific rigor, the largely unforgiving competitive nature of capitalism, the so-called Protestant conscience or Protestant work ethic and its role in economic development have been strong factors in our incomparable prosperity.

A heavy price, however, has been paid. Sigmund Freud observed that "the price of progress in civilization is paid in forfeiting happiness through the heightening of the sense of guilt."[21] One of the symptoms of unresolved guilt is depression. Widespread depression seems to have become a characteristic of our times.

Reaction to Doric discipline is a pendulum swing toward Platonic tolerance with its concerns for acceptance, tolerance, permissiveness, self-esteem, and financial bailouts of failed businesses. This toleration has marked much of Western society since World War II and characterizes the contemporary Sadducee. Great strides have been made in race relations, women's rights, and better opportunities for people previously left out of the advantages in society. Princeton sociologist Robert Wuthnow has noted this pendulum swing in which our society has moved from harsh discipline to indulgent permissiveness in recent history. He shows that religion, once stern and prescriptive, has become a tool of therapy that buttresses individual choice and encourages people to feel good about whatever code of conduct they may choose.[22] Philip Rieff's observation

---

21. Freud, *Civilization and Its Discontents*, 123.
22. Wuthnow, *God and Mammon in America*, 72–77.

was: "The new releasing insights deserve only a little less respect than the old controlling ones."[23] What needs to be understood is that our human condition without the gospel is destined always to ride the pendulum from discipline to permissiveness, from justice to mercy and back again with much pain and destruction accompanying each swing.

When the freedom of Christian faith is corrupted by the malignant law of the Pharisee, a reaction is inevitable. The current atmosphere of corrosive permissiveness is the world's poignant and inescapable reaction to the Pharisaic moralism devoid of the gospel that we have seen is present in all traditions. We, who find ourselves unable to obey the law and condemned as sinners, will not emotionally accept such rejection. In the long run we will reject the rejection and discard or redefine the demands that brought us under condemnation. Recent views concerning homosexuality are examples of this dynamic.

Another example of radical permissiveness in Western culture is the following news item:

> Is promiscuity in our genes? Yes, says a controversial British Anglican bishop. "God knew when he made us that he has given us a built-in sex drive to go out and sow our seeds. He has given us promiscuous genes," Bishop of Edinburgh (ret.) Richard Holloway said in a recent speech on sex and Christianity, warning that humans were not designed to be faithful and that man was born to have many lovers. "I think it would be wrong for the church to condemn people who have followed their instincts."[24]

Is this a privilege only for men and not women? A very large part of what is meant by civilization is that we do *not* follow our instincts. Since Cain and Abel our instincts have expressed themselves not only in sex but in murder. If Holloway were living in Baghdad, rather than Britain, would he be so enthusiastic about people following their instincts? Holloway no longer identifies himself with Christianity but he does represent the pendulum in its permissive swing about as far as it can go, we hope.

The permissiveness that characterizes our era tends to deny the reality of sin. It reduces responsibility to that which people can live with. This reduction of duty and morality becomes necessary in a culture where the knowledge of God's grace and mercy in costly forgiveness is unknown

23. Rieff, *Triumph of the Therapeutic*, 261.
24. *Post and Courier*, June 8, 1995.

and where there is no transcendent hope to enable us to bear greater responsibility. The only place where justice and mercy have been perfectly blended is the cross. Reaction against Doric discipline toward acceptance and permissiveness, that cannot endure the unforgiving demands of the law, is not a reaction to the Christian faith but to its counterfeit—the malignant Pharisee teachings in all church traditions.

The swing away from responsibility and standards of morality to unprecedented acceptance of what has traditionally been regarded as outrageous has brought some thoughtful anxiety regarding its effect on society. Robert Bartley writing in the *Wall Street Journal* issued a wise recommendation:

> Christianity has instructed us on moral issues for two millenniums, and Judaism longer still. With or without personal faith we have been living off this capital; our social pathologies mean it is being rapidly depleted. Rather than denigrating Christianity and religion in general, socially conscious elites ought to be asking what religious impulse can teach us, and how amid the winds of modernity we might start to replenish the stock of moral guidance it bequeathed us.[25]

This advice is in strong contrast to that from the *New York Times,* which printed a story of an outrageous and unmentionable episode of gross beastiality as *something strangely beautiful.*[26] The latter is of such gross and dehumanizing depravity that it underscores dramatically the wisdom of Robert Bartley's observation.

However, as cogent and timely as his recommendation is, to replenish the stock of moral guidance that Christianity and Judaism bequeathed us would simply emphasize a needed balance. This does not point to the cross, which can stop the pendulum swings as they tear our human souls and undermine society. As welcome as Bartley's recommendations are, in the long run, they will be in vain. The moral guidance of Judaism and Christianity is a fruit of faith. It is very stern stuff. Each of the aspects of Doric discipline (e.g., justice, judgment, and responsibility) brings us under some measure of condemnation. Christian judgment and responsibility (cf. Sermon on the Mount) is a heavier burden of condemnation than any other. Depriving moral guidance of its religious context is to

25. *Wall Street Journal,* December 24, 1992.
26. *New York Times,* April 1, 2007, 13.

remove the grace that grounds condemnation in God's mercy, the cross. "For God has consigned all men to disobedience, that he may have mercy upon all" (Rom 11:32).

Without its Christian context the stock of moral guidance, no matter how desperately needed (and it is), in the long run will only produce a swing away from such moral guidance. Robert Bartley is correct; but as Freud also correctly observed: religious demands in both Judaism and Christianity, as he understood them, were too heavy a burden to bear ("none is righteous, no not one . . ." Rom 3:10; Matt 5, 6, 7) and the human psyche will throw up what it cannot digest. Each is correct but neither gets us off the pendulum. We have this very tension in Scripture itself. I can recall my mother's favorite biblical text: Galatians 6:2, "Bear ye one another's burden and so fulfill the law of Christ" (KJV). But my father's favorite was three verses later, Galatians 6:5, "For everyman shall bear his own burden" (KJV). My mother was a Democrat my father a Republican. *But Scripture uses this tension to lead us to Good Friday and Easter* and the only place where justice and mercy are fulfilled and neither cheapened.

The illustration of a pendulum is limited and can be misleading. The laws of physics determine the extent of inevitable swings from either pole, whereas in history the actions and reactions are neither predictable nor inevitable. A swing in history may not reverse itself. It may end up destroying culture in its uncorrected extremes. The psychiatrist Robert Wetmore used to warn that it is easier to relax a strict conscience than it is to restrict a lax conscience. The Platonic tolerance polarity, if not corrected, can destroy Western civilization. An argument could be made that it is no less true of Doric discipline, but in this present age it is not the threat to the world that God loves as is the Platonic tolerance momentum. But either way, both grow out of the same desire to avoid the risk of trust.

We urgently need to see that the cross of Christ has freed us from the bondage to these polarities or corrections and that Christ has enabled us to accept lofty demands without the moralism of the Pharisee or the permissiveness of the Sadducee. "The odour of blood" is a shocking term. If we cannot smell the blood we will idolatrously identify either polarity with Christianity, or not perceiving the graciousness, love, and power in Good Friday and Easter, we will justify atheism. Every contemporary Christian tradition is split or in tension on this pendulum. Yeats warns us that each swing is vain. No matter how urgently necessary it is to recover the disappearing virtues of Doric discipline, Pharisaic hope in law and responsibility can never be a synonym for Christianity. The rational justification for a correction to the so-called depravity drift in Western civilization presents a great temptation for Christians to equate conservatism with Christianity. Similarly, Sadducee tolerance, with all its temporary humane reactions to the condemnation resulting from God's just demands, becomes merely another self-destructing idol.

> Since, therefore, we are now justified by his blood, much more shall we be saved by him from the wrath of God. For if while we were enemies we were reconciled to God by the death of his Son, much more now that we are reconciled, shall we be saved by his life. (Rom 5:9–10)

When the Pharisee in us gives up the heavy burden of trust in our own goodness (now or to be achieved) and it is replaced with trust in God's love symbolized by the word blood, then our hearts begin to change and we begin to see and treat others with something of the compassion with which God sees and treats us. When the Sadducee in us sees in this word blood the wounded self-exposed accessibility of God, and the corresponding power of the resurrection victory over death, then our burden of cynicism and idolatry can give way to the sure and certain hope of eternal life and a justice that we can endure and trust because of his mercy.

As St. Paul tells us, because we are "justified by blood" (Rom 5:9) we "have peace with God through our Lord Jesus Christ" (Rom 5:1). The world's horror of blood is now turned right side up. By his life outpoured we know we have a gracious God. We usually think of blood as something that stains, but the actual blood in our bodies is a life-dependent cleansing agent. Blood is at each moment being pumped to every cell in our bodies to remove the cell's refuse to the kidneys. This picture of our blood's function gives us a new way to look at the cleansing and redeeming power of blood: "we have fellowship with one another, and the blood of Jesus his Son cleanses us from all sin" (John 1:7); "The cup of blessing, is it not a participation in the blood of Christ?" (1 Cor 10:16); "But now in Christ Jesus you who once were far off have been brought near in the blood of Christ." (Eph 2:13); "how much more shall the blood of Christ . . . purify your conscience from dead works to serve the living God" (Heb 9:14); "You know that you were ransomed from the futile ways inherited from your fathers, not with perishable things such as silver or gold, but with the precious blood of Christ" (1 Pet 1:18–19).

These five texts are indicative of the Easter transformation of the word "blood" from its negative and disagreeable connotation to its function: "cleanses," "blessing," being "brought near," "purify," and "ransomed." In the Old Testament blood was the synonym for life. When bleeding in a sacrificial lamb stopped, life ended. Blood meant the life of the lamb. The blood of Christ means Jesus's life outpoured in love.

As either Pharisee or Sadducee we find it impossible to appreciate one of the most comforting texts in Scripture. When Pilate acquiesced in releasing Barabbas instead of Jesus and said, "I am innocent of this man's blood," the people answered, "His blood be on us and on our children!" (Matt 27:25). They did not know that after Easter this terrible curse would be transformed into a blessing. The Pharisee yeast has always been the source of malevolent anti-Semitism. Who killed Christ? The Jews! Failing to see our universal self-as-center as the cause and reason for Christ's crucifixion ("Twas I Lord Jesus, I it was denied thee; I crucified thee."),[27] we will not see ourselves as recipients of his forgiveness. "Father, forgive them for they know not what they do" (Luke: 23:34).

The blood that cleanses us from sin is the very blood that the people called "to be on us and on our children." Pharisees seek reassurance of our own righteousness by measuring it against the alleged wickedness of others (". . . God, I thank thee that I am not like other men, extortioners, unjust, adulterers, or even like this tax collector. Luke 18:11). This is the dynamic in all scapegoating, from gossip to the holocaust to the crucifixion. Unrepentant Pharisees who blame Jews and exclude ourselves from responsibility also exclude us from its cleansing power. The cross and resurrection transforms the blood of guilt into the blood of cleansing, the profound comfort of God's transcendent forgiveness. As repentant Pharisees we know ourselves to be complicit in the crucifixion and are being healed of this self-righteous yeast. The curse, "His blood be on us and our children," becomes after Easter the greatest of all blessings.

"Odour of blood" in modern ears is not merely shocking, although it is that and should be. It is not unlike the outrageous claim that Jesus made, "Truly, truly, I say unto you, unless you eat the flesh of the Son of Man and drink his blood, you have no life in you" (John 6:53).

To ask his disciples to eat his flesh and drink his blood was indeed outrageous and offensive, and, at best, incomprehensible. "After this many

27. Heermann, # 158, *Hymnal.*

of his disciples drew back and no longer went about with him" (John 6:66). The meaning of this hard saying was not revealed until after Easter in the Eucharistic act of communication (communion) and restoration. "When he was at table with them, he took bread and blessed and broke it, and gave it to them. And their eyes were opened and they recognized him" (Luke 24:30– 31); ". . . Jesus took bread and blessed, and broke it, and gave it to the disciples and said, 'take, eat; this is my body.' And he took the cup . . . saying, 'Drink of it, all of you for this is my blood.'"

George Herbert describes the costly transformation of Christ's sacrifice:

> Love is that liquour sweet and most divine,
> which my God feels as bloud; but I, as wine.[28]

After Easter, as Jesus's outrageous claim was revealed in the Eucharist, so Yeats's conventionally disagreeable phrase, "Odour of blood," is similarly disclosed in all its beneficent power and promise at Easter.

"Odour of blood when Christ was slain made all Platonic tolerance vain and vain all Doric discipline" are words that come from a play that Yeats wrote in 1931. The play's title is "The Resurrection."[29]

In the play are two main characters, a Greek and a Hebrew. Christ has been crucified. The disciples are huddled together hiding in a back room because they know the authorities will be hunting for anyone who followed Jesus. The Greek and the Hebrew, who had different hopes for this Jesus, plan to defend the narrow stairway until they are both killed to give the disciples time to escape over the rooftops if they have nerve enough to do so. The Hebrew seems doubtful that they do have that much nerve left. He believes they were paralyzed after Jesus was taken and crucified and could no longer believe him to be the Messiah.

Outside, a pagan mob is dancing in the streets in the annual rites believed to restore life to its eternally dying and rising god, Dionysus, the Greek god of wine and fertility. The Greek begins laughing, and the Hebrew is angered by it. He laughs because as a Greek he was what the early church called a Docetist, one who believed Jesus was divine but not fully human. Christ only seemed to be born, seemed to eat, walk, suffer, and die. The Hebrew, on the contrary, believed that Jesus was truly

---

28. Vendler, *Poetry of George Herbert*, 74.
29. Yeats, *Collected Plays of W. B. Yeats*, 371–73.

human, had truly cared for human misery, truly suffered and truly died and was simply mistaken in his belief that he was the Messiah.

A Syrian bursts in. He has met some women coming from the tomb, and they told him it was empty. The Greek says he knew all along the tomb was empty, because the Romans had killed a ghost. The Syrian wants to tell the disciples, but the Greek and the Hebrew bar the way.

Christ suddenly is in the room. The Hebrew falls to his knees in shock. The Greek again breaks out into laughter. Thinking Jesus is only a phantom, a ghost, he believes he can pass his hand right through it.

> He reaches out his hand. And he SCREAMS!
> He reached for a phantom. And touched . . . reality.
> ". . . The heart of a phantom is beating."[30]

The arguments of both the Greek philosopher, believing the mere divinity, and the Hebrew realist, believing the mere humanity, are shattered. The play quietly ends with a chorus that comes out and sings,

> Odour of blood when Christ was slain,
> Made all Platonic tolerance vain,
>   and vain all Doric discipline.[31]

30. Yeats, *Collected Poems.*
31. Ibid.

Bibliography

Adams, James R. *The Sting of Death*. New York: Seabury, 1971.

Adams, John H., ed. *The Layman*. Lenoir, NC: Presbyterian Lay Committee, October, 2005.

Albright, Madeleine. *The Mighty and the Almighty: Reflections on America, God and World Affairs*. New York: Harper Collins, 2006.

Allen, Diogenes. "What Happened to Neo-orthodoxy?" *Theology Today*. January, 1978.

Allison, C. F. *The Rise of Moralism*. Vancouver: Regent, 2003.

Anonymous. *The Whole Duty of Man*. London, 1806.

Arendt, Hannah. Review of *Pius XII* by Rolf Hochhuth in *New York Times Book Review*, 1964.

Armstrong, Brian. *Calvinism and the Amyraut Heresy*. Eugene, OR: Wipf & Stock, 2004.

Armstrong, Karen. *A History of God*. New York: Ballantine, 1993.

Auden, W. H. *Collected Poetry*. New York: Random, 1945.

———. *For the Time Being: A Christmas Oratorio*. New York: Random, 1944.

Augustine. "On Rebuke and Grace." *The Nicene and Post Nicene Fathers*. Vol. 5. Ed. Philip Schaff, New York: Christian Literature, 1885.

Bainton, Roland. *Erasmus of Christendom*. New York: Scribner, 1969.

Bartley, Robert. "The Stock of Moral Guidance," *The Wall Street Journal*. December 24, 1992.

Barrett, C. K. *The Gospel According to St. John*. London: SPCK, 1967.

Barzun, Jacques. *From Dawn to Decadence, 1500 to the Present: 500 Years of Western Cultural Life*. New York: HarperCollins, 2000.

Baxter, Richard. *Aphorisms of Justification*. London: Gooding, 1649.

Bayne, Stephen, ed. *Theological Freedom and Social Responsibility*. New York: Seabury, 1967.

Becker, Carl. *Heavenly City of the 18th Century Philosophers*. New Haven: Yale University Press, 1932.

Beeke, Joel. *The Quest for Full Assurance: The Legacy of Calvin and His Successor*. Carlisle, PA: Banner of Truth Trust, 1982.

Bennett, William. "Getting Used to Decadence: The Spirit of Democracy in America." Lecture 477, Heritage, 1993.

Bennett, William. *The Index of Leading Cultural Indicators*. New York: Simon & Schuster, 1994.

Bergman, Ingmar. "Why I Make Movies." *Horizon*, 3, No. 1. New York: American Heritage, 1960.

Bettelheim, Bruno. *Freud and Man's Soul*. New York: Knopf, 1983.

Bloom, Allen. *The Closing of the American Mind*. New York: Simon & Schuster, 1987.

Bonhoffer, Dietrich. *The Cost of Discipleship*. New York: Macmillan, 1963.

Bibliography

The Book of Common Prayer According to the use of the Episcopal Church. New York: The Church Hymnal, 1979.

Bork, Robert. *Slouching Towards Gomorrah.* New York: Harper Collins, 1996.

Bradley, Omar. "Patriot Post," Vol. 3, No. 27, June 30, 2003.

Bray, Gerald. *Biblical Interpretation.* Leiscester: IVP, 1996.

Brown, Frank Burch. "The Startling Testimony of George Steiner," *Theology Today.* December, 2003.

Bruce, Steve. *God is Dead: Secularization in the West.* Oxford: Wiley-Blackwell, 2002.

Brueggemann, Walter. *Struggling with Scripture.* Louisville, KY: Knox, 2002.

Bryce, James. *Modern Democracies.* New York: Macmillan, 1921.

Budziszewski, J. *What We Can't Not Know: A Guide.* Dallas: Spence, 2003.

Bunyan, John. *Grace Abounding.* Grand Rapids: Zondervan, 1948.

———. *Pilgrim's Progress.* New York: Collier & Son, 1909.

Calvin, John. *Institutes of the Christian Religion. The Library of Christian Classics.* London: SCM, 1960.

Carroll, T. K. *Jeremy Taylor: Selected Works.* New York: Paulist, 1990.

Carson, D. A. *Justification and Variegated Nomism.* Peabody, MA: Baker Academic, 2004.

Carter, Grayson. *Anglican Evangelicals: Protestant Secessions from the Via Media, c. 1800–1850.* Oxford: Oxford University Press, 2001.

Carter, Stephen. *The Culture of Disbelief.* New York: Basic, 1993.

Carus, William. *The Life of Charles Simeon.* New York: Carter, 1847.

Casserley, J. V. Langmead. *Toward a Theology of History.* New York: Holt Rinehart, 1965.

Catholic Encyclopedia. New York: Encyclopedia, 1913.

Chadwick, Owen. *The Secularization of the European Mind in the 19th Century.* New York: Cambridge University Press, 1991.

Cheney, Lynne. *Telling the Truth.* New York: Simon & Schuster, 1995.

Cherbonnier, E. *Hardness of Heart.* New York: Doubleday, 1955.

Chesterton, G. K. *Orthodoxy.* New York: John Lane, 1919.

Coleridge, Samuel Taylor. *The Complete Works of Samuel Taylor Coleridge.* Professor Shedd, ed. Vol. 5. New York: Harper & Brothers, 1876.

———. *Notes on English Divines.* Vol. V. *The Complete Works of Samuel Taylor Coleridge, VII Vols.* New York: Harper & Brothers, 1876.

Cook, Faith. *Selina Countess of Huntingdon.* Carlisle, PA: Banner of Truth Trust, 2001.

Cox, J. E., ed. *Miscellaneous Writings and Letters of Thomas Cranmer.* Cambridge: Parker Society, 1846.

Crain, Caleb. "Dr. Strangelove," *The New York Times*, October 3, 2004.

Cromartie, Michael. Interview with Francis Fukuyama, "Our Posthuman Future," *Books and Culture*, July/August, 2002.

Cross, F. L., and E. A. Livingstone, eds. *Oxford Dictionary of the Christian Church.* Oxford: Oxford University Press, 1997.

Dawkins, Richard. *The God Delusion.* Boston: Houghton Mifflin Harcourt, 2007.

Delbanco, Andrew. *The Death of Satan, How the Americans Have Lost Their Sense of Evil.* New York: Farrar, Straus, & Giroux, 1995.

Demant, V. A. *Religion and the Decline of Capitalism.* London: Faber & Faber. 1952.

Dewar, Lindsay, and Cyril Hudson. *Christian Morals.* London: University of London Press, 1948.

Dillistone, F. W. *Religious Experience and Christian Faith.* London: SCM, 1981.

Bibliography

Dodds, P. R. *The Greeks and the Irrational*. Los Angeles: University of California Press, 1951.

Doherty, Brian. *Radicals for Capitalism: A Freewheeling History of the Modern American Libertarian Movement*. New York: Public Affairs, 2007.

Eliot, T. S. *Selected Essays 1917–1932*. New York: Harcourt Brace, 1932.

Elkins, Stanley, and Eric McKitrick. *The Age of Federalism*. New York: Oxford University Press, 1993.

Elmen, Paul. *The Anglican Moral Choice*. Wilton, CT: Morehouse-Barlow, 1983.

Elwell, Walter, ed. *Evangelical Dictionary of Theology*. Grand Rapids: Baker, 1984.

Erasmus, Desiderus. *Discourse on Free Will*. Edited by Ernst F. Winter, New York: Continuum, 2005.

Erickson, Richard C. "The Psychology of Self Esteem: Promise or Peril," *Pastoral Psychology*. 1987.

Fenlon, D. *Heresy and Obedience in Tridentine Italy: Cardinal Pole and the Counter-Reformation*. Cambridge: Cambridge University Press, 1972.

Ferguson, Sinclair. *John Owen on the Christian Life*. Carlisle, PA: Banner of Truth Trust, 1987.

Fisher, Edward. *The Marrow of Modern Divinity*. London: Tegg & Son, 1837.

Forde, Gerhard O. *The Captivation of the Will*. Grand Rapids: Eerdmans, 2005.

Forster, E. M. *The Oxford Dictionary of Quotations*. Oxford: Oxford University Press, 1992.

Frankl, Victor. *Man's Search for Meaning: An Introduction to Logotherapy*. London: Hodder & Stoughton, 1971.

Freud, Sigmund. *Civilization and Its Discontents*. London: Hogarth, 1957.

Frey, Bishop William. *The Dance of Hope*. Colorado Springs: Waterbrook, 2003.

Friedman, Maurice. *To Deny Our Nothingness*. New York: Delacorte, 1967.

Fromm, Erich. *Psychoanalysis and Religion*. New Haven: Yale University Press, 1959.

———. *Psychology and Religion*. New Haven: Yale, 1950.

Fukuyama, Francis. *The Great Disruption: Human Nature and the Reconstitution of Social Order*. New York: Free, 1999.

Gatch, Milton. *Death*. New York: Seabury, 1969.

Gore, Charles. *The Reconstruction of Belief*. New York: Scribner, 1926.

Greer, Rowan. *Anglican Approaches to Scripture*. New York: Herder & Herder, 2001.

Guinness, Os. *Unspeakable: Facing up to Evil in an Age of Genocide and Terror*. San Francisco: Harper, 2005.

Hall, Basil. "Calvin Against the Calvinists." *John Calvin*, ed. G. E. Duffield. Grand Rapids: Eerdmans, 1966.

Hall, Joseph. *Works*. 10 vols. London: Whittingham, 1808.

Harnack, Adolph. *History of Dogma*. New York: Funk & Wagnalls, 1893.

Harris, Sam *The End of Faith: Religion, Terror, and the Future of Reason*. New York: Norton, 2004.

Harvey, Van. "Jesus and History, the Believer and the Historian." *The Christian Century*. January 26, 2000.

Hauerwas, Stanley. *After Christendom? How the Church is to Behave if Freedom, Justice, and a Christian Nation are Bad Ideas*. Nashville: Abingdon, 1991.

Heber, Reginald. *The Whole Works of the Rt. Rev. Jeremy Taylor, 15 vols*. London: 1828.

Heitzenrater, Richard. "The Tale of Two Brothers," *Christian History*, vol. XX, no. 1, issue 69.

Bibliography

Helm, Paul. *Calvin and the Calvinists.* Carlisle, PA: Banner of Truth Trust, 1982.

Hendershott, Anne. *The Politics of Deviance.* New York: Encounter, 2004.

Henry, Stuart C. *George Whitefield: Wayfaring Witness.* Nashville: Abingdon, 1957.

Hibbert, Christopher. *The French Revolution.* New York: Viking, 1980.

Hillesum, Etty. *Letters from Westerbork.* London: Grafton, 1987.

Himmelfarb, Gertrude. *The De-Moralization of Society: From Victorian Virtues to Modern Values.* New York: Knopf, 1995.

———. *Marriage and Morals Among the Victorians.* New York: Knopf, 1966.

Hitchens, Christopher. *God is not Great: How Religion Poisons Everything.* Lebanon, IN: Hachette, *2007.*

Holifield, E. Brooks. *A History of Pastoral Care in America: From Salvation to Self Realization.* Nashville: Abingdon, 1983.

Hooker, Richard. *The Works of Mr. Richard Hooker in Eight Books* of *Ecclesiastical Polity.* London: Crook, 1666.

Hovestol, Tom. *Extreme Righteousness.* Chicago: Moody, 1997.

Hughes, Trevor. *The Piety of Jeremy Taylor.* London: Macmillan, 1960.

Huntley, Frank. *Jeremy Taylor and the Great Rebellion.* Ann Arbor: University of Michigan Press, 1970.

Hutter, Reinhard. *Bound to be Free.* Grand Rapids, MI: Eerdmans, 2004.

The Hymnal 1982 according to the use of the Episcopal Church. New York: The Church Hymnal, 1982.

Inge, William. "Context," March 15, 1997.

Johnson, Luke T. "II Timothy 3: 16–17." Two unpublished lectures given in New Haven, CT, 1974.

Kahler, Martin. *The So-Called Historical Jesus and the Historic Biblical Christ.* Minneapolis: Fortress, 1964.

Kendall, R. T., and David Rosen. *The Christian and the Pharisee.* New York: Faith Words, 2006.

Ketley, Joseph, ed. *The Two Liturgies, A.D. 1549, and A.D. 1552; with other Documents set forth by Authority in the reign of King Edward VI.* Cambridge: Parker Society, 1844.

Kimel, Alvin, ed. *Speaking the Christian God.* Grand Rapids: Eerdmans, 1992.

Kipling, Rudyard. *Poems.* New York: Knopf, 2007.

Kittel, Gerhard, ed. *Theological Dictionary of the New Testament.* Grand Rapids: Eerdmans, 1974.

Koestler, Arthur. *The God That Failed.* New York: Harper & Brothers, 1949.

Kreeft, Peter. *Fundamentals of the Faith.* San Francisco: Ignatius, 1988.

Kung, Hans. *Justification.* Philadelphia: Westminster, 1981.

Kushner, Harold. *When Bad Things Happen to Good People.* New York: Schocken, 1981.

Law, William. *A Serious Call to a Devout & Holy Life.* London: Dent, 1906.

Lewis, Bernard. *What Went Wrong? The Clash Between Islam and Modernity in the Middle East.* New York: Harper, 2003.

Lewis, C. S. *Fern Seed and Elephants.* London: Fontana, Reprint in Fount Paperbacks, 1977.

———. *The Four Loves.* New York: Harcourt Brace, 1960.

———. *God in the Dock: Essays on Theology and Ethics.* Grand Rapids: Eerdmans, 1974.

———. *The Great Divorce.* New York: Macmillan, 1952.

———. *Mere Christianity.* San Francisco: Harper, 2001.

———. *Perelandra.* London: Pan, 1955.

Bibliography

Llibagiza, Immaculee with Steve Erwin. *Left to Tell: Discovering God Amidst the Rwandan Holocaust*. Hay, 2006.

Lloyd, Genevieve. *Providence Lost*. Cambridge: Harvard University Press, 2008.

Locke, John. *An Essay Concerning Human Understanding*, Bk IV, Ch. 9. New York: Oxford University Press, 1979.

Lowe, D. M. *Edward Gibbon 1737–1794*. New York: Random, 1937.

Lucas, Henry L. *The Renaissance and the Reformation*. New York: Harper & Brothers, 1934.

MacIntyre, Alasdair. *After Virtue*. Notre Dame: Notre Dame Press, 1984.

———. *Three Rival Versions of Moral Enquiry*. Notre Dame: Notre Dame, 1990.

———. *Whose Justice? Which Rationality?* Notre Dame: University of Notre Dame Press, 1988.

MacLeish, Archibald. *J. B.: A Play in Verse*. Boston: Houghton Mifflin, 1956.

Mairet, P., ed. *Christian Essays in Psychiatry*. London: Camelot, 1956.

Malia, Martin. Review of *Le Livre Noir Du Communism* in *The Times Literary Supplement*. March, 27, 1998.

Markus, Robert A. *Christianity and the Secular*. Notre Dame: University of Notre Dame Press, 2006.

Marsden, George. *The Soul of the American University: From Protestant Establishment to Established Non-Belief*. New York: Oxford University Press, 1994.

Marty, Louis, ed. *George Herbert: The Oxford Poetry Library*, 97. Oxford: Oxford University Press, 1994.

Mascall, Eric. *The Secularization of Christianity*. New York: Holt, Rinehart, & Winston, 1965.

McAdoo, H. R. *The Spirit of Anglicanism*. New York: Scribner's, 1965.

McCullough, D. W. *The Trivialization of God*. Colorado Springs: NavPress, 1995.

McDougall, Walter. *Freedom Just Around the Corner: A New American History 1585–1828*. New York: HarperCollins, 2005.

McGill, Arthur. *Sermons of Arthur C. McGill*. Edited by David Cain. Eugene, OR: Cascade, 2007.

McSorley, Harry. *Luther: Right or Wrong*. New York: Newman, 1969.

Merkin, Daphne. "A Neurotic's Neurotic." *New York Times Magazine*. December 30, 2007.

Milbank, John. *Theology and Social Theory: Beyond Secular Reason*. Oxford: Oxford University Press, 1990.

Miles, Jack. *A Crisis in the Life of God*. New York: Knopf, 2001.

Miller, Perry, and Thomas H. Johnson, eds. *The Puritans: A Sourcebook of their Writings*. New York: Harper & Row, 1965.

Minear, Paul. *Eyes of Faith: A Study in the Biblical Point of View*. London: Lutterworth, 1948.

Moulton, John Fletcher. "Laws and Manners," *Atlantic Monthly* 134 (July, 1924).

Muller, Richard A. *After Calvin Studies in the Development of a Theological Tradition*. Oxford: Oxford University Press, 2003.

———. *Post Reformation Reformed Dogmatics*. Grand Rapids: Baker, 2003.

Murray, Iain. *David Martin Lloyd Jones: The Fight of Faith 1939–1981*. Carlisle, PA: Banner of Truth Trust, 1990.

Napier, B. Davy. *From Faith to Faith*. New York: Harper & Brothers, 1955.

Nazir-Ali, Michael. *Conviction and Conflict: Islam, Christianity and World Order*. London: Continuum, 2006.

Bibliography

Neusner, Jacob. *Judaism in the Beginning of Christianity.* London: SPCK, 1984.

———. *Method and Meaning in Ancient Judaism.* Third Series. Chico, CA: Scholars, 1981.

The New Catholic Encyclopedia. Farmington Hills, MI: Gale, 2002.

Newbigin, Lesslie. *The Gospel in a Pluralist Society.* Grand Rapids: Eerdmans, 1989.

Niebuhr, Reinhold. *The Nature and Destiny of Man.* New York: Scribners, 1949.

Norman, Edward. *Secularization.* New York: Continuum, 2002.

Null, Ashley. *Cranmer's Doctrine of Repentance: Renewing the Power to Love.* New York: Oxford University Press, 2000.

O'Donovan, Oliver. *The Desire of the Nations.* Oxford: Oxford University Press, 1996.

Ollard, S. L., and Gordon Crosse. *Dictionary of English History.* Oxford: Mowbray, 1912.

Olson, Roger E. *Arminian Theology: Myths and Realities.* Downers Grove, IL: IVP, 2006.

Orme,William. The *Practical Works of Richard Baxter With a Life of the Author and the Critical Examinations of his Writings,* 23 vols. London, 1830.

Outler, Albert. *John Wesley.* New York: Oxford University Press, 1964.

Packer, J. I. *Knowing God.* Downers Grove, IL: IVP, 1973.

Packer, J. I., and O. R. Johnston. *Martin Luther on the Bondage of the Will: A New Translation.* Grand Rapids, MI: Baker, 1957.

Pascal, Blaise. *Pensees, Everyman's Library.* New York: Dutton, 1943.

Peck, M. Scott. *People of the Lie: The Hope for Healing Human Evil.* New York: Simon & Schuster, 1983.

———. *The Road Less Traveled.* New York: Simon & Schuster, 1978.

———. "The Devil Didn't Make Me Do It." David Neff interview in *Christianity Today* (February, 2005).

Pelikan, Jaroslav. *Reformation of Church and Dogma.* Chicago: University of Chicago Press, 1984.

Pike, James A. *A Time for Christian Candor.* New York: Harper & Row, 1964.

Piper, John. *Desiring God: Meditations of a Christian Hedonist.* Sisters, OR: Multnomah, 1966.

Placher, W. C. The *Domestication of Transcendent Thinking About God.* Louisville, KY: Westminster Knox, 1996.

Polanyi, Michael. *Knowing and Being.* Chicago: Chicago University Press, 1969.

———. *Personal Knowledge: Towards a Post-Critical Philosophy.* Chicago: University of Chicago Press. 1962.

Pound, Ezra. "Hugh Selwyn Mauberley," *Oxford Book of American Verse.* New York: Oxford University Press, 1950.

Priestly, J. B., and J. Spier, eds. *Adventures in English Literature.* New York: Harcourt, 1931.

Rahner, Karl, ed. *Encyclopedia of Theology.* New York: Seabury, 1975.

Rand, Ayn. *Atlas Shrugged.* New York: Signet, 1992.

Raspberry, William. *The Tuscaloosa News,* May 15, 1994.

Rogan, Donald. *Campus Apocalypse.* New York: Seabury, 1969.

Rieff, Philip. *Triumph of the Therapeutic.* New York: Harper & Row, 1966.

Rookmaaker, H. R. *Modern Art and the Death of a Culture.* Wheaton, IL: Crossway, 1973.

Rupp, E. Gordon, and Philip S. Watson, eds. *Luther and Erasmus, Free Will and Salvation.* Louisville: Westminster Knox, 2006.

Russell, Bertrand. *The Scientific Vision.* New York: Norton, 1931.

Saldarini, Anthony J. *Pharisees, Scribes and Sadducees in Palestinian Society.* Edinburgh: T. & T. Clark, 1988.

Bibliography

Sartre, Jean-Paul. *No Exit, A Play in One Act*. London: Samuel French, 1958.

Schlesinger, Arthur. *The Disuniting of America: Reflection on a Multicultural Society*. New York: Norton, 1990.

Schlossberg, Herbert. *Idols for Destruction: Christian Faith and Its Confrontation with American Society*. New York: Nelson, 1983.

Scott, David. *Christian Character: Jeremy Taylor and Christian Ethics Today*. Latimer Studies #38, Oxford: Latimer, 1991.

Seitz, Christopher, and Kathryn Greene-McCreight, eds. *Theological Exegesis, Essays in Honor of Brevard S. Childs*. Grand Rapids: Eerdmans, 1999.

Seymour, A. C. H. *The Life and Times of Selina Countess of Huntingdon*. 2 vols. London: 1839.

Smith, Christian, ed. *The Secular Revolution: Power, Interest, Conflict in the Secularization of American Public Life*. Berkeley: University of California Press, 2003.

Sommerville, C. John. *The Decline of the Secular University*. Oxford: Oxford University Press, 2006.

Southey, R. *The Life of William Cowper*. 1854.

Spong, John. Interview in *The London Times*. August 4, 1989.

———. "12 Theses," Diocese of Newark web site, 1998.

St. Anselm's Proslogion. Translated by M. J. Charlesworth. Notre Dame: University of Notre Dame Press, 1979.

Steiner, George. *Real Presences*. Chicago: University of Chicago Press, 1989.

Steinmetz, David. "The Superiority of Pre-Critical Exegesis," *Theology Today*. Vol. 37, No. l, April, 1980.

Stranks, C. J. *Anglican Devotion*. Greenwich, CT: Seabury, 1961.

Sykes, Charles. *A Nation of Victims: The Decay of the American Character*. New York: St. Martin's, 1992.

Taylor, Charles. *The Secular Age*. Cambridge: Belknap/Harvard, 2007.

Taylor, Jeremy. *The Whole Works of the Rt. Rev. Jeremy Taylor*. Ed. Reginald Heber. 15 vols. London: Rivington, 1818.

Temple, William. *Christianity and the Social Order*. Aylesbury: Penguin, 1942.

———. *Nature, Man and God*. London: Macmillan, 1951.

———. *Nature of Personality*. London: Macmillan, 1911.

Thornton, Martin. *The Rock and the River*. London: Hodder & Stoughton, 1965.

Tillich, Paul. *A History of Christian Thought*. Ed. Carl Braaten. New York: Harper & Row, 1968.

———. *Systematic Theology*. Chicago: University of Chicago Press, 1963.

Tuchman, Barbara. *A Distant Mirror*. New York: Ballantine, 1987.

———. *The March of Folly*. New York: Ballantine, 1985.

Turner, Philip. "Episcopal Authority in a Divided Church," *Pro Ecclesia*, VIII, Winter, 1999.

Tyerman, Luke. *Life and Times of John Wesley, M.A.* New York: Harper & Brothers, 1870.

Tyson, John. "John Wesley and William Law: A Reappraisal." *Wesleyan Theological Journal*. Fall, 1982.

Van Buren, Paul. *The Secular Meaning of the Gospel*. New York: Macmillan, 1965.

Vendler, Helen. *The Poetry of George Herbert*. Cambridge: Harvard University Press, 1975.

Venn, Henry. *The Complete Duty of Man*. London: Simpson, 1811.

Bibliography

Vitz, Paul. *Psychology as Religion: The Cult of Self-Worship*. Grand Rapids: Eerdmans, 1994.

Vos, Nelvin. *Eugene Ionesco and Edward Albee: A Critical Essay*. Grand Rapids: Eerdmans, 1968.

Wakeley, Joseph Beaumont. *The Prince of Pulpit Orators: A Portraiture of George Whitefield, M.A.* New York: Carlton & Lanahan, 1871.

Wall, Jerry. *Heaven: The Logic of Eternal Joy*. New York: Oxford Univ. Press, 2002.

Ward, Adolphus William. *The Poetical Works of Alexander Pope*. London: Macmillan, 1896.

Warren, Rick. *The Purpose Driven Church*. Grand Rapids: Zondervan, 1995.

———. *The Purpose Driven Life*. Grand Rapids: Zondervan, 2002.

Warren, Robert Penn. *Brother to Dragons*. New York: Random, 1953.

Wasserman, Dale. *Man of La Mancha*. New York: Random, 1966.

Weaver, Richard. *Ideas Have Consequences*. Chicago: University of Chicago, 1948.

Wells, David. *Losing Our Virtue: Why the Church Must Recover Its Moral Vision*. Grand Rapids: Eerdmans, 1998.

Wheelis, Allen. *The Quest for Identity*. New York: Norton, 1958.

Wesley, John. "A Plain Account of Christian Perfection." *Sermons on Several Occasions*. London: Waugh & Mason, 1831.

Witt, William. *Creation, Redemption, and Grace in the Theology of Jacob Arminius*. PhD unpublished dissertation. Notre Dame University, 1993.

Witte, John. "Exploring the Frontiers of Law, Religion, and Family Life." *Emory Law Journal*, No. l, Vol. 58, 2008.

———. *God's Joust, God's Justice*. Grand Rapids: Eerdmans, 2006.

Witte, John, and Frank Alexander. *The Teachings of Modern Christianity in Law, Politics, and Human Nature*. New York: Columbia University Press. 2006.

Witte, John, Jr., and Frank S. Alexander, eds. *The Weightier Matters of the Law Essays on Law and Religion*. Atlanta: Scholars,1988.

The Writings of James Arminius. Grand Rapids: Baker, 1986.

Yeats, William Butler. *Collected Poems of William Butler Yeats*. New York: Macmillan, 1937.

Index